J. G. BALLARD
a primary and
secondary bibliography

Masters of
Science Fiction and Fantasy

Editor
L. W. Currey

Advisory Acquisitions Editor
Marshall B. Tymn

Other bibliographies in the series:

Lloyd Alexander, Evangeline Walton Ensley, and Kenneth Morris
Leigh Brackett, Marion Zimmer Bradley, and Anne McCaffrey
Arthur C. Clarke
Samuel R. Delaney
Gordon R. Dickson
Ursula K. Le Guin
Andre Norton
Robert Silverberg
Clifford D. Simak
Theodore Sturgeon
Jules Verne
Jack Williamson
Roger Zelazny

J. G. BALLARD
a primary and secondary bibliography

DAVID PRINGLE

G.K.HALL &CO.
70 LINCOLN STREET, BOSTON, MASS.

Copyright © 1984 by David Pringle.

All rights reserved.

Library of Congress Cataloging in Publication Data

Pringle, David.
  J. G. Ballard : a primary and secondary bibliography.

  Includes bibliographical references and index.
  1. Ballard, J. G., 1930-   —Bibliography. I. Title.
Z8068.94.P74 1984 [PR6052.A46] 016.823'914 83-18528
ISBN 0-8161-8603-0

This publication is printed on permanent/durable acid-free paper
MANUFACTURED IN THE UNITED STATES OF AMERICA

Contents

The Author. vi
Preface vii
Introduction. xi
Checklist of Books. xxxv
Interview with J.G. Ballard 1

PRIMARY BIBLIOGRAPHY
      Part A: Fiction 27
      Part B: Miscellaneous Media 53
      Part C: Nonfiction. 57

SECONDARY BIBLIOGRAPHY
      Part D: Critical and Bio-Bibliographical Studies. 75

APPENDIXES
      1:   Foreign Language Editions. 137
      2:   Nonfiction in French 143

INDEXES
      1:   The Writings of J.G. Ballard 147
      2:   Critics, Reviewers, and Interviewers 152
      3:   Persons Referred to by Ballard and His Critics . . 154

The Author

David Pringle attended the University of Sussex, where he received a B.A. in English literature. In 1978/79 he was a research fellow at the Science Fiction Foundation, North East London Polytechnic, undertaking research into the educational usefulness of science fiction. He was elected reviews editor of Foundation: The Review of Science Fiction in 1977, and from 1980 to the present has served as the editor-in-chief. He is also coeditor of the new science fiction magazine, Interzone.

Pringle is author of Earth is the Alien Planet: J.G. Ballard's Four-Dimensional Nightmare (Borgo Press, 1979) and coeditor of J.G. Ballard: The First Twenty Years (Bran's Head Books, 1976). He has been a contributor to Peter Nicholls's Encyclopedia of Science Fiction, and has written various articles and book reviews for Foundation and other publications.

Preface

This bibliography is divided into four main sections.

Part A lists J.G. Ballard's published fiction from his prize-winning student study, "The Violent Noon," 1951, through his latest collection, Myths of the Near Future, published in 1982. I have attempted to list all anthology appearances (in the English language) for each short story, though some such appearances may have been overlooked. The entries are arranged in chronological order, according to the magazine date--or the month of publication in the case of books. When stories have appeared simultaneously, in magazines of the same date, I have generally listed them in alphabetical order of magazine title. Thus "Escapement" (A2) precedes "Prima Belladonna" (A3), although the December 1956 issue of Science Fantasy, carrying the latter story, probably appeared on the newsstands some weeks before the December 1956 New Worlds, which contained the former. "Prima Belladonna" is often cited as Ballard's "first" story, perhaps because of the aptness of the title. In point of fact, it was accepted for publication after "Escapement" (see John Carnell's statement in D62). Where a short story and a book appeared in the same month, I have placed the story before the book, on the assumption that most magazines (commercial ones, at any rate) actually appear prior to the beginning of the month. Very occasionally, the ordering of items is arbitrary--for example, I have placed Terminal Beach (American collection, A54) before The Terminal Beach (British collection, A56), although both books appeared in the same month, June 1964, and I have been unable to establish which actually has precedence. I have listed first hardcover and first paperback editions, British and American, of all Ballard's books. Subsequent reprints, or reissues by different paperback houses, are not listed.

Part B lists miscellaneous items which do not fall comfortably under the headings "Fiction" or "Nonfiction". There are sixteen of these short texts, ranging from scraps of verse and computer printouts to "advertisements" and concrete poems.

Part C lists Ballard's nonfiction from his New Worlds guest editorial in 1962 through his recent review of a Scott Fitzgerald

Preface

biography in 1982. I have provided brief annotations of many of these items--though in the case of book reviews these are limited to the authors and titles of the books under review. Also included in this section are interviews with the author (interviewers' names are listed alphabetically in Index 2). Excluded from this list are extremely brief statements by Ballard, mainly book-jacket endorsements, which are difficult to trace to a primary source (one such is his oft-reprinted endorsement for Michael Moorcock's novel, <u>Stormbringer</u>, 1964). It is possible I have overlooked other fugitive pieces, but I am confident that the ninety-seven items listed here constitute the near-totality of Ballard's published nonfiction.

Part D is headed "Critical and Bio-Bibliographical Studies"; it is in fact a list of most of the interesting references to J.G. Ballard and his work which I found. It is arranged chronologically, it is selective, and it is, unfortunately, limited to the English language (which is why one of the best critical essays on Ballard, Robert Louit's "Le chirurgien de l'apocalypse," 1980, is excluded). The items listed here range from early magazine profiles to more-or-less weighty academic papers. I have included numerous newspaper reviews, to illustrate how Ballard's books were first received. Also included are several "peer testimonials," extracts from interviews with other writers who have made off-the-cuff remarks about Ballard's work. I have annotated all the items in Part D fairly heavily, and have quoted copiously, in the hope that this section of the bibliography can be read almost as a continuous narrative of the author's career. No doubt this part of the bibliography could have been twice as long, but I chose not to include very brief or ill-informed reviews (unless written by famous names, in which case they became interesting!); also, I did not include various general books on sf which seemed to have little of interest to say about Ballard (although they invariably mention his name somewhere). Some good critical material may not have come to my attention, and I apologize here for any such notable oversights.

Throughout, the entry numbers of items I have not actually seen (e.g., Kingsley Amis's famous <u>Observer</u> review of <u>The Drowned World</u>, D8) are preceded by an asterisk, and the source of my information, usually one of the five works listed below, is given in brackets. In cases where I have seen only a cutting or photocopy, I was generally able to check dates and page numbers in the major British daily newspapers, but I was unable to consult runs of the Sunday papers (e.g., the <u>Observer</u> and <u>Sunday Times</u>); I did not have access to files of American newspapers, and the reviews from the United States that I have included usually came into my hands in the form of clippings--hence the occasional lack of page numbers and approximated publication dates.

There are three indexes to the four major sections of the bibliography. Index 1 is a straightforward alphabetical listing, by title, of all J.G. Ballard's writings--that is, of all the material

Preface

listed chronologically in Parts A, B, and C. Index 2 lists the authors, though not the titles, of all the critical and biographical comments in Part D; it also contains the names of the interviewers whose conversations with Ballard are listed in Part C. Finally, Index 3 is an alphabetical list of all the persons mentioned by Ballard and his critics in the entries of Parts B, C, and D. It should be noted that this is simply an index of the entries as given here, and it does not attempt to cover all the references in the original articles. The persons referred to in this index are, for the most part, writers, artists, and film-makers. In all three indexes reference is made to entry numbers in the main bibliography, not to page numbers.

Also included in this volume are appendixes listing foreign-language editions of Ballard's books and nonfiction material by Ballard which has appeared only in French. I believe that my information on Ballard's books in French is complete, and up to date to 1981, but I suspect that the information for other languages is far from complete. Nevertheless, I have included as many translations as I have been able to trace, in the belief that it is better to indicate the scope of the subject than to leave it completely unremarked. Ballard is a much-translated author, and his books have appeared in at least twelve languages other than English. Almost all of his fiction has now been translated into Dutch, French, German, Italian, Japanese, and Spanish. I have not attempted to list translations of individual short stories, although I know that they are many and wide-spread. A Russian correspondent, Vladimir Gopman, informs me that several Ballard stories have appeared in magazines in the USSR, and his books are reviewed there regularly. One interesting point arising from the subject of translations: thanks to the labors of Jannick Storm, the editio princeps of The Atrocity Exhibition is actually the Danish translation, which appeared in Copenhagen in 1969, months before the first English-language edition. (Similarly, the first full edition of Vermilion Sands, incorporating "The Singing Statues" and a foreword by Ballard, appears to be the Norwegian translation of 1972, lovingly edited by Jon Bing.)

Elsewhere in this volume is an interview with J.G. Ballard which I recorded in 1979, some months before the publication of The Unlimited Dream Company. A shorter version of this has already been published in the magazine Thrust (C87). It is included here because it contains a certain amount of biographical and bibliographical information, as well as interesting comments by Ballard on critics and editors. Also, I hope that the interview will make this book of greater value to readers.

In compiling this volume I have used a number of general bibliographical sources in addition to the primary sources of information. These include The British National Bibliography and The Times Index for the appropriate years. Like all recent bibliographers of

Preface

science-fiction authors, however, I owe a special debt to the following invaluable works:

    CLARESON, THOMAS D. <u>Science Fiction Criticism: An Annotated Checklist</u>. Kent, Ohio: Kent State University Press, 1972.
    CONTENTO, WILLIAM. <u>Index to Science Fiction Anthologies and Collections</u>. Boston: G.K. Hall, 1978.
    HALL, HAL W. <u>Science Fiction Book Review Index, 1923-1973</u>. Detroit: Gale Research, 1974. Annual Supplements. Bryan, Tex.: H.W. Hall, 1975-1978.
    NEW ENGLAND SCIENCE FICTION ASSOCIATION. <u>Index to the Science Fiction Magazines, 1966-1970</u>. Cambridge, Mass.: NESFA Press, 1971. Annual Supplements, 1972-1977.
    STRAUSS, ERWIN S. <u>The MIT Science Fiction Society's Index to the SF Magazines, 1951-1965</u>. Cambridge, Mass.: MIT SF Society, 1966.

    I also owe thanks to many people and institutions for the help they gave me in tracing much of the information in this book. In particular, I should like to say thank-you to: John Wolfers, J.G. Ballard's agent, who provided me with foreign editions, and who gave me access to his clippings-file; James Goddard, who published the first bibliography of Ballard's works back in 1970, and who collaborated with me on a second (contained in <u>J.G. Ballard: The First Twenty Years</u>, 1976); my former employers, Leeds City Libraries, and the members of staff who allowed me to browse through the closed-access stacks, consulting everything from <u>New Scientist</u> to <u>Punch</u>; the Science Fiction Foundation, North East London Polytechnic, which possesses invaluable runs of sf magazines and fanzines; Malcolm Edwards, who allowed me to consult his private magazine collection; John Brady, Colin Greenland, Maxim Jakubowski, Nick Pratt, and Patrick Lepetit, who all provided me with snippets of information; and, of course, J.G. Ballard himself, who answered all my questions and wished me well.

    Finally, I should like to thank my wife, Ann, for her patience, and my editor, Lloyd Currey, for his forbearance.

Introduction

J.G. Ballard is not merely a "Master of Science Fiction and Fantasy"; he is one of the most important figures in English fiction today. His international reputation is growing--he has been translated copiously into over a dozen languages--so an exhaustive bibliography, such as this, is not untimely. Ballard has been writing seriously for some twenty-five years, and although by no means prolific he has built up a solid body of work. It is work with a unique appeal and an undoubted relevance. In the words of Michael Moorcock, editor of New Worlds in the crucial period 1964-1970, "For all his invention and wonderful exoticism, his paradoxes and the beauty of his imagery, Ballard is primarily concerned with human beings. He is one of the few writers capable of dealing profoundly with the problems unique to contemporary mankind."[1]

Ballard has gained peer recognition not only from Moorcock but from such sf writers and editors as Brian Aldiss, Damon Knight, Judith Merril, Harlan Ellison, and Barry Malzberg. Aldiss wrote one of the first substantial critical articles on Ballard's work (D27). Damon Knight was editorial adviser to Berkley Books in the early 1960s, and hence was responsible for Ballard's first book publications. Judith Merril was the first to anthologize Ballard's stories, including his "Prima Belladonna" in her 1957 best-of-the-year collection and later reprinting two of his works in her SF: The Best of the Best anthology in 1967. She also wrote a long and rapturous appreciation of his fiction for the Magazine of Fantasy and Science Fiction in 1966 (D39). More recently, Barry Malzberg has acclaimed Ballard as "perhaps the major figure in Western Literature of our time" (D118). No other writer associated with genre science fiction has received accolades quite as lavish as those which Ballard's admirers have given him.

The enthusiastic praise has come from outside the sf field too. Kingsley Amis, Graham Greene, Anthony Burgess, William Burroughs, Robert Nye, Angela Carter, and Malcolm Bradbury have all endorsed his work on various occasions, as has the sculptor Eduardo Paolozzi, the poet George MacBeth and the critic Susan Sontag. "I have admired Ballard's work for many years," says the last-named. "He is one of

Introduction

the most important, intelligent voices in contemporary fiction."[2] Even his detractors, such as H. Bruce Franklin (D139) and Martin Amis (D95), feel the need to refer in passing to Ballard's "brilliant imagination" and his "awesome visual imagination and verbal intensity." What almost all these accolades have in common is that they do not refer to Ballard primarily as a science-fiction writer but as one of "our finest writers of fiction <u>tout court</u> period," in Anthony Burgess's words (D135).

It is clear that we are dealing with an author who transcends genre stereotyping. His admirers see him primarily as a writer, an artist, perhaps even a prophet (in the moral sense). He is accepted as one who speaks for his age, not merely for a certain section of the fiction-reading public. Interviews with Ballard have appeared widely, in everything from <u>Transatlantic Review</u> and <u>Penthouse</u> to <u>Street Life</u> and <u>Search and Destroy: Rebel Youth Culture</u>. He is one of a kind, and it is impossible to confuse him with any other author. Ballard is Ballard, just as, say, Dali is Dali. He defines the terms of the discourse which surrounds him. In this sense he is the most charismatic figure which science fiction has so far produced.

James Graham Ballard was born on 15 November 1930 in Shanghai, China, the only son of James Ballard and Edna (Johnstone) Ballard. His father was the managing director of a subsidiary of a British firm in Shanghai, and the family lived in the International Settlement of the "large, polyglot city" where Ballard remembers being brought up largely by servants. "My memories of childhood are of wandering around the Chinese areas of the city on my own or of being driven out by the Russian chauffeur to visit the abandoned battlefields a few miles away in the countryside. Since the Sino-Japanese hostilities of 1937 the city had been surrounded by Japanese troops, and these years passed against a background of intermittent fighting and political excitement. I have a vague memory of being introduced to Madame Sun Yat-sen."[3]

In 1937 the Japanese had invaded China, although they did not enter the Shanghai International Settlement until the day after Pearl Harbor in December 1941. Ballard recalls: "I was going to do the scripture exam at the end-of-term examinations at the school I went to. Pearl Harbor had just taken place, the previous night, and I heard tanks coming down the street. . . . The Japanese took over the place, and they segmented Shanghai into various districts with barbed wire, so you couldn't move from Zone A to Zone B except at certain times. They'd block off everything for security reasons, and on certain days the only way of going to school was to go to the house of some friends of my parents who lived on one of these border zones--between, I think, the French Concession and the International Settlement. There was an abandoned nightclub, a gambling casino called the Del Monte . . . a huge building in big grounds. We'd climb over the fence . . . and go up the main driveway on the other side of the

Introduction

border zone, and go to school."[4] Such dislocations undoubtedly left a mark on the eleven-year-old boy, and in later years his fiction was to be full of zones of transition, empty buildings, and strange psychological reversals.

After some months the Ballard family was interned by the Japanese in a civilian prisoner-of-war camp, some miles from Shanghai. They were to be held there for almost three years, from 1942 to 1945. Ballard remembers: "Our camp was a former university campus, occupying I suppose about one square mile. In fact, we occupied about two thirds of the campus. There was a section of buildings which for some arbitrary reason--maybe the Japs were short of wire--they'd left out. Something like 15 buildings were on the other side of the wire. You can imagine a little township of big two- and three storey buildings, the nearest of which was about 20 yards away. A complete silent world, which I looked out on every morning and all day from my block. After about a year the Japs agreed to allow these buildings to be used as a school, so we used to enter this place every day and walk through these abandoned rooms. Military equipment was lying around all over the place. I saw rifles being taken out of a well. All rifles were taken away, but spent ammunition, ammunition boxes and bayonets, all the debris of war, was lying around. We used to walk through this totally empty zone. It had been deserted for years. I'm sure that must have had a great impact on me. . . ."

Ballard lived with his parents and young sister in one small room throughout the period of internment. They suffered food shortages and other privations, but in general were not ill-treated. The greatest danger came from American bombers: towards the end of the war an adjacent Japanese airfield was bombed almost continuously. After the Japanese surrender in 1945 the family was released and returned to live in Shanghai: "During this unusual period, an interregnum of two months or so, I made a number of visits to our camp, walking across this empty landscape where units of Japanese, American and both Kuomintang and Communist Chinese forces were busy rounding each other up. During this return to peace Shanghai was one of the most exhilarating places in the world."[5] In his 1968 afterword to the story "End-Game" (C27) Ballard recounts some of the curious incidents of this period in his life: his interest in the psychology of imprisonment was born out of these experiences.

Ballard was sent to England with his mother and sister in 1946. He became a boarder at the Leys School in Cambridge, where he had an early induction into university undergraduate life. His father remained in China until 1950, and for a time Ballard lived with his maternal grandparents in West Bromwich, near Birmingham. He was not favorably impressed by Britain, and recalls: "England was a place that was totally exhausted; the war had drained everything. It seemed very small, and rather narrow mentally. . . . I remember when I landed at Southampton in '46 looking around at the little roads and mean houses by the docks. It was a sad place. The British working

Introduction

class, I suddenly realized, existed. They were nine-tenths of the population and they were appallingly treated. The little side streets away from the docks were lined with what seemed to be black perambulators with doors--too large for perambulators--which I assumed were some sort of mobile coal-scuttle used for bunkering ships. Because cars were all black, you see. English cars were black, whereas American cars were every colour under the sun. . . ." He had grown up in a partly Americanized world. The Europeans in Shanghai drove American cars, bought American magazines and listened to commercial radio stations of an American type. After this, and all the upheaval of war and imprisonment, the placid repressed "home-country" was something of a shock. This teenager must have felt very much an alien.

At school he developed passionate interests in modern literature, in surrealist painting, and in psychoanalysis. He began to write experimental fiction, influenced by Joyce, Kafka, Hemingway. Deciding that he would like to become a psychiatrist, he went up to King's College, Cambridge, to study medicine in 1949. Here he continued writing in his spare time, and in May 1951 succeeded in winning a prize for his short story "The Violent Noon." This prize was awarded by the student newspaper <u>Varsity</u>, which also published the story. "The Violent Noon" is a tale of terrorism in Malaya. It begins:

> Rank and turgid, the morning sweltered in the sunlight. The road turned roughly through the jungle and the dense matted undergrowth swarmed in a tangled mass along the verge of the narrow track. The heavy fetid stench of growth and decay hung in the humid air, slowly swirling round the car as it laboured over the bumps and potholes towards Kuala Lumpur.

It is a crude and over-adjectival description, yet it provides a foretaste of many Ballardian jungles to come (compare the opening of <u>The Drowned World</u>, 1962). Although the style is immature, "The Violent Noon" is an interesting story. The car is ambushed by terrorists and two of its occupants killed. The survivors, the quiet Mrs. Allison (who has lost her husband and child) and the loud-mouthed Hargreaves, are asked to point out their attackers at a police identity parade. Hargreaves is convinced that the men on view are innocent, but Mrs. Allison denounces them all as terrorists. Despite his ultraimperialistic opinions and his expressed contempt for "natives," Hargreaves is deeply disturbed. He and Mrs. Allison have exchanged roles. She, the formerly "soft voiced and gentle," is now advocating indiscriminate revenge, a terrorism in reverse, while he is paralyzed by doubt. A weak character, he eventually concedes:

> The justice of vengeance, he thought. These innocent men must pay for the deaths of others, yield their lives to give a little consolation to this grieving widow. . . .

Introduction

> He turned to the Inspector: "Yes," he said,
> looking sternly at the limp pathetic line of prisoners,
> "these are the bandits, I'm quite sure of it now."[6]

Clearly, at the age of twenty, Ballard was already highly conscious of psychological paradox, a theme which was to emerge in most of his later science fiction and fantasy.

After this small success, Ballard decided to abandon his medical studies. He dropped out of Cambridge in the summer of 1951 and enrolled as a student of English literature at the University of London. "I would have qualified as a doctor, without any doubt, but for the fact that the imaginative pressure to write was so strong. I was beginning to neglect medicine altogether. I was primarily interested in anatomy and physiology--these were the subjects that I did for two years. Once I had covered the basic course in those subjects I found more advanced medicine so technical that it didn't relate to the system of metaphors that, say, anatomy is so rich in. . . . Once you've dissected the cadaver--thorax, abdomen, head and neck, etc.--you go on to more exhaustive anatomy of, say, the inner ear, and the metaphors aren't so generously forthcoming. So I'd had enough of it in two years." Nevertheless his experience as a medical student was not wasted and was to make itself apparent in his later fiction. Ballard soon had enough of London University too, and gave up his English course after just one year. He then embarked on a series of short-term jobs--copywriting, door-to-door selling, etc.-- while living in a bedsitter in London and writing in his spare time. He recalls submitting "experimental" short stories to such journals as Cyril Connolly's <u>Horizon</u>, with no success. In 1953 he joined the Royal Air Force and was sent to Canada to train as a pilot: "I was in a bit of a dead end. I hadn't started reading sf. I was writing short stories, planning a novel like any novice, but I wasn't organized. It struck me--I was very interested in aviation--that it might be worth going into the service for a couple of years, one of those short-service commissions they had then." In fact he did not enjoy RAF life and the most notable result of his stay in Canada was his discovery of the American science-fiction magazines.

Ballard recalls: "There was nothing to do, nothing to read on the newsstands. There were no national papers, just local papers. <u>Time</u> magazine was regarded as wildly highbrow. The only intelligent reading-matter was science fiction! I suddenly devoured it. This was the heyday of these magazines, there were dozens of them. Magazines like <u>Fantastic Universe</u> published some great stuff. Plus <u>Galaxy</u>, which I thought was the best, the most tuned-in to me, and <u>Astounding</u>. . . . A lot of American writers were very good. Ray Bradbury above all--I thought he was head and shoulders above everybody else. He had that wider dimension to his writing which the others, however good, didn't really achieve. I liked Sheckley very much--very droll and witty. Pohl, too, I liked. Matheson I liked-- very much, actually, because he showed you why sf wasn't about outer

Introduction

space, wasn't about the future. So many of his stories were psychological twist stories--I liked those."

This discovery of American sf soon bore fruit. Back in England in 1955, while waiting to be discharged from the RAF, Ballard wrote his first sf story, "Passport to Eternity." As he said of it in his notes to The Best of J.G. Ballard (1977), "this is out-and-out widescreen super-science, wringing every variant I could conceive from the repertory of interplanetary sf. In fact, the original draft was written well before the first science fiction story of mine to be published. Just before I left the RAF in 1955 I tapped this out on a borrowed typewriter at RAF Booker, where cashiered air-crew sat around in underheated huts at a disused airfield."[7] Apparently he did not think to submit the story at the time, though it eventually appeared, slightly revised, in Amazing Stories in 1962 (A29). "Passport to Eternity" is a jeu d'esprit, and one which clearly shows the influence of such Galaxy-magazine writers as Frederik Pohl and Robert Sheckley. Curiously, certain sections also prefigure the tone and concerns of William Burroughs's novels, especially The Ticket That Exploded (1962) and Nova Express (1964). For example:

> (5) SLEEP TRADERS. Unregistered.
> A somewhat shadowy group who handle all dealings on the Blue Market, acting as a general clearing house and buying and selling dreams all through the Galaxy.
> Sample: Like to try a really new sort of dream? The Set Corrani Priests of Theta Piscium will link you up with the sacred electronic thought pools in the Desert of Kish. These mercury lakes are their ancestral memory banks. Surgery is necessary but be careful. Too much cortical damage and the archetypes may get restive. In return one of the Set-Corrani (polysexual delta-humanoids about the size of a walking dragline) will take over your cerebral functions for a long weekend. All these transactions are done on an exchange basis and SLEEP TRADERS charge nothing for the service. But they obviously get a rake-off, and may pump advertising into the lower medullary centres. Whatever they're selling I wouldn't advise anybody to buy.[8]

Years later Ballard was to hail Burroughs as "true genius and first mythographer of the mid-20th century" (C3). The affinity between them, particularly the paranoid sense of fun which they share, is readily apparent in this very early Ballard story.

In the midfifties, however, the immediate literary influence on Ballard's developing sense of the possibilities of science fiction was a large, blackly humorous (and much underrated) novel by Bernard Wolfe called Limbo (1952; published in Britain in 1953 as Limbo '90). Like Ballard, Wolfe combined a strong interest in psychoanalysis (he

Introduction

gained a B.A. in psychology from Yale in 1935) with a passionate concern for the problems of the present day, particularly the problems of war, institutionalized violence, and humanity's possible capacity for self-destruction. Limbo, a dystopian vision of the late twentieth century, is a book which goes gloriously over the top: it is replete with puns, philosophical asides, satire on the American way of life, comments on drugs, sex, and nuclear war, doodles and typographical jokes, medical and psychoanalytical jargon, and landscapes of destruction:

> Miami was part shambles, part ghost town. Through Jerry's binoculars Martine could see that the town had suffered a relatively light and haphazard bombing. . . .
> Here and there along the ragged skyline, jutting up senselessly from the rubble like an oversight, he could make out a lopsided villa, an upended hot-dog stand, the corkscrewed framework of a beach-front luxury hotel, a sagging night club with a fragment of neon tubing on its facade. . . .
> Martine rubbed his eyes and looked again. The thing he had seen was still there, it was moving: it was a giraffe and it seemed to be nibbling at the neon letters on top of the night club.
> The place was not quite deserted. Now he became aware of other movements in and around the debris--an undeniable camel here, an indisputable llama there, what could only be an okapi sprinting improbably down the avenue just beyond. Chewing its cud idiotically alongside a tiled swimming pool, a yak. Further on, standing guard outside a tilted real-estate office, a zebra.
> Flashes of violent colour. Flamingos, pink and preenful, were waddling on erector-set legs along the pock-marked pavements, poking their aristocratic beaks into piles of--what?--one could only guess--sandals and sun-lotion bottles, contraceptives and cash registers.[9]

In his recent comic novel Hello America (1981) Ballard pays a belated tribute to Bernard Wolfe (and to that giraffe!), but in his early years as an sf writer he was certainly influenced by Limbo in several ways. It provided him with a mature and exciting example of what could be achieved in the sf mode. It encouraged him to explore psychological and biological themes, and to write a science fiction which was essentially about the world of the present even if ostensibly set at some future date ("I am writing about the overtone and undertow of now," said Wolfe in a postscript to Limbo, "in the guise of 1990 because it would take decades for a year like 1950 to be milked of its implications."[10]).

On leaving the RAF Ballard once more undertook a series of short-

Introduction

term jobs. Among other things he was a librarian, and a scriptwriter for a scientific film company. He married Helen Mary Matthews--"a great-niece of Cecil Rhodes," according to biographical information contained in Ballard's first British paperback.[11] They soon had a son, James, to be followed in the later 1950s by two daughters, Fay and Beatrice. Meanwhile Ballard continued to write, working on a novel (apparently called <u>You and Me and the Continuum</u>, a title he was to revive ten years later for a short story) and trying his hand at further sf tales. In the summer of 1956 he completed two stories, "Escapement" and "Prima Belladonna," and sent them to John Carnell, then editor of the two leading British sf magazines, <u>New Worlds</u> and <u>Science Fantasy</u>. Carnell promptly bought them and published them, one in each magazine, in December of that year. Thus was Ballard's career as an sf writer launched; Carnell was never to reject a single story of his.

"Prima Belladonna" is the more memorable of the two pieces, and has been reprinted several times since Judith Meril picked it for her 1957 anthology. It is a light tale, set during "the Recess, that world slump of boredom, lethargy and high summer which carried us all so blissfully through ten unforgettable years." The location is Vermilion Sands, a near-future desert resort inhabited by artists and layabouts. The story concerns a beautiful nightclub singer, Jane Ciracylides, and her power over the musical plants which the narrator breeds. It is a witty story, full of delightful technical conceits:

> I was in the shop tuning up a Khan-Arachnid orchid with the UV lamp. It was a difficult bloom, with a normal full range of twenty-four octaves, but like all the tetracot K3 + 25 C5 A9 chorotropes, unless it got a lot of exercise it tended to lapse into neurotic minor key transpositions which were the devil to break. And as the senior bloom in the shop it naturally affected all the others. Invariably when I opened the shop in the mornings it sounded like a madhouse, but as soon as I'd fed the Arachnid and straightened out one or two pH gradients the rest promptly took their cues from it and dimmed down quietly in their control tanks, two-time, three-four, the multi-tones, all in perfect harmony.

And a pleasant lyricism:

> Sometimes in the late afternoons we'd drive out along the beach to the Scented Desert and sit alone by one of the pools, watching the sun fall away behind the reefs and hills, lulling ourselves on the heavy rose-sick air. And when the wind began to blow cool across the sand we'd slip down into the water, bathe ourselves and drive back to town, filling the streets and cafe terraces with jasmine and musk-rose and

Introduction

>   helianthemum.
>   On other evenings we'd go down to one of the quiet
> bars at Lagoon West, and have supper out on the flats,
> and Jane would tease the waiters and sing honeybirds
> and angelcakes to the children who came in across the
> sand to watch her.¹²

This story immediately established Ballard's credentials as a writer. Few other contributors to Carnell's magazines could exhibit the ease, the fluidity, the range of reference and the wealth of invention of the young Ballard. In retrospect, "Prima Belladonna" is a minor story, but, appearing when and where it did, it must have had considerable impact on those that read it. (A small irony: Cyril Connolly, reviewing Judith Merril's The Best of the Best for a British newspaper, circa 1968, picked out this particular story for praise. It is unlikely that he recognized the hand of a writer whose work he had rejected from Horizon.¹³)

Ballard met John Carnell shortly after he began writing for the latter's magazines, and Carnell succeeded in finding him an editorial job with the parent company, McLaren's. After about six months Ballard moved on to become Assistant Editor of Chemistry and Industry, the weekly publication of a leading chemical society. He was to work there for about four years, his longest stint of regular employment. During this period he continued as a weekend writer of short stories, though he would occasionally try his had at other creative ventures. A collage which he produced in 1958, made up partly of clippings from American scientific journals, was eventually published in 1978 (B15). This is an interesting item, as it carries references to several Ballard "characters" (e.g., "Coma, the million-year girl," later to appear in "The Voices of Time") and contains phrases ("Mr F. is Mr F.," "beach Hamlet," etc.) which crop up in later work. Although Ballard was constrained by the traditional short-story formula of the sf magazines he was already interested in producing fiction of a more unconventional kind. In part, he was inspired at this time by the early pop artists, Eduardo Paolozzi and Richard Hamilton among others, whose work he saw at the Institute of Contemporary Arts and elsewhere. Certainly there was little to stimulate him in the sf field of this period, and he appears to have lost interest in magazine sf by the end of the 1950s.

Ballard recalls: "I began writing in '56, '57, round about the time of Sputnik 1--which seemed to confirm everything that the sf fans, writers and publishers in America believed in: this was the Millennium, it had arrived. It would have seemed, superficially, the worst time for moving away from writing a science-fictional art based on space, interplanetary travel, the far future and what-have-you. It would have seemed the worst time to stop writing that kind of thing, and yet [Carnell] encouraged me, said go ahead. One tends to forget how resistant to change and experiment of any kind sf is. That's the paradox: it ought to be dedicated to change and

Introduction

novelty and experiment. You found in the 50s and 60s in the States an absolute resistance to any kind of novelty. Carnell was unique in giving me this freedom to write anything I wanted to."

Most of Ballard's stories were resolutely earthbound. Tales like "Build-Up" and "Manhole 69" contain no images of space-travel and rocketry, much less robots and ray-guns. By pursuing his own concerns, into the human mind and its perceptions of time and environment, he was single-handedly creating what would later be known as the sf New Wave. However, he did write one interplanetary story in this period, and a spectacular one it is too. "The Waiting Grounds" (1959) is about two men on a far planet who stumble upon a sort of Galactic Temple. The narrator experiences a vision of all time and space and the future evolution of intelligent life into "a vast mantle of ideation." This story, slightly reminiscent of Olaf Stapledon's Star Maker (1937) was almost like a purging from Ballard's system of all the grander cosmic themes of sf. It was probably necessary for him to have written it.

Nineteen-sixty saw a marked increase in the number (and the overall quality) of Ballard's stories. The long pieces "The Sound-Sweep" and "The Voices of Time" appeared in that year, together with a number of lesser tales. Many would agree that "The Voices of Time" really represents Ballard's arrival as a major author. It is a dense, imaginative, and very moving exploration of biological themes, desert landscapes, and humanity's sense of its place in the universe. Many Ballardian "properties" are evoked--drained swimming pools, Jungian mandalas, eccentric architecture, "terminal documents"--and the whole piece works (as Charles Nicol has pointed out, D116) in the manner of poetry. It is one of the masterpieces of modern imaginative writing. And it was immediately followed by another masterpiece: "Studio 5, the Stars" (1961) was a return to the Vermilion Sands setting of "Prima Belladonna," and is probably the best story he has written in that particular mode. It combines the humor and light inventiveness of the earlier tale with the hallucinatory desert landscapes of "The Voices of Time." The next story, "Deep End," is almost as haunting. By this time, mid-1961, Ballard had established his terrain. It was clear that he was an image-maker of phenomenal power, capable of producing pictures in the reader's mind as original and as "valid" as the paintings of the surrealists he so admired: Dali, Ernst, Tanguy, Delvaux.

In 1960 Ballard had moved with his wife and three young children to Shepperton, a quiet suburb some miles to the west of London. He was still working in central London, though, and finding it increasingly difficult to devote as much time as he might wish to writing. He remembers: "I was thirty or thereabouts, and I realized I was getting nowhere. We'd come to live here, out of necessity. We were driven out of London--once you had small children you were anathema. I had this very long railway journey up to central London to my office every day. There I was, coming home with these small

Introduction

children running around--and I was absolutely exhausted. My wife had had all these babies and she was tired. I knew the one thing I had to do was make a complete break and become a full-time writer. I knew I'd never write a novel--a serious novel--while I was not getting home till 8 o'clock in the evening. I was just too tired. But I had this fortnight's holiday coming up, and my wife, as a joke, said 'why don't you write a novel in a fortnight?' So I thought: 'Good, that's sensible talking.' I'd already got, through Carnell, certain contacts with the American paperback people and I had a feeling that if I wrote a novel I could sell it, even if I wasn't going to get very much money. So I said: 'I'll write a novel in ten days, six thousand words a day, during this holiday,' and I thought 'what shall I do?' So I had this idea about a whirlwind. I thought I'd use all the clichés there are, the standard narrative conventions, and I sat down at the typewriter and I wrote the book. Six thousand words a day, which is quite a lot. I kept it up, and when I got back to the office I had the manuscript of a novel, which Carnell sold."

The Wind from Nowhere was serialized in New Worlds in September/ October 1961 (as "Storm-Wind"), then published in book form by Berkley paperbacks of New York in January 1962. It is a potboiler, a disaster story in the mode of John Wyndham's The Kraken Wakes (1953) and John Christopher's The Death of Grass (1956), popular sf thrillers which had sold well in Britain. Although the characterization and the plot are perfunctory some of the descriptions of devastation are extremely vivid. The eponymous wind is felt. But in this novel Ballard scarcely uses the disaster as an analogue for a state of mind, as he had already done in such short stories as "Deep End" and was to continue to do so successfully in his next three novels. The important fact about The Wind from Nowhere is that it did allow him to give up his job and become a full-time writer. It cemented his early relationship with Berkley Books, who promptly followed the novel with a collection of Ballard's short stories, The Voices of Time, in February 1962. The income from these books, and from increased magazine sales, was enough to fund the writing of his first serious novel, The Drowned World.

Ballard's first books coincided with his first story sales to America. "The Garden of Time" was published in The Magazine of Fantasy and Science Fiction, and he went on to sell half a dozen stories to Amazing and Fantastic over the next year (magazines edited by Cele Goldsmith, a percipient lady who in that same annus mirabilis, 1962, was to discover such important new American writers as Thomas M. Disch, Ursula Le Guin, and Roger Zelazny). Ballard's first two years as a freelance writer were to be the most productive of his whole career. Brilliant stories were spilling out of him at an extraordinary rate: "Billennium" and "The Cage of Sand" in New Worlds, "The Watch-Towers" in Science Fantasy, "The Thousand Dreams of Stellavista" and "The Singing Statues" in Amazing and Fantastic, plus others. At the same time he was working on his novel.

Introduction

<u>The Drowned World</u> was published by Berkley in August 1962, and by Victor Gollancz, London, in January 1963. In America it went unnoticed (just another garish "paperback original") but in Britain, where it had the dignity of hard covers and of reviews in the <u>Observer</u>, the <u>Times Literary Supplement</u> and elsewhere, it created something of a stir. Kingsley Amis called Ballard "one of the brightest new stars in postwar fiction" (<u>not</u> "science fiction," as the frequent misquotation has it), and likened the novel to the work of Joseph Conrad (D8). Ballard remarks: "It's a funny thing, but when <u>The Drowned World</u> was published people said it was heavily influenced by Conrad. Oddly enough, though I was 31 or 32, I'd never read a word of Conrad. I remember Victor Gollancz the publisher, taking me out to lunch after they'd bought <u>The Drowned World</u>, and turning to me jokingly and saying 'well, you stole the whole thing from Conrad.' I thought 'oh, what's this?,' and going away and actually reading some Conrad--which I found rather heavy going, though he's obviously a great writer with a unique evocative style--I could see a resemblance. But that's partly because if you're going to try and build up the atmosphere of steaming jungles, there's only one way of doing it."

Whether or not there's only one way of doing it, there is no doubt that in <u>The Drowned World</u> Ballard did it supremely well. The tropical jungle and fetid swamps, which in this novel are depicted as having overtaken London, are among the finest imaginary landscapes in modern literature. They shade into the surrealist landscapes of Ernst and Delvaux, which Ballard explicitly evokes, and they make a felt reality of the "metabiological" theme--of human devolution, and a night-time descent down the spinal column. Although the author's concerns are metaphysical, his fictions are solidly there and brilliantly lit. The language throughout is rich and evocative, dense with similes and asides, and the characters, while emblematic to a degree, are vividly drawn. The behaviour of the characters worried some readers, however: they seem to conspire with the disaster which is overtaking their world, and instead of fighting against it they accept it.

Ballard says, of this and later novels: "When <u>The Drowned World</u> was accepted by my American publisher he said 'yes, it's great, but why don't we have a happy ending? Have the hero going north instead of south into the jungle and sun.' He thought I'd made a slight technical mistake by a slip of the pen and had the hero going in the wrong direction. I said: 'No. God, this <u>is</u> a happy story. . . .' Usually disaster stories are treated straight, and everyone is running for the hills or out of the hills or whatever. If it's going to be cold they're all putting on overcoats. I use the form because I deliberately want to invert it--that's the whole point of the novels. The heroes, for psychological reasons of their own, embrace the particular transformation. These are stories of huge psychic transformations, and I use this external transformation of the landscape to reflect, and marry with, the internal transformation, the psycho-

Introduction

logical transformation, of the characters. This is what the subject-matter of these books is; they're transformation stories rather than disaster stories. In The Day of the Triffids I think it's probably fair to say that there's absolutely no psychological depth. The characters react to the changes that are taking place, but they are not in any psychological way involved with the proliferating vegetation or whatever else is going on. My novels are completely different, and they only use the form superficially."

The modest financial success of The Drowned World (Gollancz had to reprint it within a month) led to the publication of Ballard's first British volume of short stories later in 1963. It was entitled The Four-Dimensional Nightmare and contained a mix of the best stories from the three American paperback collections The Voices of Time, Billenium and Passport to Eternity. This also received praise, Kingsley Amis referring to it in the Observer as proof of Ballard's standing as "an imaginative talent of great depth and originality" (D12). Meanwhile Ballard's output of new short stories was as fecund as ever. "The Subliminal Man" in New Worlds proved that he could write admonitory sf of the Galaxy type as well as anyone. "A Question of Re-Entry" in Fantastic contains a superb description of the Amazon rain-forest and is also an ironic commentary on the space program. "The Time-Tombs" in Worlds of If and "Now Wakes the Sea" in F & SF are atmospheric tales of the mysteries of time. "The Encounter" in Amazing (later to be retitled "The Venus Hunters") is a witty commentary on the sf genre itself and on the obsessions of UFO-spotters. In all he published ten new stories in 1963, and each has something to commend it.

Earlier, in the May 1962 issue of New Worlds, Ballard had published his first nonfiction statement. This guest editorial (C1) is in fact a manifesto for the as-yet-unchristened New Wave. In clear tones Ballard enunciates a credo:

> I think science fiction should turn its back on space, on inter-stellar travel, extraterrestrial life forms, galactic wars and the overlap of these ideas that spreads across the margins of nine-tenths of magazine sf. . . .
> I've often wondered why sf shows so little of the experimental enthusiasm which has characterized painting, music and the cinema during the last four or five decades, particularly as these have become wholeheartedly speculative, more and more concerned with the creation of new states of mind, new levels of awareness, constructing fresh symbols and languages where the old cease to be valid. Similarly, I think science fiction must jettison its present narrative forms and plots. Most of these are far too explicit to express any subtle interplay of character and theme. Devices such as time travel and telepathy,

Introduction

for example, save the writer the trouble of describing the inter-relationships of time and space indirectly. And by a curious paradox they prevent him from using his imagination at all. . . .

The biggest developments of the immediate future will take place, not on the Moon or Mars, but on Earth, and it is <u>inner</u> space, not outer, that needs to be explored. The only truly alien planet is Earth. In the past the scientific bias of sf has been towards the physical sciences--rocketry, electronics, cybernetics--and the emphasis should switch to the biological sciences, particularly to imaginative and fictional treatments of them, which is what is implied by the term science <u>fiction</u>. Accuracy, that last refuge of the unimaginative, doesn't matter a hoot. What we need is not science fact but more science fiction. . . .

More precisely, I'd like to see sf becoming abstract and "cool," inventing completely fresh situations and contexts that illustrate its theme obliquely. For example, instead of treating time like a sort of glorified scenic railway, I'd like to see it used for what it is, one of the perspectives of the personality, and the elaboration of concepts such as the time zone, deep time and archaeo-psychic time. I'd like to see more psycho-literary ideas, more meta-biological and meta-chemical concepts, private time-systems, synthetic psychologies and space-times, more of the remote, sombre half-worlds one glimpses in the paintings of schizophrenics, all in all a complete speculative poetry and fantasy of science.[14]

One can see Ballard practicing what he preaches in two important works which appeared in 1964--the story "The Terminal Beach" (<u>New Worlds</u>, March) and the novel <u>The Burning World</u> (Berkley Books, August; retitled <u>The Drought</u> when published in Britain the following year). "The Terminal Beach" is a meditation on the theme of nuclear Armageddon; it contains no overt "statements," yet it is one of the most memorable works of fiction to be inspired by The Bomb. Set on the Pacific Island of Eniwetok, where the United States carried out nuclear tests during the 1950s, the story is told in "nonlinear" fashion. Traven, an ex-bomber-pilot, arrives at the island, where he has evidently decided to maroon himself among the concrete blocks, fused sand and wrecked aircraft. He seems to be seeking some kind of solace, for he carries the burdens of the world on his shoulders:

> The Pre-Third: the period was characterized in Traven's mind above all by its moral and psychological inversions, by its sense of the whole of history, and in particular of the immediate future--the two decades, 1945-65--suspended from the quivering

Introduction

>   volcano's lip of World War III. Even the death of his
>   wife and six-year-old son in a motor accident seemed
>   only part of this immense synthesis of the historical
>   and psychic zero, the frantic highways where each
>   morning they met their deaths the advance causeways
>   to the global armageddon.[15]

Little happens, but Traven's environment, a sombre half-world indeed, is gradually revealed to the reader in a slow, progressive description which builds to quite stunning poetic effect. In a sense, the island is Traven's mind: he is stranded on a terminal beach of his own soul. Here Ballard creates a synthetic psychology and space-time, a cool abstract context which illustrates his theme obliquely. In some ways this is the supreme Ballard short story.

His novel The Drought is rather like a drier, more stripped-down version of The Drowned World. Once more a biospheric disaster provides the sf rationale, but the significance of this novel is not to be found in any passing comments Ballard makes on the topic of environmental pollution. The significance lies in the fantastic landscapes of sand and salt and ash, and in the strange psychodramas which the characters enact in the foreground. An sf device merely serves the purpose of creating a truly alien Earth.

Nineteen sixty-four was another rich year. In addition to the works just mentioned he published eight short stories, including such small masterpieces as "The Drowned Giant" and "The Gioconda of the Twilight Noon" (both original in his second Gollancz collection, The Terminal Beach, published in June of that year). He also published "Equinox," a short novel later to be expanded into The Crystal World (1966). But 1964 brought a major change in Ballard's personal life. Mary Ballard died, and he was left with the sole care of their three children. He appears to have written nothing during the latter part of 1964, and comparatively little throughout 1965. His first phase as a writer was ending, a second about to begin.

In May 1964 the magazine New Worlds had changed publishers and editors. Michael Moorcock, the twenty-four-year-old editor-designate, was a great admirer of Ballard's work. He was determined to change the character of Carnell's magazine but equally determined that Ballard should remain its leading contributor. Ballard explains the genesis of his fourth novel, The Crystal World: "Originally I wrote it as a short story, 'The Illuminated Man.' Then Mike Moorcock, when he took over New Worlds as a small-format magazine, asked me to write a lead serial. I didn't want to write a novel at that point. My mind was already beginning to change, I was starting to think about the Atrocity Exhibition type of approach. . . . So I said to him: 'I'll expand this short story if you like'—because I'd got a lot more ideas. I felt that the short version was incomplete; it was too much of a science-fiction fantasy. I wanted to develop more of the serious implications of the idea—which I did, I think, in that

serial ['Equinox']. When I'd done that it occurred to me--or it
occurred to my agent--that I'd got a novel. So I then expanded it
even further. It was a peculiar way of writing a novel, but it just
happened that way."

The Crystal World seems to have marked Ballard's "arrival" in
America, in the way that The Drowned World had in Britain three years
earlier. It was his first book to be published initially as a hardcover in the United States, and it garnered serious reviews. In the
pages of F & SF Judith Merril hailed Ballard as sf's foremost artist.
The novel was also well reviewed in Britain, where it was Ballard's
second book to be published by Jonathan Cape (a publisher who, unlike
Gollancz, did not label his work as science fiction). The novel's
attraction lies in its striking imagery. Where The Drought had seemed
a comparatively flat and arid book, The Crystal World offered a
sumptuous visual feast. The descriptions of jeweled forests, animals,
and men appealed at a time when "psychedelic" was a newly fashionable
term. Suddenly the world (a part of it at any rate) had caught up
with Ballard. He was already beginning to influence younger writers.
Moorcock's New Worlds carried occasional stories which aped his
manner, and others which simply took advantage of the possibilities
he had opened up. By 1966 the New Wave was in full swing in Britain
(it reached America slightly later). Ballard helped it along with
his critical writing, as well as by his creative example. He had
begun to review sf regularly for the Guardian newspaper in the spring
of 1965, and his occasional articles in New Worlds (on William
Burroughs, Wyndham Lewis, the surrealist painters, and other topics)
broadened the horizons of many sf readers.

Ballard recalls, with reference to New Worlds: "The late 1960s
was a period of totally unprecendented excitement in almost every
field. I think by the time the change from a small to a large-format
magazine took place [July 1967] it was really the final break with
the American-dominated sf of the 40s and 50s--the break was complete,
the battle had been won. The group of writers that Moorcock published in New Worlds, myself included, had proved their point, and
the old guard had run out of gas. At that time New Worlds was not
just the most exciting sf magazine in the world--it made all the
American mags like Analog seem terribly dull--it was one of the most
exciting magazines of any kind in this country and was extremely
lucky to have Mike Moorcock running it. I think, with the benefit of
hindsight, it ceased to be an sf magazine at all, even within my
elastic definition of the term, and became something much closer to
avant-garde experimental writing. Perhaps that was inevitable."
But it wasn't just New Worlds: suddenly Ballard was writing for
literary periodicals, small poetry magazines, counter-culture papers.
He became the prose editor of Ambit in 1966 (a post he still retains);
he contributed pieces to Encounter, Transatlantic Review, The Running
Man, Ronald Reagan: The Magazine of Poetry, and International Times
during the latter 1960s. He also had two stories in Playboy.

Introduction

His principal work in these years was the series of fifteen pieces which went to make up The Atrocity Exhibition, published by Cape in 1970. This began with "You and Me and the Continuum" in Impulse (the retitled Science Fantasy) for March 1966. Most of these pieces, which Ballard was later to term "condensed novels," were non-linear stories chopped up into headlined half-page paragraphs. They constituted a new form of prose poetry, and were in terms of technique as much of an advance on "The Terminal Beach" as that story had been on "The Voices of Time." Most of them featured the same lead character--a doctor, perhaps suffering from a nervous breakdown, whose name varied but always began with a "T": Traven, Tallis, Travers, Talbot, etc. Through the crazed vision of this protagonist we see the world of the 1960s media landscape on a number of different levels and from several peculiar angles. He is obsessed with motorways and multi-storey car-parks; with the bodies of film-stars and politicians; with "the time-music of the quasars" and with strange "assassination weapons" and "fusing devices." He is also haunted by other characters, who often seem like figments of his own mind. Here is an example from "The Death Module" (New Worlds, July 1967; later retitled "Notes Towards a Mental Breakdown"):

> Algebra of the Sky. At dawn Trabert found himself driving along an entry highway into the deserted city: terrain of shacks and filling stations, overhead wires like some forgotten algebra of the sky. When the helicopters appeared he left the car and set off on foot. Sirens wailing, white-doored squad cars screamed past him, neuronic icons on the spinal highway. Fifty yards ahead, the young man in the astronaut's suit plodded along the asphalt verge. Pursued by helicopters and strange police, they took refuge in an empty stadium. Sitting in the deserted stand, Trabert watched the young man pace at random around the pitch, replicating some meaningless labyrinth as if trying to focus his own identity. Outside Kline walked in the sculpture garden of the air terminal. His aloof, cerebral face warned Trabert that his rendezvous with Coma and Xero would soon take place.[16]

It is powerful, mysterious stuff, and this form of writing excited some readers--for example the poet George MacBeth, who produced a BBC radio program devoted to Ballard in 1967[17]--while it offended others, particularly the sf traditionalists. One piece, provocatively titled "Why I Want to Fuck Ronald Reagan," was produced as a little booklet in 1968 and was cited for obscenity in a court case against the Unicorn Bookshop, Brighton (run by the Canadian poet Bill Butler, himself a contributor to New Worlds).

The Atrocity Exhibition received rather poor reviews when it was published in Britain in July 1970. Some reviewers found it obscure,

Introduction

others thought it pretentious. Ballard comments: "Obviously a book like that is not going to be as popular as a conventionally-written book. . . . [But] I found those stories in The Atrocity Exhibition produced more response from people than anything else I've written. People whom I'd never had any contact with, from all over the world, took the trouble to get in touch with me, which is a sure test of something. I felt the response to that book was better and larger than anything else I've ever had. In fact I was encouraged to go on, because as I wrote the stories over a period of four or five years the response grew. . . . People questioned me about why I broke everything up. I tended to exaggerate a bit in the hope of getting something through--I may have made over-large claims for nonlinear narrative, or whatever you want to call it--but basically I still feel that the subject-matter comes first and the technique you adopt comes second. It was the subject-matter of those stories that defined the way in which they were written. At the same time it's true that once you develop an approach like that it, of itself, opens up so much more territory. I once said those condensed novels (as I called them) are like ordinary novels with the unimportant pieces left out. But it's more than that: when you get the important pieces together, really together--not separated by great masses of 'he said, she said,' opening and shutting of doors, 'following morning' and all this stuff, the great tide of forward conventional narration--it achieves critical mass as it were, it begins to ignite and you get more things being generated. You're getting crossovers and linkages between unexpected and previously totally unrelated things, events, elements of the narration, ideas that in themselves begin to generate new matter. . . . It was very exciting to do. But those stories were written very much about their period, which was the middle-to-late 60s."

In the four years following The Atrocity Exhibition Ballard wrote no new short stories. A number of conventional stories had appeared at intervals during the late sixties, including such notable pieces as "Storm-Bird, Storm-Dreamer," "The Cloud-Sculptors of Coral D," "The Dead Astronaut," and "The Killing Ground," but no major new story-collection had been published--The Disaster Area (Cape, 1967) consisted for the most part of old, pre-"Terminal Beach" material. In 1971 Ballard gathered together his Vermilion Sands stories, two of which had appeared in The Four-Dimensional Nightmare, and they were published as a paperback-original collection by Berkley Books. This was eventually issued in revised form in Britain by Cape in 1973. Throughout this period Ballard was at work on his first new novel in half a dozen years: Crash. And when that book appeared, in June 1973, it came as a shock.

In Crash Ballard had taken some of the subject-matter of The Atrocity Exhibition and reworked it exhaustively into a long, more-or-less conventional narrative. It is told in the first person and the protagonist's name is "James Ballard." Many British and American readers found it extremely discomfiting. Crash is not merely an "exposé" of our indifference to death and destruction on the roads:

Introduction

it is a no-holds-barred confrontation of our most ambiguous attitudes to such events. It explores the "attractions" of automobile accidents, using the car and our modern road-systems as symbols of the convergence between humanity's secret desires and its technological artifacts. The result is a persistent, irritating, and nettling book; it gets under the skin, and is, as they say, unforgettable. Ballard explains his intentions: "When I set out to write Crash I wanted to write a book in which there was nowhere to hide. I wanted the reader, once I'd got him inside the book, never to lose sight of the subject-matter. It would have been very easy to write a conventional book about car-crashes, in which it was quite clear that the author was on the side of sanity, justice, and against injuring small children, deaths on the road, bad driving, etc. What could be easier? I chose to completely accept the demands of the subject-matter, which was to provoke the reader by saying that these car-crashes are good for you, you thoroughly enjoy them, they make your sex-life richer, they represent part of the marriage between sex, the human organism and technology. I say all these things in order to provoke the reader and also to test him. There may be truth in some of these sentiments, disagreeable though they are to consider. Nobody likes that: they'll think 'God, the man's mad'--but any other way of writing that book would have been a cop-out I think."

Most English-language critics were duly horrified (although one detects a slowly growing admiration for the novel over the past decade, as though it literally takes years to sink in). In France, however, the reaction was completely different. A number of Ballard's books had been translated into French but had attracted little serious attention. When Crash appeared there in 1974, in a translation by Robert Louit, it took the French by storm. It was reviewed at length in most of the leading newspapers, and hailed by some as a masterpiece. French journalists began to cross the Channel to interview Ballard repeatedly. The novel sold more copies than any previous work of his had done, in any language, and it was bought by Livre de poche, the leading French reprint publisher. There was a rush to obtain translation rights to Ballard's other books, and The Drought, Vermilion Sands, The Atrocity Exhibition, and even The Wind from Nowhere were all issued in swift succession. The French saw Crash and its immediate successors, Concrete Island (1974) and High-Rise (1975), as determined attempts to make literary use of the new technological landscapes of Europe, to comment on the psychopathology of everyday life in the 1970s. They seem to have been much less fazed by Ballard's departure from the bourgeois norms of what constitutes "a good novel." Also, being less familiar with his early work, they probably had fewer preconceptions about Ballard the fantasist, Ballard the exotic landscape artist.

Concrete Island and High-Rise, both urban nightmares (though somewhat less intense than Crash), brought to an end Ballard's second phase as a writer. In late 1974 he began to write short stories once more. He also began to abandon the contemporary concrete scene, and

Introduction

to produce stories more easily definable as sf. The novella "The Ultimate City" (published as an original in the collection Low-Flying Aircraft, 1976) is a curiously mellow work, full of images of birds and flowers. During this period Ballard became an associate editor of the new literary magazine Bananas (begun by his friend, the novelist Emma Tennant) and the series of stories which he published there showed a return to more speculative themes. "Low-Flying Aircraft" (1975) is a straight sf story, about mutant children and a population implosion in a future Europe. Some pieces are horrifying--for example, "The Air Disaster," about the crash of a giant airliner--while others are jokey--for example, "The Index" (1977), about a shadowy figure who has influenced public events through his contacts with all the great persons of the century.

By this time Ballard had long since given up the sf magazines, and his stories appeared solely in low-circulation avant-garde periodicals. The sf field had ossified during the 1970s, New Worlds and the New Wave were no more, and Ballard seemed to be increasingly out of touch with the American scene. Although he has influenced numerous younger writers (including some Americans) the sf establishment has never rewarded him in any way. He has never come within striking distance of a Hugo Award; and while three of his works were nominated for Nebula Awards in the 1960s ("The Drowned Giant," The Crystal World and "The Cloud-Sculptors of Coral D") none succeeded in winning. No doubt this causes him little concern; he seems to relish an anti-establishment stance, and enjoys confounding expectations. Certainly his 1979 novel, The Unlimited Dream Company, came as a surprise. It is an out-and-out fantasy, a tale of magical transformations, of mysticism and flight.

The Unlimited Dream Company will probably come to be seen as one of the masterpieces of the Ballard canon. Set in the present day, in Ballard's home town of Shepperton, it is a magnificent rhapsody on the absurd ambitions of the Self, and it is (in Anthony Burgess's words) "as basic as a dream of the whole human race."[18] The narrator, a twenty-five-year-old misfit, crashes his stolen airplane into the River Thames. He apparently dies and is reborn. Quickened by strange powers, he finds himself unable to leave Shepperton and he begins to remould the lives of its inhabitants. There is some suggestion that this is all a split-second fantasy in the dying brain of the illicit aviator, but Ballard does not drive home any "rational" explanation. The situation allows Ballard to give full rein to his inventive powers. Shepperton is remade as a jungle town, filled with colorful birds and animals. The hero teaches the townsfolk to fly, absorbing them into his body then expelling them once more. There is a continual dark undertone: love and hate merge and become indistinguishable, giving of oneself becomes the ultimate selfishness. It is a novel full of paradox, utterly original and baffling. It also contains much humor.

The latest novel, Hello America (1981), is intended as a light

xxx

Introduction

entertainment. Ballard originally meant it to be a novella, to be published as a large-format illustrated book. But the publisher who commissioned it went bankrupt, and meanwhile the novel grew. It is Ballard's wry tribute to the American Dream, an exploration of a future United States where everything has been inverted. It is his most science-fictional novel in many years, and also his slightest. Although it contains much good writing and some excellent scene-painting, it also displays a number of Ballard's weaknesses as a novelist: his difficulties with "conventional" characterization and plot-structuring. Some of the jokes are rather rote and flat. In a novel such as this the weaknesses are thrown into relief because the main thrust of the work doesn't have the urgency, the carefully controlled "madness" of so much of the earlier work. In books like Crash and The Unlimited Dream Company Ballard's failings, judged by conventional novelistic yardsticks, scarcely matter: the works are carried along by the power of the central obsessions. This is untrue of Hello America, though no doubt many readers will find it enjoyable and it may even turn out to be one of his more popular novels.

Ballard's most recent book, at this time of writing, is a collection of short stories which Cape published in September 1982. It is entitled Myths of the Near Future and it is perhaps his best new collection since The Terminal Beach in 1964. Ballard still excels in the short-story form, and his recent works are as pointed and disturbing, and as sharply engaged with contemporary reality, as the stories of his "classic" period of the early 1960s. He still has the unerring ability to pick out valid themes--themes which often seem more cogent three or four years later than they did at the time of writing. Thus "Theatre of War" (1977), about a strife-torn Britain of the near future, anticipated in some ways the serious street-riots of summer 1981; and "Having a Wonderful Time" (1978), the ultimate unemployment story, predated by some two years the soaring rate of those out of work in the United Kingdom and elsewhere.

Some readers, including the present bibliographer, believe J.G. Ballard to be a great writer, a potential classic (as Julian Rathbone claims, D164) whose works may still be read 200 years from now. He is certainly the most significant author to emerge from genre science fiction. Why? There are many reasons: he astonishes; he entertains; he disturbs; he brings wide intellectual resources to bear on commonplace genre materials, transforming them; he turns memorable phrases; he creates truly haunting landscapes; he transforms the everyday furniture of our lives into resonant literary symbols; he dramatizes the neuroses and paranoias of our age, often before we are fully aware of them; he brings previously taboo subjects, especially the psychological implications of scientific and technical advance, into the purview of the modern novel; he is relentlessly iconoclastic, forever twisting the blade; he punctures complacency and "normality," opening unexpected imaginative vistas and thus enriching our lives;

Introduction

above all (as I have written elsewhere) he returns our world to us, vivid and estranged. Ballard's overall message could be grossly simplified as: Be aware, and perhaps beware, of your own secret desires. Which could be further boiled down to the classical injunction: Know thyself.

Notes

1. J.G. Ballard. Chronopolis (New York: Berkley, 1972). The endorsement by Moorcock appears on the flyleaf.
2. J.G. Ballard, The Best Short Stories of J.G. Ballard (New York: Holt, Rinehart & Winston, 1978). Susan Sontag's endorsement appears on the back cover.
3. John Wakeman, ed., World Authors, 1950-1970 (New York: H.W. Wilson, 1975), p. 109. The entry on Ballard contains some autobiographical quotation.
4. James Goddard and David Pringle, "An Interview with J.G. Ballard, 4 January 1975," in J.G. Ballard: The First Twenty Years, ed. Goddard and Pringle (Hayes, Middlesex: Bran's Head Books, 1976), pp. 8-35. In this introduction all the subsequent quotations from Ballard are taken from this 1975 interview, unless otherwise indicated.
5. Wakeman, World Authors, p. 109.
6. J.G. Ballard, "The Violent Noon," Varsity, 26 May 1951, p. 9.
7. J.G. Ballard, The Best of J.G. Ballard (London: Futura, 1977), p. 288.
8. The Best of J.G. Ballard, pp. 300-301.
9. Bernard Wolfe, Limbo (New York: Ace Books, n.d.), pp. 87-88.
10. Wolfe, Limbo, p. 413.
11. J.G. Ballard, The Drowned World (Harmondsworth: Penguin, 1965). The biographical information on the flyleaf also contains this statement: "He believes that science fiction is the apocalyptic literature of the 20th century, the authentic language of Auschwitz, Eniwetok and Aldermaston. He also believes that inner space, not outer, is the real subject of science fiction."
12. J.G. Ballard, The Four-Dimensional Nightmare (Harmondsworth: Penguin, 1965), pp. 83, 86, 94-95. In the revised version of "Prima Belladonna" which Ballard later included in Vermilion Sands (1973) some of this youthful exuberance is thinned down.
13. I don't have a reference for this and am relying on memory. The newspaper was probably the Sunday Times.
14. J.G. Ballard, "Which Way to Inner Space?" New Worlds 40, no. 118 (May 1962), pp. 117-18.
15. J.G. Ballard, The Terminal Beach (London: Gollancz, 1964), pp. 136-37.
16. J.G. Ballard, The Atrocity Exhibition (London: Panther, 1972), pp. 55-56.
17. Again, I'm relying on memory here. The whole of "You and Me and the Continuum" was read out, as I recall, and it came across very well indeed.
18. J.G. Ballard, The Unlimited Dream Company (London: Cape, 1979).

Introduction

Burgess's endorsement appears on the dust-jacket flap.

For all the other biographical information given here I am indebted to the interviews with J.G. Ballard listed in Part C of this bibliography, and to my own conversations with J.G. Ballard and with his agent, John Wolfers.

Checklist of Books

This is a quick-reference chronological listing of J.G. Ballard's books. The numbers on the left refer to the appropriate entries in the main fiction bibliography, which follows.

A23   The Wind from Nowhere. 1962. Novel.

A26   The Voices of Time. 1962. Collection.

A34   The Drowned World. 1962. Novel.

A35   Billenium. 1962. Collection.

A41   The Four-Dimensional Nightmare. 1963. Collection.

A46   Passport to Eternity. 1963. Collection.

A54   Terminal Beach (U.S.). 1964. Collection.

A56   The Terminal Beach (U.K.). 1964. Collection.

A62   The Burning World. 1964. Novel.

A67   The Drought (revised edition of The Burning World). 1965.

A71   The Crystal World. 1966. Novel.

A72   The Impossible Man. 1966. Collection.

A83   The Day of Forever. 1967. Collection.

A85   The Disaster Area. 1967. Collection.

A88   The Overloaded Man. 1967. Collection.

A107 The Atrocity Exhibition. 1970. Collection.

A110 Vermilion Sands. 1971. Collection.

Checklist of Books

A111 Chronopolis. 1971. Collection.

A112 Love and Napalm: Export USA (retitle of The Atrocity Exhibition). 1972.

A114 Crash. 1973. Novel.

A116 Concrete Island. 1974. Novel.

A122 High-Rise. 1975. Novel.

A127 Low-Flying Aircraft. 1976. Collection.

A131 The Best of J.G. Ballard. 1977. Collection.

A139 The Best Short Stories of J.G. Ballard. 1978. Collection.

A140 The Unlimited Dream Company. 1979. Novel.

A143 The Venus Hunters. 1980. Collection

A146 Hello America. 1981. Novel.

A149 Myths of the Near Future. 1982. Collection.

Interview with J. G. Ballard

I interviewed J.G. Ballard at his home in Shepperton, Middlesex, on 14 June 1979. We began by talking about science-fiction criticism and about the journal Foundation in particular. . . .

JGB: I thought the piece by Michael Moorcock, that long article on the history of New Worlds under him, was a remarkable effort of accurate recall. Bearing in mind that memory plays most of us false, particularly in the case of something like the whole New Wave in the midsixties--I mean, it's so easy to romanticize and mythologize the entire episode. But in fact I thought that was absolutely accurate in every detail--remarkably accurate too about the whole spirit of the enterprise, written with all Mike's great generosity and so on. That was a first-class piece. If only these magazines dedicated themselves a little more to that sort of thing. . . .

DP: One of the problems with academic journals is that they're not written by creative writers. What was notable about New Worlds in its heyday is that the criticism and polemic was written by practicing writers like yourself and Moorcock. . . .

JGB: The critical writing, the polemical writing in New Worlds throughout the sixties wasn't in any way academic or analytic. It was exhortatory, it was inspirational in its intention. It was kite-flying. The object of the exercise was to mark out terrain--not to look back over one's shoulder at well-ploughed fields but to look forward to the raw new terrain ahead. The trouble with academic critics is that, for all the apparent academic approach, most of them soon revert to the status of fans, and you see exactly the same sort of machinery unwinding that you get in fanzines. I mean, a total collapse of any sense of scale, you don't know whether you're looking at a mountain or a mole-hill. You know: the greatest writers of the twentieth century are James Joyce, T.S. Eliot, and John Brunner! Those sorts of slippages. Also, you get what I call hopscotch criticism, a quick jumping from one writer to the next, taking a little bit from each one in order to make whatever pattern is

Interview with J.G. Ballard

required.

DP: You've been writing for about twenty-three years now. Do you think critical attention has been a long time coming to you? Beyond reviews in the press, of course?

JGB: I'm grateful for any intelligent criticism I get, whether in newspapers or in specialist journals. It doesn't really influence me very much. I'm not a literary man, I don't work within a literary frame of things at all. Over the last five years, from France in particular, there's been a great flood of theses. . . . You'd be amazed. Frankly, I find it a little bit _funny_. Although my younger daughter is reading English at university, I regard the subject itself as a sort of pseudosubject, actually. You know, the whole attempt to impose . . . to make the study of English a kind of moral discipline, and the sort of elaborate textual analysis that goes on. . . . I think some of the scholastic approach to a novel by Henry James or a play by Samuel Beckett is rather akin to looking at a painting by Leonardo Da Vinci from a distance of three centimetres with a magnifying glass, tracking from left to right across a piece of drapery and analyzing at enormous length the texture of impasto. It seems to me that a novel, like a painting, needs to be read within an intelligent and informed set of values but you can go _too far_. One's in danger of that sort of guide-book mentality. I've seen friends of mine sitting in the lobby of a hotel in Venice, one reading James Morris's _Venice_ and the other reading another guide-book, when what they should be doing is walking around the place! I mean, now and then glancing at the guide-book to see what on earth this statue or church is. . . .

DP: But readers are always asking for guidance, and this is one of the things that _New Worlds_ did so well. It did it for me.

JGB: _New Worlds_ was rather different, wasn't it? As I was saying earlier, there's a complete difference between something like _Science-Fiction Studies_, the whole new academic approach to sf, and the sort of polemical writing in _New Worlds_, which was inspirational, trying to define and mark out a new set of territories, lay out a completely new direction for sf. If you read the critical writing in _New Worlds_ in the midsixties—Moorcock's editorials, book reviews by various people, articles on painters by various people including myself—what _that_ writing had was something that seems to be missing from so much academic critical writing. . . . That is, all the references are to the world beyond science fiction, whereas too much of present-day heavy academic criticism refers _only_ to the world of sf. Now and then you get a reference to Lucian's _True History_ or _Gulliver's Travels_ or what have you, but basically. . . . I mean, this criticism is being written by a new kind of _fan_. These are fans who don't move their lips when they read.

Interview with J.G. Ballard

DP: Did you coin the phrase "lumpen-intelligentsia" which occurs in your story "The University of Death" in 1968?

JGB: As far as I know. That describes these people! I don't want to spend all my time knocking these people--I'm not interested in them. I'm told by people like Moorcock that there's a huge flood of books hitting the market all the time.

DP: Mainly in America. . . .

JGB: The American academic approach to sf makes me profoundly uneasy, as it makes as far as I know most of the American writers of my generation. It shares a lot with that kind of once-fashionable criticism you got in architectural journals in the sixties. You had people like Reyner Banham writing endlessly about the architecture of American filling-stations. The whole of the consumer-goods society was treated as a great pop artifact. A set of academic disciplines previously used to discuss the architecture of the past were applied to supermarkets, filling-stations, airport lobbies. It was quite fascinating in a way, but but it can go too far.

DP: It's precisely what you love to do yourself, in your fiction!

JGB: Well. . . . Exactly, it's the imaginative writer's job to make those connections.

DP: I see you've got a copy of Banham's Los Angeles over there.

JGB: Yes, I enjoyed it. A fine book, I loved it. He doesn't go too far there. He is really an imaginative writer. I don't object to that. In a way it doesn't really matter, because I think anybody who's drawn to science fiction, or to this particular kind of imaginative fiction interested in the present day, is not going to be affected by an over-zealous academic approach in universities or in journals of review. Thank God. . . . Because sf springs from something very deep, and it'll come out whatever happens.

DP: Do you not think academic criticism can be damaging to writers?

JGB: I don't think it is, because how many writers are going to read that? [Pointing to my copy of Science-Fiction Studies.]

DP: Well, take Ursula Le Guin, for example. It may be unfair to say it, but she seems to have dried up a bit since this immense amount of attention she started to receive a few years ago.

JGB: Well, I don't know. I met her once, she seemed awfully nice. Her fiction isn't my kind of sf. It's all set on alien planets. It seems to me to go backwards rather than forwards. It strikes

Interview with J.G. Ballard

me as being part of that so-called American New Wave which in fact had nothing to do with the English New Wave--writers like Zelazny, Delany, Ursula Le Guin. It's all baroque fantasy using the old standbys of interplanetary sf, time-travel and all the rest of it, all the conventions of forties and fifties sf but with a slightly more ironic and literary flare. A couple of years ago I was sent a book of hers to review for the New Statesman, and it had the most extraordinary introduction by Ursula Le Guin describing her own creative processes. I'm only speaking from memory--check me out--but she referred to Einstein, Churchill, Shakespeare, Chaucer, Milton, quoted various pieces from Keats, Blake I think. . . . It was quite extraordinary--I was staggered at the delusions of grandeur. [The introduction referred to is in the British edition of The Word for World is Forest, and the names invoked by Le Guin are in fact those of: Freud; Ernest Hemingway; Emily Bronte; Solzhenitsyn; Winston Churchill; Plato; Shelley; Charlotte Bronte; God; Harlan Ellison; and Dr. Charles Tart, in that order--DP.] There must be something in the rainy weather in Portland, Oregon, that has this effect on people. I mean, thank God, one never feels that the great American writers of sf--Bradbury, Pohl, Sheckley, even in their way people like Asimov--would have succumbed to all that nonsense. All that fiction wouldn't exist! I don't think English writers of sf suffer from those sorts of delusions. When you ask do I feel any critical attention I'm receiving now is overdue, the answer is I don't--because the difference between British and American writers is that the British writer has always had a much more intelligent critical atmosphere than the American writer. It's only recently that the American writer has begun to receive this huge. . . . The siege-gun of academia is being rolled out and pointed at him. I think probably everything I've written has been reviewed in, say, the Times Literary Supplement, whereas I don't know how many sf writers even now are regularly reviewed in, say, the nearest equivalent of the TLS, which would be the New York Review of Books--my guess is very few.

DP: It's beginning to happen.

JGB: Yes, it will. So I think we've always had a more intelligent critical climate, partly because British sf is so different from American sf and always has been. American sf is so much a product of commercial magazine fiction in the 1930s and forties. Modern American sf was generated during a very brief period. That isn't the case over here. Here sf has been a part of the broad stream of imaginative fiction--let's say, if you go back to the English contemporaries of Verne in the 1870s, 1880s, and then on through Wells. There is this strong stream of imaginative fiction, some romantic sf, some more serious, some of it written by the greatest writers like Wells, Huxley, Orwell, some by lesser writers. I remember I read a long sf story by Kipling once. And also there are so many exceptions, writers who have no counterparts in

Interview with J.G. Ballard

America as far as I know, like David Lindsay, author of <u>A Voyage to Arcturus</u>, or C.S. Lewis. So the English writer comes to sf with a completely different background to what he's going to write than his American counterparts. The young American writer comes to sf against a background of people like Asimov, Heinlein, Bradbury and the commercial magazines that produced them. I mean, somebody like that illiterate editor, whatever his name was--Campbell--is an important figure to the American writer, and his influence is still strong. But he has no counterpart over here. I regard American sf--much as I admire individual writers-- as really a kind of cul-de-sac, a minor tributary of the great stream of imaginative fiction. I regard the Americans, modern commercial sf which extends from, say, Asimov at one end of the spectrum to <u>Star Trek</u> at the other, as having done an enormous disservice to the possibility of the emergence of, you know, a serious science fiction.

DP: Did you always agree, though, with Mike Moorcock that this serious sf must also try to be popular?

JGB: Absolutely. I made that clear when I first knew Moorcock. I felt this before I knew him. This was one of the reasons why I started writing sf. I still believe this. Although I've written for literary magazines over the years--<u>Ambit</u>, <u>Bananas</u>, and one or two others--they're not by any means typical of literary magazines as a whole. <u>Bananas</u>, for example, has always tried to be a commercial magazine, it's tried to sell across the newsagent's counter. I don't think I would have ever wanted to be a literary writer, writing just for literary magazines. Right from the start I felt that you had to appeal to people who would buy your fiction in the same sort of spirit as they would buy a newspaper, a news-magazine. You know, they might buy a copy of <u>Vogue</u>, a copy of <u>Time</u>, the <u>Guardian</u> <u>and</u> a science fiction magazine.... This is what it was all about. I wouldn't have wanted to write for the <u>London Magazine</u> or what-have-you.

DP: So what about the relative failure of <u>New Worlds</u>? Eventually it had to fold for financial reasons, and some people say this was because it wasn't a commercial sf magazine, it strayed too far from the <u>Analog</u> type of thing....

JGB: I don't think that was the reason at all. It became extremely difficult by the end of the sixties for any kind of specialist magazine to survive in the market-place, simply because the major distributors like Smith's wouldn't handle a periodical unless it had a guaranteed circulation well above anything that any of the sf magazines had ever had. I think that was part of the reason. And obviously a taste for imaginative fiction of any kind is rather a limited one. You know, the ghost story is a popular form of fiction. We all read ghost stories in our adolescence; they form part of the whole repertory of classic fiction. On the other hand, if you started a magazine called Ghost Stories it would get nowhere. That's purely a marketing thing. I think there was another factor in the case of New Worlds. It ceased-- I've said this before and I don't intend it as any criticism whatever--it ceased to be a science fiction magazine even in the very elastic sense in which I use the term. It became something much closer to a magazine of alternative fiction or whatever you want to call it. I think New Worlds was drawing much closer to magazines like Frendz and IT, the counter-culture magazines. They happened to have very small circulations. Some of them managed to be commercial but only in a very restricted sense. That, I think, is what happened to New Worlds. I don't think it had anything to do with not being like Analog because New Worlds never was, even in the days of Carnell. . . .

DP: It did start off trying to be something like a British version of Astounding or Galaxy, in the early fifties. . . .

JGB: By the time I started writing, Carnell stated quite openly that he did not want to try to copy the American magazines, which were, from his point of view, too inbred to appeal to the larger audience that he wanted to attract to sf.--I've urged Mike recently. . . . I think now the time is ripe for a magazine, rather like the small-format New Worlds as opposed to the large-format magazine. With a minimum of illustrations now, and publishing nothing but short stories and perhaps just a few book reviews. And adopting a fairly cool and calm approach rather than the extravagant approach of the large-format New Worlds. We are now, at the end of the seventies, in a situation rather similar to that in which we were at the end of the fifties. I mean, the last fifteen years have created a completely new. . . . The terrain of our everyday lives has been created anew. A lot of new developments are popping up--the energy crisis, this, that and the other--and the whole transformation of society has been proceeding apace in a largely invisible way. I'm thinking particularly of the developments in computers, data-processing devices, communications satellites, which are changing the character of life, our whole relationship to what is real and what isn't. We've got a new world around us, rather similar to the one which twenty years ago I began writing about. I think the time has come for a new New Worlds, let's say, to start looking closely at the world in which we live, and science fiction is the perfect tool to do this. Incidentally, one associates with the New Wave in the midsixties so-called "experimental" writing. The sort of stories I visualize, which I would love to see in a small-format New Worlds, would not be experimental. I think of them as absolutely straight because that is the best technique to deal with what is going on around us. It's a completely different sort of landscape to that of the midsixties.--I think the time is urgent and I'd love to see that happen.

Interview with J.G. Ballard

DP: So there hasn't really been much change in your attitudes over the last twenty years? You still feel that a serious sf is as urgent, as important, as it was then?

JGB: Yes, I do. I think it's _more_ important in a sense now, because so many of the transformations made in our lives by science and technology are not visible ones, people aren't aware of the changes that have taken place. Not just the physical landscape has changed, nor its hidden dangers of the kind I've written about in Crash, Concrete Island, and High-Rise, but a whole new sensibility is being created that people aren't aware of. Particularly as we're on the edge of the VHS revolution--you know, these video home systems hooked into your TV set which are going to transform everybody's home into a TV studio before long. . . . Plus all these things like CEEFAX, PRESTEL and God knows what else coming along. . . . Everything's going to be coming off your TV screen over the next ten years, whether you like it or not. We're going to be drowning in electronic possibilities. This is exactly the sort of climate, this tsunami of possibilities heading towards us two miles high. . . . This is the sort of storm-climate, as it were, that the sf writer writes his best out of. I think there's something about the immediacy of publication in a magazine, particularly a monthly magazine, that gives the writer a sort of jet-assisted take-off every time he sits down to write. That's why I've always gone on writing for magazines. But writing, say, for your own probable publication in two or three years time in a collection of your own stories in hardback, and then waiting another year or two for the paperback when you reach a real audience, the time factor militates against an aggressive approach.

DP: So if there were a British sf magazine now you would be encouraged to write a continual stream of new stories yourself?

JGB: Yes, I think I would. That's probably been a great gap in my life. The curious thing is that a close friend of mine, Emma Tennant, began Bananas in 1975, at which point I wrote a story for almost every one of the issues which she edited. At that point I had not written any short stories at all for something like four years, largely because there was nowhere to publish. This is nothing to do with payment, by the way. I never was paid a penny for any of the stories I wrote for Bananas, nor for any that I've ever written for Ambit. Mike was very generous, but in the latter years of New Worlds he wasn't able to pay either. So it's nothing to do with payment. If Emma Tennant had not started Bananas it's probably not an exaggeration to say that none of those ten stories would have been written.

DP: Why don't you, or why doesn't your agent, submit stories to the sf magazines in America at all these days?

Interview with J.G. Ballard

JGB: He doesn't handle my short stories, actually. I don't think I've had a short story published in a commercial magazine for years and years. . . . He handled the story I wrote for Christopher Priest, whatever it was called--"Utah Beach," or something. "The Ultimate City" was published in an American magazine as a two-part serial, a magazine called CoEvolution Quarterly. My agent handled that, but all the other stories I've written--something like ten or eleven for Bananas and possibly two or three over the last four years for Ambit--were written in response to the editors, whom I know very closely.

DP: Has your association with Bananas ended now that Emma Tennant has left?

JGB: Well, I wrote one story for the new editor, Abigail Mozeley. I suppose, to be honest, I wasn't happy about the sort of direction she plans to take the magazine in. I haven't written anything over the last six months for her. But the reason is simply that I think I've come to the end of a certain phase of short story writing. I want to move about a bit and start writing a different kind of story. Maybe a fresh start is necessary and a fresh look at what is going on.

DP: Do you think you're a better short story writer than a novelist?

JGB: I don't compare the two, actually. They're such totally different forms. I mean, it is much easier to write a good short story than a good novel. Many hundreds of perfect short stories have been written--perfect in the sense that a good carpenter can construct a perfectly made table. Hundreds of perfect short stories have been written by, you know, the masters of the short story--Maupassant, Chekhov, O. Henry, the Edwardian ghost story writers, Saki. . . . and the masters of modern sf. People like Bradbury have probably written twenty perfect short stories. It's much easier to achieve formal perfection in the short story, and this is the sort of yardstick which you just can't apply to the novel. Has anyone written a perfect novel? One doesn't think of the novel in those terms. It's such an open structure, it defies any kind of definition--whereas the short story is actually extremely hostile to innovation. The novel, in a sense, invites innovation. The novel doesn't exist--no novel exists in a defined, formal sense. That's something unique to the novel. You can say that The Importance of Being Ernest is a perfect play, its structure is perfect. You can say that about many of Shakespeare's plays--Macbeth, which I've read over the last few years several times helping my three children through 'O' levels and 'A' levels, strikes me as being a perfect play. You can't say that about any novel. What I think I can say about my own fiction is that my novels and my short stories are very different. Something like Crash bears no relation to any of the short fiction

Interview with J.G. Ballard

I've written. I think that's a good sign.

DP: You mentioned TV a little while ago. Did you happen to see the program Bombers on BBC TV a couple of days ago? [This was a World War II documentary broadcast on 12 June 1979.]

JGB: Yes, I did. That was interesting. I was very impressed. There have been a lot of similar films on TV over the last four or five years, during the big World War II boom, but. . . . There's something about an air war over Germany, like the air war over China during World War II that I did witness, that's profoundly moving. There's something about the human scale of those machines that I think we've lost in the years since. It may have come back during the Vietnam War, but that was such a grim nightmare that one can't visualize a similar film about being a gunship pilot in the Mekong Delta--though I daresay it'll come.

DP: What other sorts of things do you watch on television?

JGB: I have appallingly good taste. I don't watch any of the programs that critics seem to watch and review. I like these American crime serials because they are total stylization-- programs like Hawaii 5-0, where the plots and even the characters are merely pegs onto which to hang a stylized flow of images. Without delivering a full-length critique on TV, I think it is important. So many of the television reviewers take the line that it's a joke basically--you know, as long as you can write a few funny paragraphs about Come Dancing or It's a Knockout you're doing your job. . . . But I think TV is so important to people in this world that it ought to be taken more seriously than it is. One gets all sorts of perceptions into what the future is going to be like watching TV. Watching something like the Olympic Games on TV I always find fascinating. I'm totally uninterested in athletics, I couldn't give a damn who can hurl a fifty-pound iron ball the furthest, but what is interesting is the TV presentation. I mean the TV presentation gives you an idea, the nearest idea that I can see, as to what the future is going to be like. That tremendously stylized competition in the media city that's created especially for the event. . . . Very much at variance with conventional views of what the future is going to be like, which tend to visualize an absence of competition, an absence of individualism, with soft technology. I think that is the wrong view of the future: I think we're going to have a high-technology future. We'll be living in a media landscape, with intense individual competition of a very stylized kind, of the kind that athletes have, which lasts as long as they're bursting down the track or hurling their javelin. Now TV provides that sort of perception. You won't get that sort of perception by going to the Festival Hall and listening to a Brahms symphony-- which most people say one should do rather than watch telly.

Interview with J.G. Ballard

DP: So, do you think we're heading towards some sort of post-industrial microprocessor paradise where few people have to work for a living? What about the energy and resources collapse that many predict?

JGB: I think both are going to come true. There is obviously going to be an energy and resources collapse, and one can see signs already. . . . Over the last couple of months, watching the TV newsreels from California during the gasoline shortage, I felt that this is what I was writing. . . . I invented all this twenty years ago, in a sense. It's uncanny, it's like a film made of some of my fiction. There is going to be an energy crisis, obviously. The supply of oil is finite, and the whole notion--particularly in the United States and Western Europe--that the essence of the good life resides precisely in its abundance and in a casually spendthrift approach to everything is going to have to be revalued. There's no question about that. It may be that the era of cheap travel will come to an end, and that travel will become extremely expensive again. As it was, say, in the Middle Ages when for an artisan or a parish priest to journey from Edinburgh to London, or from Frankfut to Paris, a journey of a few hundred miles, he probably consumed a year's income. That may happen again. All these transformations are going to take place, but at the same time I think we're moving into a high-technology era centered on the proliferation of communications devices of every conceivable kind--a superextension of TV, quadrophonic sound, the whole video-cassette explosion that will burst at any time--which will transform just about everything. You're not using up any vital resources sitting in front of a TV tube. Probably the most economically beneficial act you can perform on behalf of society at large is to watch Hawaii 5-O!

DP: Are you awaiting the fall of Skylab with interested anticipation?

JGB: It would be tragic if it actually landed on Falmouth or Miami or some village in Sinkiang and killed people. That would be appalling.--But I don't really have any strong feelings either way. I've said endlessly that I think the space age is over, or at least an early phase of the space age is over. I don't think people are going to be very interested in this large piece of junk hurtling down into the Atlantic or wherever. I don't think they're going to see it as a symbolic act or that it'll touch their imaginations in any way. I thought the man-powered flight across the Channel the day before yesterday was a far more moving experience, a remarkable event. That in a sense is a sort of high technology--the technology of these extremely light metals, extremely light but strong plastics, coupled with the high technology of a highly trained modern athlete. This is the nature of things that you'll see in the future more and more. We won't all be piloting around some huge Buick that's consuming vast quantities of fossil fuel, rare chromes and all the rest of it used purely for ornament. We'll be pedaling these beautiful man-powered high-technology gliders around the place. That strikes me as marvelous! We can all become birds. That'll touch the human soul far more.

DP: What you say about the first phase of the space age being over implies that there may be a second, and what you say about these high-technology materials ties in with what a number of people have been saying recently: that we should develop space as an industrial area. . . .

JGB: These O'Neill cylinders? I think they're mad. Yes, I know about them—these cylinders seven miles long, a mile in diameter, with windows the size of wheatfields. . . .

DP: Does this not touch your imagination?

JGB: No, it doesn't. It's just a nightmare. I've read about his projects in some detail, and it strikes me that the whole thing is a huge, almost Victorian, fantasy of giant engineering structures. The sort of goals that the whole thing is designed to fulfill are those of the great Victorian engineers and industrialists. He thinks in terms of mining ore on the surface of the moon, and of the transfer of vast amounts of raw energy directly from the sun by microwave to the surface of the earth. . . . These are straight from the popular science encyclopedias of the 1920s and 1930s which sold the glories of giant dams and fast trains and so on. I mean, he's not interested in space in any sort of psychological sense at all. This seems to me partly why the space program failed to touch people—this was potentially one of the most significant events in the whole of human history which was approached purely as an engineering project. . . . But there won't be any space age until there's a cheap and efficient means of getting large numbers of people into space. The damn thing isn't cost-effective at present. No industrialized society at present, not even the United States, can really afford it. Also . . . I mean, nobody has looked into what life in these huge O'Neill colonies would be like. I see chewing-gum on plastic floors and scuffed rusting rails, and a funny smell in the air from the air-conditioning, and a background of what other people have termed "airplane fear"—you know, a whole lot of flying DC-10s orbiting over your head. When is metal fatigue going to suddenly pump the atmosphere out?—I'm not interested actually in whether it comes about or not—what I'm interested in is how it touches our imaginations. It seems to me that the pioneer years of flight at the turn of the century, let's say from the 1850s onwards, ballooning and all this sort of thing, to the Wright Brothers and then on until the 1930s, was when aviation was still built around the dimensions of the man. It touched people's imaginations in consequence, in the most

Interview with J.G. Ballard

powerful sense. It provided some of the most potent metaphors that human beings have ever responded to. I suppose World War II was the last fling, but since then aviation is just Skytrain, which lacks any sort of imaginative dimension whatever.

DP: But the sort of speculations you were just making about what life would be like in an O'Neill colony is precisely what sf writers should do. . . .

JGB: Have they done that? You get the odd rusty tramp spaceship bucketing through the fiction of Harry Harrison and people like that, but on the whole sf writers of the forties and fifties had a tremendously optimistic view, really rather an adolescent view, which circumstances have shown to be wrong.

DP: So it's unlikely that you'd ever write a story set on an O'Neill colony yourself?

JGB: I wouldn't.—It seems to me that the tremendous publicity that the NASA flights got, the live radio transmissions, the live TV from the surface of the moon, and all the flight-control expertise that was poured out, has had an intimidating effect on some sf writers. You know, you can't just say: "he looked into the viewscreen at the surface of the planet"; you've got to have more of that "AOK Mission Control" stuff. And that's difficult to do if you've never taken part in it. I don't know. To be honest, I haven't seen a copy of Analog in about ten years. They're probably all doing it marvelously.

DP: To change the subject: what sort of turn is your life taking now that your children have grown up?

JGB: It's an interesting question to me. My younger daughter left for her university two years ago, in October '77. She left . . . not she in particular, but the absence of those three children left a colossal vacuum in my life. I was married rather early, at 23, and I was really a glorified schoolboy when I did get married. I've spent my entire adult life with a large busy family around me. It is very strange—all parents go through this—to find oneself in this huge vacuum that I've absolutely no training to deal with. So I've been asking that question for at least a year—what the hell do I do now? I could point my life in almost any direction. I could go and live in Tahiti if I wanted to, I could live almost anywhere in the world rather than in Shepperton. I don't know—these changes, these sort of seismic waves, move slowly through one's life, but maybe over the next five years I'll find somewhere. I ought to travel more, but I seem to be going through quite a productive phase. Writing takes priority over everything else, but I suppose I ought to close the typewriter, put it away for a while, and perhaps travel.

Interview with J.G. Ballard

DP: A year or two ago you told an interviewer that you were thinking of perhaps going back to China. . . .

JGB: Oh, I'd like to. But I think there's no point in going until the regime is sufficiently liberalized for me to be able to go anywhere I want to go. It would be ridiculous to go all that way to Shanghai and then not be able to visit the houses where I lived, the schools that I went to, the country club, the camp where I was imprisoned for three years. My impression, from the people I know who've been there, is that one's still very restricted. You can't hail a cab and say "take me to such-and-such a place ten miles away from Shanghai." That camp may well be a military installation now. They might decide that the entire zone south of Shanghai is forbidden to visitors. Till there's a fair degree of liberalization there's not much point in going. But I intend to go, I'm waiting for that. I ought to make a book out of it . . . but I think all my fiction is probably about China in a way, or some of it anyway. . . .

DP: Did you and your parents have a horrified attitude to the Communist regime when it took over? Were they bogey-men to the Europeans in Shanghai?

JGB: I'm sorry to say that my parents, like all the people of their generation, like all the old Far East hands, were absolutely convinced that the zealous Maoist phase would last all of the time it took the commissars to put away their guns, climb down from their tanks and walk into the bars and brothels of downtown Shanghai. It was a big shock when that didn't happen. The thing about the Chinese--for whom I have an enormous respect, as I do the Japanese--is that they're enormously industrious people. If people are naturally tremendously industrious, if their work-tempo is three times ours, they're going to find sooner or later some means of expressing this. It sounds crazy to say this, but maybe the Hong Kong style of capitalism actually serves the Chinese temperament better than the more puritanical and restricted economic life that communism offers. I don't know. I guess things will liberalize there, I'd be very surprised if they didn't--over the years.

DP: After your wife died how did you manage to write and to rear three children at the same time? Isn't it unusual for a writer to have done this?

JGB: I suppose that's true. I think Orwell, at one phase in his life, looked after his son by himself--admittedly, only for something like a year or two.--I was able to. It wasn't as difficult, actually, as it may seem. I was tremendously involved with my children and they were a great source of strength. I genuinely like children--I like being with children, other people's as well as my own. As for finding the time to write: they went to

Interview with J.G. Ballard

school. Even when they were here I was able to work with three children playing in the next room. That never bothered me. I drank a great deal of alcohol, to be honest. I used to have my first large whisky at nine in the morning, and I would <u>stop</u> drinking round about the time I start now. That helped.

DP: Do you think if this hadn't happened your career would have been very different? Would you have written more?

JGB: I think I kept up. I haven't looked at this, but my impression is that I kept up a fairly steady tempo over the, whatever it is, twenty-two years that I've been writing.

DP: Well, there was a falling-off in quantity in the latter sixties. . . .

JGB: I don't think that had anything to do with my children. After my wife died I wrote <u>The Crystal World</u>--that was 1965--then I started writing the <u>Atrocity Exhibition</u> stories, but I was also writing other short stories at the same time. I'd come to the end of a phase--although even now I'm still writing short stories of a kind that I wrote twenty years ago. I mean, I wouldn't have wanted to go on endlessly producing variants of <u>The Crystal World</u>, particularly in the atmosphere of the midsixties. You won't remember what it was like in England <u>before</u> the midsixties. The transformation was so radical, it was so extraordinary. Not just the transformation of England, but of Western Europe and of the United States to a large extent. So much was happening, one could see the shape of things to come. Things <u>had</u> come to a large extent. It seemed to me that--this was nothing to do with my wife's death or bringing up children--whatever had happened, even if I'd been a bachelor or happily married, by something like 1965 I'd have wanted to have a hard look at what I was doing as a writer of science fiction. I was moving in that direction anyway, with <u>The Drought</u> and then my story "The Terminal Beach." With the benefit of hindsight, I can see that I was reaching towards something like the <u>Atrocity Exhibition</u> pieces, and that was the gateway to <u>Crash</u> and the other novels. The sort of technique I used in <u>The Atrocity Exhibition</u> to deal with that huge media explosion of Vietnam, the Apollo program, the Kennedy assassinations, the whole youth and drug explosion, was the right one as far as I was concerned. What I would have written if the sixties hadn't occurred, if the sixties had been like the fifties or the seventies, I don't know. Maybe I would have gone on writing <u>The Crystal World</u>. I'm glad I didn't have to.

DP: There was obviously a big shift at that point in your writing, from a first phase to a second phase. Do you agree with me that you're now moving into a third phase, starting about 1975 or '76?

JGB: Yes, I think I am. You're right. The book I finished in

Interview with J.G. Ballard

December, <u>The Unlimited Dream Company</u>, is stage one, I think.

DP: Well, I see this latest phase as beginning with "The Ultimate City," and in this phase of your writing images of <u>flight</u> seem to be coming to predominate over images of <u>imprisonment</u>. . . .

JGB: That's very true, I'm glad you said that. It's all about flying. I noticed, starting to write these stories for Emma Tennant and <u>Ambit</u> about three years ago, that a flying machine or some reference to flight has been in almost every bloody story! Even one I wrote about a man who's having a mental breakdown, without realizing it elements that refer to flight or flying in some way were coming through all the time. It's a funny thing, that. And this novel, <u>Unlimited Dream Company</u>, is partly about man-powered flight, oddly enough. It's funny that this man-powered flight across the Channel has just taken place. What I would love to do—I won't, because this sort of thing requires actual practical experience—is to write a novel about a man-powered flying machine. Not exactly <u>Zen and the Art of Man-Powered Aircraft</u>, because I didn't like that book particularly, but you know what I mean—the whole private mythology. There's something about it, I don't know what. . . .

DP: I don't know whether you do, but I associate these images of flight with a happier. . . .

JGB: Escape! Yes, a happier frame of mind. I think that's absolutely true.

DP: Do you think you're becoming mellower?

JGB: I don't know about that. It may be the case. The brain does settle down after the age of forty, physiologically. Nobody becomes psychopathic, I gather, after the age of forty. The brain quietens. A lot of people with long-standing mental problems do emerge into some sort of calm plateau after the age of forty. But I don't know . . . I've always tried to follow accurately, like a cruise missile, the contours of the period in which I'm living. Perhaps if images of flight have begun to appear in my fiction they may reflect something in the atmosphere that we all breathe. You know—we're all looking for some sort of vertical route out of the particular concrete jungle that we live in. It's just possible.

DP: Do you think you'll ever write books as black as <u>The Atrocity Exhibition</u> and <u>Crash</u> again?

JGB: I don't see them as black. I think they're true to their subject-matter. If you're going to write a novel about, say, war, you can do it in a romantic way, like all that <u>Boy's Own Paper</u> fiction based on the First and Second World Wars. You can do the

Interview with J.G. Ballard

Sands of Iwo Jima thing. You can glorify heroism and comradeship and play down the reality of the experience, or else you can try to tell the truth. The truth is that in wars people get mutilated, depraved, and demoralized, blown to pieces, and all values go down the drain. It's hell, literally. If you're going to write about that truthfully what you write will tend to be a bit black. It seems to me that the kind of world I was describing in Atrocity and Crash, the emergence of a new kind of logic, is . . . you know. Those books are true to the world we live in. You could hardly write an optimistic book about the car-crash, could you--a cheerful book?

DP: Did you happen to read Susan Sontag's book On Photography, or have you seen the TV program based on it?

JGB: No, neither.

DP: It seemed to me a lot of the ideas about the way we use cameras had been anticipated in your fiction, in stories like "The Sixty-Minute Zoom" for instance.

JGB: Oh, yes. No, I haven't read that. I'd like to because I like the sound of her. She's been extremely generous about my fiction, said the most complimentary things about it. From what I've read of her criticism she's a first-class critic, with a very rare sensibility, absolutely in tune with a lot of the goals that I think writers and critics should set themselves and few do. I admire her enormously. I'm happy that there are correspondences.

DP: Do you get much inspiration from following world affairs? Do things like the upheavals in Iran or the situation in Rhodesia interest you in a political way?

JGB: Yes, they do. I read a lot of news-magazines and I'm a keen reader of newspapers. I am interested in the world.

DP: But you've rarely said anything overtly political in your fiction.

JGB: I suppose there just hasn't been room for political statements in my fiction. You could take a novella like "The Ultimate City"-- that makes a number of what I suppose you could call implicit political points, about conservation on the one hand and the pitfalls of limitless opportunist capitalism on the other. There are built-in implicit political standpoints in High-Rise and Crash and Atrocity, aren't there? A lot of those short stories I was writing in the sixties, like "The Subliminal Man" on advertising--I don't know whether you'd call that a political comment. . . .

DP: In a way, obviously. The trouble with High-Rise is that it got a glowing review in such a right-wing newspaper as the <u>Daily Telegraph</u>. . . .

JGB: Did it? It's news to me. I've always had good reviews in the <u>Daily Telegraph</u> and often very hostile ones in the liberal papers like the <u>Guardian</u>--although I've had some very good reviews there. It's funny, but I think the reason is that the traditionalist right-wing conservative standpoint on life is much more tolerant of Original Sin, the intolerance of man to man, than the liberal conscience will allow. Many of the reactions to <u>High-Rise</u>, as to <u>Crash</u>, were "it couldn't happen because it <u>shouldn't</u> happen." The place where those books of mine, <u>Crash</u> in particular, received the greatest critical attention and praise was France, where presumably, again, there's a much more tolerant view about human nature and the unpleasant byways it may lead us into.

DP: <u>High-Rise</u> was compared to Golding's <u>Lord of the Flies</u>, which is a novel left-wing people love to hate because it's apparently all about Original Sin and how we can never make ourselves any better. . . .

JGB: There's a big difference, of course. I've heard the comparison made. There's all the difference in the world because Golding is saying, and his characters at the end endorse this, "this is Original Sin and we regret it." Whereas in <u>High-Rise</u> the whole point of the book, as in <u>Crash</u>, is that the characters eagerly embrace these revelations about themselves and the new life that technology has made possible. The whole logic of the book and their behaviour only makes sense if you assume that they <u>want</u> this apparent descent into barbarism. It is willed by them all, either consciously or unconsciously. In the last paragraph I think the character who's my mouthpiece more or less says this. He looks forward to this world because it's one he wants. And that's completely different from Golding's approach.

DP: The other big difference is that Golding has an idyllic desert island whereas in your novel it's the environment that's partly to blame.

JGB: Not to <u>blame</u>: the environment makes possible the whole set of unfolding <u>logics</u>, like those that unfold on the highway in <u>Crash</u>. The technology as a whole has a sort of alienating effect. . . .

DP: Have you discovered any new imaginative writers, say in the last five years, who have excited you?

JGB: Difficult to say. . . . I was tremendously impressed by Ian Watson's first novel, <u>The Embedding</u>. I've read three of his novels, the first three now, and I think--who cares what I think?--there is a slight falling-off, successively, in those novels. But they're still tremendously stimulating and exciting

Interview with J.G. Ballard

and clever in a way that I don't see in almost any other sf writer. As novels of ideas, the only previous novel that I can think of in sf is Bernard Wolfe's Limbo 90 in 1952, a long time ago.

DP: What about some of your New Worlds colleagues? The recent work of Moorcock or M. John Harrison?

JGB: I haven't read anything by them recently. I'm a bit out of touch there. I look forward to reading Moorcock, actually, reading his recent stuff.

DP: There's a book you praised highly in a review in the New Statesman a couple of years ago. . . .

JGB: A sure sign that I hadn't read it! But go on.

DP: That was Man Plus by Frederik Pohl.

JGB: What the hell was that about?

DP: It's the one about the astronaut who's rebuilt to survive on Mars.

JGB: When I took up reviewing for the Statesman I was very reluctant to do it, so I said that--I annoyed Tom Disch for some reason when I told him this--I would only criticize or find fault with a book if I'd read it. If I hadn't read it, I'd always give it a good review. It was only fair. . . . Maybe Pohl's book was one I hadn't read.--I vaguely remember it, I think. It was rather well done, quite exciting. I do remember it now, and it was rather good. Marvelous ideas. Pohl has always been a good writer, actually, with excellent ideas. But I can't think of anybody who's had the same impact on me that Ian Watson has. I found The Embedding tremendously exciting to read, particularly as it begins in a very quiet way and then suddenly--wham! Particularly as I knew nothing about him beforehand. I'd read a marvelous article by him, about Japan, in the old New Worlds which was brilliantly written.

DP: That was about the first thing he had published.

JGB: Yes. But then I knew nothing about him at all until The Embedding, which was a knockout.

DP: So you're still, to put it crudely, an "ideas" man rather than a "style" man? Some people have faulted Watson as a literary stylist.

JGB: He's got a good style, hasn't he? Pacy? He's a good descriptive writer. I think he's got great pace and verve. He can set a scene. His descriptions of the whales talking to each other I think is marvelously done, in <u>The Jonah Kit</u>. I think he's got a good style. What sort of impact has he had in the States? I would have thought they would be able to accommodate him because he, unlike myself, does embrace all the conventions of interplanetary travel and all the hardware--there are spaceships and beings from another planet. You know, I can totally understand them not liking my stuff but I would have thought they would like his.

DP: Well, he's had a few good reviews but he's not exactly sold a lot--yet.

JGB: I wasn't thinking of big sales, I was just thinking that if they had any sense they'd hail him as a new discovery. He's much more interesting than Delany, for example. Vastly superior.

DP: I detect a certain sourness on the part of <u>New Worlds</u> writers like M. John Harrison and Michael Moorcock over the fact, as they see it, that the real gains of the so-called New Wave have been cheapened by second-rate imitators. Avant-garde sf has become a subgenre in its own right and thus it's been sanitized and robbed of its power. Do you ever share this anger?

JGB: What sort of writers are Harrison and Moorcock talking about?

DP: Well, mainly certain younger British writers. Watson may well be one of them.

JGB: I don't feel that. I wasn't aware that process was going on, frankly. I'd be very surprised to find, given the sort of entropic climate in which we live now, a New Wave sf as questing and vivid as it was between '65 and '70. I'm sure any period of great change and transformation summons up from somewhere writers to deal with it, and I think they'll come. It's just that the seventies has been a desperately dull decade--very like the fifties, actually. Perhaps more interesting than one realizes because things have been happening--the beginnings of a huge transformation have certainly been taking place. But on the whole it's been desperately dull, and it's difficult to write. . . . The sf writer in particular is very much dependant on the external world, unless he's going to write what is at heart fantasy--and by that I mean something like <u>The Drowned World</u> is a fantasy.

DP: If you recall, I sent you a pastiche "Vermilion Sands" story by an American authoress called Lee Killough. . . .

JGB: Oh, yes, that. I didn't think it was very good.

DP: But it's interesting that it exists. She's written three or

Interview with J.G. Ballard

four of them for F&SF. Do you want to make any comment?

JGB: I didn't really read it, to be honest. I read the first page. It didn't strike me as being very interesting so I'm afraid I heaved it in the wastebasket. I could see what you meant. . . . Well, that sort of thing goes on, doesn't it? I take it as a compliment. That doesn't worry me. Good, I've got through! At least one American has responded to me!

DP: Do you ever reread your own older work? How do you feel now about the stuff you wrote in, say, the early 1960s?

JGB: I find it very difficult to reread my early stuff. In fact, I find it difficult to reread anything within a few months of having written it. Reading the proofs of this latest novel, I found even that a strange experience. It's just that as a writer I get intensely involved with something and then the moment it's finished it's sort of dead for me. I had a big collection of my short stories published recently in the States and I had to read the proofs of that--these are stories from the late fifties up till about 1969. I found it very strange, because one changes. . . . I didn't think the stories had dated in any way, it's just that they seemed to be written by somebody else. The first of those stories were written when I was still in my twenties. So--I try not to read my old stuff is the answer. You can see the mistakes coming off the page every other line! Ooh, how did I write so badly! You know. . . . It's a terrible thing.

DP: I compared the texts recently of the original magazine appearances of a couple of your "Vermilion Sands" stories with the slightly amended versions you used in the book, and they were improvements, I found. You'd obviously cut out phrases which were a little too flowery, adjectives which were too much. . . .

JGB: Yes. I think the reason I touched up some of those stories was: a) they had been written over a great span of time and I wanted a bit more consistency of style within the book, and b) because, unlike my other collections which have tended to appear within a fairly short space of time after the stories themselves were written, in the case of Vermilion Sands there was some sort of hold-up. When was that book published?

DP: Nineteen-seventy-three in this country, but you had a paperback edition in 1971 in America.

JGB: Yes. I only retouched them for the English edition. But in '73 it was already something like five years since the last story had been written. Also, God--many of those stories were just tossed off very quickly without any real thought to them ever being published again. Terrible thing to say, but . . . it's

Interview with J.G. Ballard

like doing a quick review. It's like writing an exam paper that nobody else is ever going to read and that's never going to surface. I tried to do a decent job on the idea, but--again, it's a terrible thing to say--back in the late fifties I didn't feel that the readers of Science Fantasy and New Worlds were going to give me any marks for a fine style. Also, I didn't have the time, I was in a rush. Some of those stories were written in a day. So they were a bit slapdash. I'd rewrite the whole bloody lot if I had the energy. . . . I think one can actually give too high a value to a perfect style. What counts is whether the story as a whole works. You can get short stories written by popular American writers in mass magazines that are written in really rather a crude style, and yet have got such force or such an original twist that they work. You could never set the story as an 'A' level text but that doesn't matter. They've got energy and all the rest of it. So I'm not too concerned about that.

DP: Your earlier novels tended to group into two loose trilogies. Do you think The Unlimited Dream Company will be the first of another three novels?

JGB: I don't know, to be honest. It may be that I just needed to make a break, because The Unlimited Dream Company is an out-and-out piece of imaginative fiction. It's not in any way a critique of life today, etc. The American publisher describes it on his blurb as a "fable." I hadn't thought of it like that, but it's a fable in the way that a short story like "The Drowned Giant" is a fable. It's that sort of thing. Maybe I needed to write a novel that would act as a dividing-line between the past and whatever is to come in the future. I don't know what will come-- hard to say. Though I do have an idea, as it happens, another imaginative idea, not similar but in the same sort of terrain as Unlimited Dream Company.

DP: Do you think The Unlimited Dream Company is likely to be more popular with readers who didn't like things like Crash?

JGB: I suppose it's an upbeat book. There's no doubt happy endings are more popular than unhappy endings. I'm not a fool, I can see that a book like The Atrocity Exhibition is indecipherable to all but a small minority of people, and a book like Crash is profoundly upsetting to even the few people who can get beyond the first ten pages. I can see that. One of my most popular books, I guess, is something like Crystal World because it seems to be upbeat or at least it has a positive message. . . . I hope, you know, that people will respond to Unlimited Dream Company on its own terms. If they like it, that'd be great. Both the British and American publishers have been very generous with it. In fact, they were, without exaggerating, wildly enthusiastic. Whereas the French publisher has been very cool. "This is a new departure for you, Jim," he said to me on the phone. It's not really, but

Interview with J.G. Ballard

there we are, what you lose on the roundabouts you gain on the swings. Funny that. There is a different national sensibility--twenty miles of English Channel and there's a complete new landscape. Very, very curious.

DP: So, with luck, it might even be a success over here or in America?

JGB: Oh, I haven't the faintest idea--it could be a total flop. I hope as a novel it's a success--in imaginative terms.

DP: By the time this interview is published the book will have been out a while.

JGB: You can put a P.S.: "it was <u>not</u> a success--dash!" Or, you know, it sold nine million copies! I'm not that concerned about whether it's a success or not. It sounds corny, but I hope it works imaginatively, and I don't expect it's another <u>Watership Down</u>. I've been around long enough to know that my stuff isn't everybody's cup of tea.

DP: Your stuff does get an intense reaction from many people. Readers either love it or loathe it. . . .

JGB: Yes, I've always had that. It doesn't surprise me, actually, because most people don't like imaginative fiction in fact--though, paradoxically, it is imaginative fiction that survives the best. Most of the popularly read classic fiction tends to be imaginative fiction. <u>Treasure Island</u> outsells . . .

DP: Henry James?

JGB: Henry James--even though Henry James and Jane Austen are doing very well, thank you. The fact is, the classics of imaginative fiction, <u>Alice in Wonderland</u>, <u>Treasure Island</u>, the novels of . . . you know . . .

DP: Rider Haggard?

JGB: Rider Haggard and Conan Doyle . . . are among the most successful fiction ever produced. <u>But</u>, with a few exceptions like <u>Watership Down</u> and Tolkien, in fact most people don't like imaginative fiction. It's too personal, you can see the writer's damn nerve-endings, whereas realist fiction a) has the reassurance of the ordinary and familiar and everyday, and b) the writer is much more self-effacing--I know there are exceptions, but on the whole he doesn't intrude in the same way that, say, Mervyn Peake intrudes into <u>his</u> fiction. I mean, you've got the hot breath of Mervyn Peake in your face as you read <u>Gormenghast</u>. The same is true of Ray Bradbury, let's say, and the same is true of my stuff. If you don't like being inside the particular writer's head, the

Interview with J.G. Ballard

one thing you want to do is to close the book and forget him forever.--I'm aware of that. In a way, it's a proof of something. If they dislike you enough, you must have something.

Primary Bibliography

Part A: Fiction

1951

A1 "The Violent Noon." Varsity [Cambridge University student newspaper], 26 May, p. 9.

    Joint-winner of the Varsity Crime Story Competition. Photograph and brief profile of the author, "J. Graham Ballard," on the same page.

1956

A2 "Escapement." New Worlds 18, no. 54 (December):27-39.

    in Passport to Eternity, 1963.
    in The Overloaded Man, 1967.
    in The Venus Hunters, 1980.

A3 "Prima Belladonna." Science Fantasy 7, no. 20 (December):63-75.

    Judith Merril, ed. SF: 57, the Year's Greatest Science-Fiction and Fantasy. New York: Gnome Press, 1957.
    in Billenium, 1962.
    in The Four-Dimensional Nightmare, 1963.
    Judith Merril, ed. SF: The Best of the Best. New York: Delacorte, 1967.
    in Vermilion Sands, 1971 [in the British edition of Vermilion Sands, 1973, the text of this story is revised.]

1957

A4 "Build-Up." New Worlds 19, no. 55 (January):52-70.

    in Billenium, 1962.
    Tom Boardman, ed. Connoisseur's SF. Harmondsworth:

Penguin Books, 1964 [paper].
in <u>The Disaster Area</u>, 1967 [as "The Concentration City"; text revised].
in <u>Chronopolis</u>, 1971.
*Charles W. Sullivan, ed. <u>As Tomorrow Becomes Today</u>. Englewood Cliffs, N.J.: Prentice-Hall, 1974 [paper]. [Source: Contento]
in <u>The Best of J.G. Ballard</u>, 1977 [as "The Concentration City"].
in <u>The Best Short Stories of J.G. Ballard</u>, 1978 [as "The Concentration City"].

A5 "Mobile." <u>Science Fantasy</u> 8, no. 23 (June):35-49.

in <u>Billenium</u>, 1962.
<u>Worlds of If</u> 17, no. 9 (September 1967):75-85 [as "Venus Smiles"; text considerably revised].
in <u>Vermilion Sands</u>, 1971 [as "Venus Smiles"].

A6 "Manhole 69." <u>New Worlds</u> 22, no. 65 (November):45-67.

*<u>New Worlds</u> [American edition] (July 1960). [Source: Strauss]
in <u>The Voices of Time</u>, 1962.
Edmund Crispin, ed. <u>Best Tales of Terror</u>. London: Faber & Faber, 1962.
in <u>The Disaster Area</u>, 1967 [text revised].
in <u>Chronopolis</u>, 1971 [text revised].
in <u>The Best of J.G. Ballard</u>, 1977 [text revised].
in <u>The Best Short Stories of J.G. Ballard</u>, 1978 [text revised].

1958

A7 "Track 12." <u>New Worlds</u> 24, no. 70 (April):62-67.

Brian Aldiss, ed. <u>Penguin Science Fiction</u>. Harmondsworth: Penguin Books, 1961 [paper].
in <u>Passport to Eternity</u>, 1963.
in <u>The Overloaded Man</u>, 1967.
Alex Hamilton, ed. <u>Best Horror Stories 3</u>. London: Faber & Faber, 1972.
in <u>The Venus Hunters</u>, 1980.

1959

A8 "The Waiting Grounds." <u>New Worlds</u> 30, no. 88 (November):41-69.

Part A: Fiction   1960

  *New Worlds [American edition] (June 1960). [Source:
   Strauss]
  in The Voices of Time, 1962.
  in The Day of Forever, 1967.
  in The Best of J.G. Ballard, 1977.
  Robert Silverberg, ed. Galactic Dreamers. New York:
   Random House, 1977.

A9 "Now:Zero." Science Fantasy 13, no. 38 (December):61-73.

  in Billenium, 1962.
  in The Overloaded Man, 1967.
  Michael Ashley, ed. The Best of British SF 2. London:
   Futura, 1977 [paper].
  in The Venus Hunters, 1980.

          1960

A10 "The Sound-Sweep." Science Fantasy 13, no. 39 (February):2-39.

  Judith Merril, ed. The 5th Annual of the Year's Best SF.
   New York: Simon & Schuster, 1960.
  in The Voices of Time, 1962.
  in The Four-Dimensional Nightmare, 1963.
  Judith Merril, ed. SF: The Best of the Best. New York:
   Delacorte, 1967.
  in Chronopolis, 1971.
  Damon Knight, ed. Tomorrow and Tomorrow. New York: Simon
   & Schuster, 1973.
  in The Best of J.G. Ballard, 1977.

A11 "Zone of Terror." New Worlds 32, no. 92 (March):52-69.

  in The Voices of Time, 1962.
  in The Disaster Area, 1967 [text revised].
  in Chronopolis, 1971.

A12 "Chronopolis." New Worlds 32, no. 95 (June):64-87.

  in Billenium, 1962.
  in The Four-Dimensional Nightmare, 1963.
  Christopher Cerf, ed. The Vintage Anthology of Science
   Fantasy. New York: Vintage Books, 1966 [paper].
  in Chronopolis, 1971.
  in The Best of J.G. Ballard, 1977.
  in The Best Short Stories of J.G. Ballard, 1978.

A13 "The Voices of Time." New Worlds 33, no. 99 (October):91-123.

  in The Voices of Time, 1962.

Kingsley Amis and Robert Conquest, eds. Spectrum III.
   London: Victor Gollancz, 1963.
in The Four-Dimensional Nightmare, 1963.
Damon Knight, ed. One Hundred Years of Science Fiction.
   New York: Simon & Schuster, 1968.
[Michael Moorcock], ed. The Inner Landscape. London:
   Allison & Busby, 1969.
Robert Silverberg, ed. Alpha 2. New York: Ballantine
   Books, 1971 [paper].
in Chronopolis, 1971.
Norman Spinrad, ed. Modern Science Fiction. Garden City:
   Anchor Books, 1974 [paper].
in The Best of J.G. Ballard, 1977.
in The Best Short Stories of J.G. Ballard, 1978.

A14   "The Last World of Mr Goddard." Science Fantasy 15, no. 43
      (October):67-82.

      in Terminal Beach (U.S.), 1964.
      in The Day of Forever, 1967.

1961

A15   "Studio 5, the Stars." Science Fantasy 15, no. 45 (February):
      69-103.

      in Billenium, 1962.
      in The Four-Dimensional Nightmare, 1963.
      in Vermilion Sands, 1971 [in the British edition of
         Vermilion Sands, 1973, the text of this story is revised].

A16   "Deep End." New Worlds 36, no. 106 (May):111-22.

      in The Voices of Time, 1962.
      in The Terminal Beach (U.K.), 1964 [text revised].
      in Chronopolis, 1971.
      in The Best Short Stories of J.G. Ballard, 1978.

A17   "The Overloaded Man." New Worlds 36, no. 108 (July):28-40.

      in The Voices of Time, 1962.
      in The Overloaded Man, 1967.
      in The Four-Dimensional Nightmare [2d ed.], 1974.
      in The Best of J.G. Ballard, 1977.
      Michael Ashley, ed. The History of the Science Fiction
         Magazine, Part 4. London: New English Library, 1978.
      in The Best Short Stories of J.G. Ballard, 1978.

A18   "Mr F. is Mr F." Science Fantasy 16, no. 48 (August):39-56.

Part A: Fiction 1961

in The Disaster Area, 1967 [text revised].
Michael Moorcock, ed. The Traps of Time. London: Rapp & Whiting, 1968.

A19 "Storm-Wind." New Worlds 37, no. 110, Part One (September): 4-48; no. 111, Part Two (October):83-125.

The Wind from Nowhere. New York: Berkley, 1962 [paper].
in The Drowned World and The Wind from Nowhere, 1965.
The Wind from Nowhere. Harmondsworth: Penguin Books, 1967 [paper].
The book version, The Wind from Nowhere, differs considerably from the magazine version, "Storm Wind." The chapter order differs, and the magazine version has an epilogue which is missing from the book.

A20 "Billenium." New Worlds 38, no. 112 (November):43-58.

in Billenium, 1962.
in The Terminal Beach (U.K.), 1964 [as "Billennium"].
Amabel Williams-Ellis and Mably Owens, eds. Out of This World 4. London: Blackie, 1964.
Edmund Crispin, ed. Best of SF Six. London: Faber & Faber, 1966.
Damon Knight, ed. Cities of Wonder. Garden City: Doubleday, 1966.
Richard Curtis, ed. Future Tense. New York: Dell, 1968 [paper].
Edmund Crispin, ed. The Stars and Under. London: Faber & Faber, 1968.
*Rob Sauer, ed. Voyages: Scenarios for a Ship Called Earth. New York: Ballantine Books, 1971 [paper]. [Source: Contento]
in Chronopolis, 1971.
*Robert Silverberg, ed. Windows Into Tomorrow. New York: Hawthorn, 1974. [Source: Contento]
M.H. Greenberg, J.W. Milstead, J.D. Olander, and Patricia Warrick, eds. Social Problems Through Science Fiction. New York: St. Martin's Press, 1975 [paper].
Ralph Clem, M.H. Greenberg, and J.D. Olander, eds. The City: 2000 AD. New York: Fawcett, 1976 [paper].
*Bernard C. Hollister, ed. You and SF: a Humanistic Approach to Tomorrow. Skokie, Ill.: National Textbook Co., 1976. [Source: Contento]
Sheila Schwartz, ed. Earth in Transit. New York: Dell, 1976 [paper].
in The Best of J.G. Ballard, 1977 [as "Billennium"].
Patricia Warrick, M.H. Greenberg, and J.D. Olander, eds. Science Fiction: Contemporary Mythology. New York: Harper & Row, 1978.
in The Best Short Stories of J.G. Ballard, 1978 [as

"Billennium"].
Ralph Clem, M.H. Greenberg, and J.D. Olander, eds. No Room for Man: Population and the Future Through Science Fiction. Totowa, N.J.: Littlefield, Adams, 1979 [paper].
Malcolm Edwards, ed. Constellations. London: Victor Gollancz, 1980.

A21 "The Gentle Assassin." New Worlds 38, no. 113 (December):29-40.

in Billenium, 1962.
in The Day of Forever, 1967.

1962

A22 "The Drowned World." Science Fiction Adventures 4, no. 24 (January):2-56.

The Drowned World. New York: Berkley, 1962 [paper; considerably expanded].
London: Victor Gollancz, 1963. [Note: title page dated 1962; published in January 1963.]
in The Drowned World and The Wind from Nowhere, 1965.
Harmondsworth: Penguin Books, 1965 [paper].
The book version of The Drowned World is expanded to about twice the length of the original magazine novella.

A23 "The Insane Ones." Amazing Stories 36, no. 1 (January):36-46.

in Billenium, 1962.
Judith Merril, ed. The 8th Annual of the Year's Best SF. New York: Simon & Schuster, 1963.
in The Day of Forever, 1967.
*Great Science Fiction (November 1967), pp. 95-? [Source: NESFA]
in The Best of J.G. Ballard, 1977.

A24 The Wind from Nowhere. See "Storm-Wind," 1961 (A19).

A25 "The Garden of Time." Fantasy and Science Fiction 22, no. 2 (February):5-12.

in Billenium, 1962.
in The Four-Dimensional Nightmare, 1963.
Avram Davidson, ed. The Best from Fantasy and Science Fiction, Twelfth Series. Garden City: Doubleday, 1963.
Brian Aldiss, ed. Introducing SF. London: Faber & Faber, 1964.
in Chronopolis, 1971.

Part A: Fiction   1962

   *Thomas E. Sanders, ed. Speculations: An Introduction to
       Literature Through Fantasy and Science Fiction. Beverly
       Hills, Calif.: Benziger, Bruce & Glencoe, 1973 [paper].
       [Source: Contento]
   Lee Harding, ed. Beyond Tomorrow. Melbourne: Wren, 1976.
   in The Best of J.G. Ballard, 1977.
   in The Best Short Stories of J.G. Ballard, 1978.

A26 The Voices of Time and Other Stories. New York: Berkley
    [paper; "The Voices of Time," 1960; "The Sound-Sweep," 1960;
    "The Overloaded Man," 1961; "Zone of Terror," 1960; "Man-
    hole 69," 1957; "The Waiting Grounds," 1959; "Deep End,"
    1961].

A27 "The Thousand Dreams of Stellavista." Amazing Stories 36, no.
    3 (March):48-68.

       in Passport to Eternity, 1963.
       *Great Science Fiction (November 1967), pp. 64-? [Source:
          NESFA]
       in Vermilion Sands, 1971 [in the British edition of
          Vermilion Sands, 1973, the text of this story is revised].

A28 "Thirteen to Centaurus." Amazing Stories 36, no. 4 (April):
    24-47.

       in Passport to Eternity, 1963.
       *The Most Thrilling SF Ever Told (Winter 1967), pp. 4-?
          [Source: NESFA]
       in The Overloaded Man, 1967.
       Thomas D. Clareson, ed. A Spectrum of Worlds. Garden
          City: Doubleday, 1972.
       *Roger Elwood, ed. The Learning Maze and Other Science
          Fiction. New York: Messner, 1974. [Source: Contento]
       in The Four-Dimensional Nightmare, 1974.
       in The Best of J.G. Ballard, 1977.
       in The Best Short Stories of J.G. Ballard, 1978 [as
          "Thirteen for Centaurus"].

A29 "Passport to Eternity." Amazing Stories 36, no. 6 (June):56-
    74.

       in Passport to Eternity, 1963.
       in The Overloaded Man, 1967.
       *The Most Thrilling SF Ever Told (Spring 1968), pp. 109-?
          [Source: NESFA]
       in The Best of J.G. Ballard, 1977.
       in The Venus Hunters, 1980.

A30 "The Cage of Sand." New Worlds 40, no. 119 (June):55-78.

in The Four-Dimensional Nightmare, 1963.
in Passport to Eternity, 1963.
Robert Silverberg, ed. Dark Stars. New York: Ballantine Books, 1969 [paper].
in Chronopolis, 1971.
Thomas M. Disch, ed. The Ruins of Earth. London: Hutchinson, 1973.
in The Best of J.G. Ballard, 1977.
in The Best Short Stories of J.G. Ballard, 1978.

A31 "The Watch-Towers." Science Fantasy 18, no. 53 (June):51-78.

in The Four-Dimensional Nightmare, 1963.
in Passport to Eternity, 1963.
Christopher Evans, ed. Mind at Bay: Eleven Horror Stories. London: Panther Books, 1969 [paper].
in Chronopolis, 1971.

A32 "The Singing Statues." Fantastic Stories 11, no. 7 (July):6-18.

*Great Science Fiction (November 1966), pp. 4-? [Source: NESFA]
in Vermilion Sands, 1973 [text revised; this story was not included in the American edition of Vermilion Sands, 1971].

A33 "The Man on the 99th Floor." New Worlds 40, no. 120 (July): 36-43.

in Passport to Eternity, 1963.
in The Day of Forever, 1967.

A34 The Drowned World. See "The Drowned World," 1962 (A22).

A35 Billenium. New York: Berkley [paper; "Billenium," 1961; "The Insane Ones," 1962; "Studio 5, the Stars," 1961; "The Gentle Assassin," 1961; "Build-Up," 1957; "Now: Zero," 1959; "Mobile," 1957; "Chronopolis," 1960; "Prima Belladonna," 1956; "The Garden of Time," 1962].

1963

A36 "The Subliminal Man." New Worlds 42, no. 126 (January):109-26.

in Terminal Beach (U.S.), 1964.
G.D. Doherty, ed. Stories from Science Fiction. London: Nelson, 1966.
Douglas Hill, ed. Window on the Future. London: Rupert Hart-Davis, 1966.

Part A: Fiction   1963

>   in The Disaster Area, 1967 [text revised].
>   Robert Silverberg, ed. The Mirror of Infinity: A Critics'
>   Anthology of Science Fiction. New York: Harper & Row,
>   1970.
>   John Stadler, ed. Eco-Fiction. New York: Washington
>   Square Press, 1971 [paper].
>   Bonnie L. Heintz, Frank Herbert, Donald A. Joos, and Jane
>   Agorn McGee, eds. Tomorrow, and Tomorrow, and Tomor-
>   row . . . New York: Holt, Rinehart & Winston, 1974
>   [paper].
>   H.A. Katz, Patricia Warrick, and M.H. Greenberg, eds.
>   Introductory Psychology Through Science Fiction. New
>   York: Rand McNally, 1974 [paper].
>   M.H. Greenberg and J.D. Olander, eds. Tomorrow, Inc.: SF
>   Stories about Big Business. New York: Taplinger, 1976
>   [paper].
>   *Bernard C. Hollister, ed. You and SF: A Humanistic
>   Approach to Tomorrow. Skokie, Ill.: National Textbook
>   Co., 1976 [paper]. [Source: Contento]
>   Sheila Schwartz, ed. Earth in Transit. New York: Dell,
>   1976 [paper].
>   in The Best of J.G. Ballard, 1977 [text revised].
>   in The Best Short Stories of J.G. Ballard, 1978.

A37 "The Sherrington Theory." Amazing Stories 37, no. 3 (March):
     102-13.

>   in The Terminal Beach (U.K.), 1964 [as "The Reptile En-
>   closure"].
>   in The Impossible Man, 1966 [as "The Reptile Enclosure"].
>   *The Most Thrilling SF Ever Told (November 1966), pp. 45-?
>   [Source: NESFA]

A38 "A Question of Re-Entry." Fantastic Stories 12, no. 3
     (March):46-77.

>   in Passport to Eternity, 1963.
>   in The Terminal Beach (U.K.), 1964.
>   in The Best of J.G. Ballard, 1977.

A39 "The Time-Tombs." Worlds of If 13, no. 1 (March):6-21.

>   in Terminal Beach (U.S.), 1964.
>   in The Overloaded Man, 1967.
>   Frederik Pohl, ed. The Second If Reader of Science Fiction.
>   Garden City: Doubleday, 1968.
>   in The Venus Hunters, 1980.

A40 "Now Wakes the Sea." Fantasy and Science Fiction 25, no. 5
     (May):76-85.

in Terminal Beach (U.S.), 1964.
Avram Davidson, ed. The Best from Fantasy and Science Fiction, Thirteenth Series. Garden City: Doubleday, 1964.
in The Disaster Area, 1967 [text revised].
in Chronopolis, 1971.

A41 The Four-Dimensional Nightmare. London: Victor Gollancz ["The Voices of Time," 1963; "The Sound-Sweep," 1960; "Prima Belladonna," 1956; "Studio 5, the Stars," 1961; "The Garden of Time," 1962; "The Cage of Sand," 1962; "The Watch-Towers," 1962; "Chronopolis," 1960].

Harmondsworth: Penguin Books, 1965 [paper].
London: Victor Gollancz, 1974 [revised contents: "The Voices of Time," 1960; "The Sound-Sweep," 1960; "The Overloaded Man," 1961; "Thirteen to Centaurus," 1962; "The Garden of Time," 1962; "The Cage of Sand," 1962; "The Watch-Towers," 1962; "Chronopolis," 1960].
Harmondsworth: Penguin Books, 1977 [paper; contents follow 1974 edition].

A42 "The Encounter." Amazing Stories 37, no. 6 (June):88-118.

in Terminal Beach (U.S.), 1964 [as "The Venus Hunters"].
in The Overloaded Man, 1967 [as "The Venus Hunters"].
in The Venus Hunters, 1980 [as "The Venus Hunters"].

A43 "End-Game." New Worlds 44, no. 131 (June):31-51.

in Terminal Beach (U.S.), 1964.
in The Terminal Beach (U.K.), 1964.
Harry Harrison, ed. Backdrop of Stars. London: Dobson, 1968. Published in America as SF: Author's Choice. New York: Berkley, 1968 [paper].
in Chronopolis, 1971.
in The Best Short Stories of J.G. Ballard, 1978.

A44 "Minus One." Science Fantasy 20, no. 59 (June):75-86.

in Terminal Beach (U.S.), 1964.
in The Disaster Area, 1967 [text revised].

A45 "The Sudden Afternoon." Fantastic Stories 12, no. 9 (September):38-51.

in Terminal Beach (U.S.), 1964.
in The Day of Forever, 1967.
*Strange Fantasy (Spring 1970), pp. 24-? [Source: NESFA]

A46 Passport to Eternity. New York: Berkley [paper; "The Man on the 99th Floor," 1962; "Thirteen to Centaurus," 1962;

Part A: Fiction 1964

"Track 12," 1958; "The Watch-Towers," 1962; "A Question of Re-Entry," 1963; "Escapement," 1956; "The Thousand Dreams of Stellavista," 1962; "The Cage of Sand," 1962; "Passport to Eternity," 1962].

A47 "The Screen Game." Fantastic Stories 12, no. 10 (October): 6-29.

in The Impossible Man, 1966.
Peter Haining, ed. The Hollywood Nightmare: Tales of Fantasy and Horror from the Film World. London: Macdonald, 1970.
in Vermilion Sands, 1971 [in the British edition of Vermilion Sands, 1973, the text of this story is revised].

1964

A48 "Time of Passage." Science Fantasy 21, no. 63 (February):85-96.

in The Impossible Man, 1966.
in The Overloaded Man, 1967.
M.H. Greenberg and J.D. Olander, eds. Time of Passage: SF Stories about Death and Dying. New York: Taplinger, 1978.
in The Venus Hunters, 1980.

*A49 "Prisoner of the Coral Deep." Argosy (March). [Source: D62]

New Worlds 48, no. 150 (May 1965):82-88.
in The Day of Forever, 1967.

A50 "The Lost Leonardo." Fantasy and Science Fiction 26, no. 3 (March):112-28.

in The Terminal Beach (U.K.), 1964.
Terry Carr, ed. New Worlds of Fantasy. New York: Ace Books, 1967 [paper].

A51 "The Terminal Beach." New Worlds 47, no. 140 (March):4-24.

in Terminal Beach (U.S.), 1964.
in The Terminal Beach (U.K.), 1964 [text revised].
Judith Merril, ed. The Year's Best SF: 10th Annual Edition. New York: Delacorte, 1965.
Michael Moorcock, ed. The Best of New Worlds. London: Compact Books, 1965 [paper].
Robert Silverberg, ed. Alpha One. New York: Ballantine Books, 1970 [paper].
in Chronopolis, 1971.

1964   Primary Bibliography

           Total Effect [Leonard Allison, Leonard Jenkin, and Robert
              Perrault], eds. Survival Printout. New York: Vintage
              Books, 1973 [paper].
           in The Best of J.G. Ballard, 1977 [text revised].
           in The Best Short Stories of J.G. Ballard, 1978.
           James Gunn, ed. The Road to Science Fiction, #3: From
              Heinlein to Here. New York: New American Library, 1979
              [paper].

     A52   "The Illuminated Man." Fantasy and Science Fiction 26, no. 5
           (May):5-31.

           in The Terminal Beach (U.K.), 1964.
           Avram Davidson, ed. The Best from Fantasy and Science Fic-
              tion, Fourteenth Series. Garden City: Doubleday, 1965.

     A53   "Equinox." New Worlds 48, no. 142, Part One (May-June):4-47;
           no. 143, Part Two (July-August):86-128.

           The Crystal World. London: Jonathan Cape, 1966 [con-
              siderably expanded].
           New York: Farrar, Straus & Giroux, 1966.
           New York: Berkley, 1967 [paper].
           London: Panther Books, 1968 [paper].

     A54   Terminal Beach. New York: Berkley [paper; "End-Game," 1963;
           "The Subliminal Man," 1963; "The Last World of Mr. Goddard,"
           1960; "The Time-Tombs," 1963; "Now Wakes the Sea," 1963;
           "The Venus Hunters," 1963; "Minus One," 1963; "The Sudden
           Afternoon," 1963; "The Terminal Beach," 1964].

     A55   "The Venus Hunters." See "The Encounter," 1963 (A42).

     A56   The Terminal Beach. London: Victor Gollancz ["A Question of
           Re-Entry," 1963; "The Drowned Giant," 1964; "End-Game,"
           1963; "The Illuminated Man," 1964; "The Reptile Enclosure,"
           1963; "The Delta at Sunset," 1964; "The Terminal Beach,"
           1964; "Deep End," 1961; "The Volcano Dances," 1964;
           "Billennium," 1961; "The Gioconda of the Twilight Noon,"
           1964; "The Lost Leonardo," 1964].

     A57   "The Delta at Sunset." In The Terminal Beach (U.K.), 1964
           (A56).

           in The Impossible Man, 1966.

     A58   "The Drowned Giant." In The Terminal Beach (U.K.), 1964 (A56).

           Playboy (May 1965) [as "Souvenir"].
           in The Impossible Man, 1966.
           Damon Knight, ed. Nebula Award Stories: 1965. Garden

Part A: Fiction   1965

              City: Doubleday, 1966.
        Judith Merril, ed. The Year's Best SF: 11th Annual Edi-
              tion. New York: Delacorte, 1966.
        *Anon, ed. The Playboy Book of Science Fiction and Fantasy.
              Chicago: Playboy Press, 1966 [as "Souvenir"]. [Source:
              Contento]
        Anon, ed. Transit of Earth. Chicago: Playboy Press, 1971
              [paper; as "Souvenir"].
        in Chronopolis, 1971.
        *Terry Carr, ed. Into the Unknown. New York: Nelson,
              1973. [Source: Contento]
        in The Best Short Stories of J.G. Ballard, 1978.

A59   "The Gioconda of the Twilight Noon." In The Terminal Beach
      (U.K.), 1964 (A56).

      in The Impossible Man, 1966.

A60   "The Reptile Enclosure." See "The Sherrington Theory," 1963
      (A37).

A61   "The Volcano Dances." In The Terminal Beach (U.K.), 1964
      (A56).

        Judith Merril, ed. The Year's Best SF: 11th Annual Edi-
              tion. New York: Delacorte, 1966.

A62   The Burning World. New York: Berkley [paper].

        The Drought. London: Jonathan Cape, 1965 [revised].
           Harmondsworth: Penguin Books, 1968 [paper].
        L. Peterson and D. Bolton, eds. Other Worlds. London:
           Heinemann Educational Books, 1979 [paper; a brief ex-
           tract from chapter 6 of the Cape edition; entitled "The
           Drought"].
        The Drought is the definitive version of The Burning World,
      considerably revised. The Burning World is divided into fifteen
      chapters, The Drought into forty-two.

                                1965

A63   The Drowned World and The Wind from Nowhere. Garden City:
         Doubleday [The Drowned World, 1962; The Wind from Nowhere,
         1962].

A64   "Dune Limbo." New Worlds 48, no. 148 (March):52-68 [an ex-
         tract from The Drought; chapters 25-27 of the Cape edition].

A65   "The Draining Lake." Ambit, no. 23 [Spring?], pp. 34-40 [an
         extract from The Drought; chapters 1-3 of the Cape edition].

A66   "Souvenir." See "The Drowned Giant," 1964 (A58).

A67   The Drought. See The Burning World, 1964 (A62).

1966

*A68 "Confetti Royale." Rogue (January/February). [Source: D62]

   New Worlds, no. 189 (April 1969), pp. 27-31 [as "The Beach
      Murders"].
   Michael Moorcock, ed. Best SF Stories from New Worlds 7.
      London: Panther Books, 1971 [paper; as "The Beach
      Murders"].
   in Low-Flying Aircraft, 1976 [as "The Beach Murders"].

A69   "You and Me and the Continuum." Impulse 1, no. 1 (March):53-
      60.

   Judith Merril, ed. England Swings SF. Garden City:
      Doubleday, 1968.
   in The Atrocity Exhibition, 1970 [text revised].
   Judith Merril, ed. The Space-Time Journal. London:
      Panther Books, 1972 [paper].

A70   "The Assassination Weapon." New Worlds 49, no. 161 (April):
      4-12.

   Michael Moorcock, ed. Best SF Stories from New Worlds.
      London: Panther Books, 1967 [paper].
   in The Atrocity Exhibition, 1970 [text revised].
   *James B. Hall and Elizabeth C. Hall, eds. The Realm of
      Fiction: 74 Short Stories. New York: McGraw-Hill,
      1977.

A71   The Crystal World. See "Equinox," 1964 (A53).

A72   The Impossible Man and Other Stories. New York: Berkley
      [paper; "The Drowned Giant," 1964; "The Reptile Enclosure,"
      1963; "The Delta at Sunset," 1964; "Storm-Bird, Storm-
      Dreamer," 1966; "The Screen Game," 1963; "The Day of For-
      ever," 1966; "Time of Passage," 1964; "The Gioconda of the
      Twilight Noon," 1964; "The Impossible Man," 1966].

A73   "The Day of Forever." In The Impossible Man, 1966 (A72).

   New Worlds 50, no. 170 (January 1967):10-28.
   in The Day of Forever, 1967.
   in The Best of J.G. Ballard, 1977.

A74   "The Impossible Man." In The Impossible Man, 1966 (A72).

Part A: Fiction   1966

           in The Disaster Area, 1967.

   A75   "Storm-Bird, Storm-Dreamer." In The Impossible Man, 1966
         (A72).

           New Worlds 50, no. 168 (November 1966):4-25.
           in The Disaster Area, 1967.
           in Chronopolis, 1971.

   A76   "You: Coma: Marilyn Monroe." Ambit, no. 27 [Spring?], pp.
         3-6.

           New Worlds 50, no. 163 (June 1966):66-71.
           Michael Moorcock, ed. Best SF Stories from New Worlds 2.
             London: Panther Books, 1968 [paper].
           Judith Merril, ed. The Year's Best SF: 12th Annual Edi-
             tion. New York: Delacorte, 1968.
           in The Atrocity Exhibition, 1970 [text revised].

   A77   "The Atrocity Exhibition." New Worlds 50, no. 166 (September):
         91-102.

           Encounter 27, no. 3 (March 1967):3-9.
           Michael Moorcock, ed. Best SF Stories from New Worlds 3.
             London: Panther Books, 1968 [paper].
           in The Atrocity Exhibition, 1970 [text revised].
           in The Best Short Stories of J.G. Ballard, 1978 [text
             revised].

   A78   "Tomorrow is a Million Years." Argosy (October).

           New Worlds 50, no. 169 (December):139-52.
           in The Day of Forever, 1967.
           Joseph Elder, ed. The Farthest Reaches. New York: Trident
             Press, 1968.

   A79   "The Assassination of John Fitzgerald Kennedy Considered as a
         Downhill Motor Race." Ambit, no. 29 [Autumn?]:3-4.

           New Worlds 50, no. 171 (March 1967):119-21.
           in The Day of Forever, 1967.
           Harry Harrison and Brian Aldiss, eds. Best SF: 1967.
             New York: Berkley, 1968 [paper]. Published in Britain
             as The Year's Best Science Fiction. London: Sphere
             Books, 1968 [paper].
           Judith Merril, ed. England Swings SF. Garden City:
             Doubleday, 1968.
           in The Atrocity Exhibition, 1970.
           Evergreen Review 17, no. 96 (Spring 1973):149-52.
           *J.D. Olander, M.H. Greenberg, and Patricia Warrick, eds.
             American Government Through Science Fiction. New York:

Rand McNally, 1974 [paper]. [Source: Contento]
Brian Aldiss and Harry Harrison, eds. Decade: The 1960s.
London: Macmillan, 1977.
in The Best Short Stories of J.G. Ballard, 1978.

1967

A80 "Plan for the Assassination of Jacqueline Kennedy." Ambit, no. 31 [Spring?]:9-11.

  Judith Merril, ed. England Swings SF. Garden City: Doubleday, 1968.
  in The Atrocity Exhibition, 1970.
  Leslie Fiedler, ed. In Dreams Awake: A Historical-Critical Anthology of Science Fiction. New York: Dell, 1975 [paper].
  in The Best Short Stories of J.G. Ballard, 1978.

A81 "The Death Module." New Worlds, no. 173 (July), pp. 21-24.

  Michael Moorcock, ed. Best SF Stories from New Worlds 5. London: Panther Books, 1969 [paper].
  in The Atrocity Exhibition, 1970 [as "Notes Towards a Mental Breakdown"; text revised].

A82 "Venus Smiles." See "Mobile," 1957 (A5).

A83 The Day of Forever. London: Panther Books [paper; "The Day of Forever," 1966; "Prisoner of the Coral Deep," 1964; "Tomorrow is a Million Years," 1966; "The Man on the 99th Floor," 1962; "The Waiting Grounds," 1959; "The Last World of Mr Goddard," 1960; "The Gentle Assassin," 1961; "The Sudden Afternoon," 1963; "The Insane Ones," 1962; "The Assassination of John Fitzgerald Kennedy Considered as a Downhill Motor Race," 1966].

  London: Panther Books, 1971 [paper; in this second edition "The Assassination of John Fitzgerald Kennedy Considered as a Downhill Motor Race" is omitted and "The Killing Ground," 1969, is added].

A84 "Cry Hope, Cry Fury!" Fantasy and Science Fiction 33, no. 4 (October):114-28.

  in Vermilion Sands, 1971.

A85 The Disaster Area. London: Jonathan Cape ["Storm-Bird, Storm-Dreamer," 1966; "The Concentration City," 1957; "The Subliminal Man," 1963; "Now Wakes the Sea," 1963; "Minus One," 1963; "Mr F. is Mr F.," 1961; "Zone of Terror," 1960;

Part A: Fiction 1968

"Manhole 69," 1957; "The Impossible Man," 1966].

London: Panther Books, 1969 [paper].

A86 "The Concentration City." See "Build-Up," 1957 (A4).

A87 "The Recognition." In <u>Dangerous Visions</u>. Edited by Harlan Ellison. Garden City: Doubleday, 1967.

A88 <u>The Overloaded Man</u>. London: Panther Books [paper; "Now: Zero," 1959; "The Time-Tombs," 1963; "Thirteen to Centaurus," 1962; "Track 12," 1957; "Passport to Eternity," 1962; "Escapement," 1956; "Time of Passage," 1964; "The Venus Hunters," 1963; "The Coming of the Unconscious," 1966 (non-fiction; see C17); "The Overloaded Man," 1961].

For a much revised edition of this collection see <u>The Venus Hunters</u>, 1980 (A143).

A89 "The Cloud-Sculptors of Coral D." <u>Fantasy and Science Fiction</u> 33, no. 6 (December):113-27.

    Judith Merril, ed. <u>The Year's Best SF: 12th Annual Edition</u>. New York: Delacorte, 1968.
    Roger Zelazny, ed. <u>Nebula Award Stories Three</u>. Garden City: Doubleday, 1968.
    Edward L. Ferman, ed. <u>The Best from Fantasy and Science Fiction, Eighteenth Series</u>. Garden City: Doubleday, 1969.
    in <u>Vermilion Sands</u>, 1971.
    in <u>The Best Short Stories of J.G. Ballard</u>, 1978.
    Frederik Pohl, M.H. Greenberg, and J.D. Olander, eds. <u>The Great Science Fiction Series</u>. New York: Harper & Row, 1980.

<u>1968</u>

A90 "The Dead Astronaut." <u>Playboy</u> (May), pp. 118-20, 166-68.

    Christopher Evans, ed. <u>Mind in Chains</u>. London: Panther Books, 1970 [paper].
    Anon, ed. <u>The Dead Astronaut: 10 Stories of Space Flight</u>. Chicago: Playboy Press, 1971 [paper].
    in <u>Low-Flying Aircraft</u>, 1976.

A91 "Love and Napalm: Export USA." <u>The Running Man</u> 1, no. 2 [July/August]:48-49.

    in <u>The Atrocity Exhibition</u>, 1970.

A92 "Why I Want to Fuck Ronald Reagan." Ronald Reagan: The Magazine of Poetry [no. 1?, Summer?], pp. 10-12.

   Why I Want to Fuck Ronald Reagan. Brighton: Unicorn Bookshop, 1968 [paper].
   in The Atrocity Exhibition, 1970.
   in The Best Short Stories of J.G. Ballard, 1978.
   Official Republican 1980 Presidential Survey. Washington: National Republican Congressional Committee, 1980 [reprinted without the title].

A93 "The University of Death." Transatlantic Review, no. 29 (Summer), pp. 68-79.

   in The Atrocity Exhibition, 1970.
   *Jerome Klinkowitz and John Somers, eds. Writing Under Fire: Stories of the Vietnam War. New York: Dell, 1978 [paper].

A94 "The Great American Nude." Ambit, no. 36 [Summer?], pp. 39-43.

   in The Atrocity Exhibition, 1970.

A95 "The Generations of America." New Worlds, no. 183 (October), pp. 13-14.

   in The Atrocity Exhibition, 1970.

A96 "The Comsat Angels." Worlds of If 18, no. 12 (December):54-66.

   in Low-Flying Aircraft, 1976.

1969

A97 "The Summer Cannibals." New Worlds, no. 186 (January), pp. 19-23.

   in The Atrocity Exhibition, 1970.

A98 "The Killing Ground." New Worlds, no. 188 (March), pp. 47-50.

   Harry Harrison and Brian Aldiss, eds. Best SF: 1969. New York: Berkley, 1970 [paper]. Published in Britain as The Year's Best Science Fiction 3. London: Sphere Books, 1970 [paper].
   Michael Moorcock, ed. Best SF Stories from New Worlds 6. London: Panther Books, 1970 [paper].
   in The Day of Forever, 1971.

Part A: Fiction

in The Venus Hunters, 1980.

A99 "The Beach Murders." See "Confetti Royale," 1966 (A68).

A100 *"Crash!" I.C.A. Eventsheet [program leaflet of the Institute of Contemporary Arts, London]. [Source: D62]

in The Atrocity Exhibition, 1970.

A101 "Tolerances of the Human Face." Encounter 33, no. 3 (September):3-14.

in The Atrocity Exhibition, 1970.

A102 "A Place and a Time to Die." New Worlds, no. 194 (September/October), pp. 2-5.

Michael Moorcock, ed. New Worlds Quarterly. London: Sphere Books, 1971 [paper].
in Low-Flying Aircraft, 1976.
Robert Holdstock and Christopher Priest, eds. Stars of Albion. London: Pan Books, 1979 [paper].

1970

A103 "Coitus 80: A Description of the Sexual Act in 1980." New Worlds, no. 197 (January), pp. 16-17.

A104 "Journey Across a Crater." New Worlds, no. 198 (February), pp. 2-5.

Michael Moorcock, ed. New Worlds Quarterly. London: Sphere Books, 1971 [paper].

A105 "Princess Margaret's Face Lift: An Intersection of Fiction and Reality." New Worlds, no. 199 (March), p. 8.

A106 "Mae West's Reduction Mammoplasty." Ambit, no. 44 [Summer?], pp. 9-11.

A107 The Atrocity Exhibition. London: Jonathan Cape ["The Atrocity Exhibition," 1966; "The University of Death," 1968; "The Assassination Weapon," 1966; "You: Coma: Marilyn Monroe," 1966; "Notes Towards a Mental Breakdown," 1967; "The Great American Nude," 1968; "The Summer Cannibals," 1969; "Tolerances of the Human Face," 1969; "You and Me and the Continuum," 1966; "Plan for the Assassination of Jacqueline Kennedy," 1967; "Love and Napalm: Export USA," 1968; "Crash!," 1969; "The Generations of America," 1968; "Why I Want to Fuck Ronald Reagan," 1968; "The Assassination of John Fitzgerald Kennedy Considered as a Downhill Motor Race," 1966].

Love and Napalm: Export USA. New York: Grove Press, 1972 [preface by William S. Burroughs].
The Atrocity Exhibition. London: Panther Books, 1972 [paper].
An edition which was to have been published by Doubleday in the United States in 1970 (as The Atrocity Exhibtion) was destroyed immediately prior to distribution. Only a handful of copies are known to exist. This edition contains drawings by Michael Foreman and a dedication--"To the insane"--which was omitted from all other editions.

A108 "Notes Towards a Mental Breakdown." See "The Death Module," 1967 (A81).

A109 "Say Goodbye to the Wind." Fantastic Stories 19, no. 8 (August):36-45, 134.

in Vermilion Sands, 1971.
Terry Carr, ed. New Worlds of Fantasy 3. New York: Ace Books, 1971 [paper].

1971

A110 Vermilion Sands. New York: Berkley [paper; "Prima Belladonna," 1956; "The Thousand Dreams of Stellavista," 1962; "Cry Hope, Cry Fury!," 1967; "Venus Smiles," 1957; "Studio 5, the Stars," 1961; "The Cloud-Sculptors of Coral D," 1967; "Say Goodbye to the Wind," 1970; "The Screen Game," 1963].

London: Jonathan Cape, 1973 [revised contents: Preface; "The Cloud-Sculptors of Coral D," 1967; "Prima Belladonna," 1956; "The Screen Game," 1963; "The Singing Statues," 1962; "Cry Hope, Cry Fury!," 1967; "Venus Smiles," 1957; "Say Goodbye to the Wind," 1970; "Studio 5, the Stars," 1961; "The Thousand Dreams of Stellavista," 1962].
London: Panther Books, 1975 [paper; follows Cape edition].

A111 Chronopolis and Other Stories. New York: G.P. Putnam's Sons ["The Voices of Time," 1960; "The Drowned Giant," 1964; "The Terminal Beach," 1964; "Manhole 69," 1957; "Storm-Bird, Storm-Dreamer," 1966; "The Sound-Sweep," 1960; "Billenium," 1961; "Chronopolis," 1960; "Build-Up," 1957; "The Garden of Time," 1962; "End-Game," 1963; "The Watchtowers" (sic), 1962; "Now Wakes the Sea," 1963; "Zone of Terror," 1960; "The Cage of Sand," 1962; "Deep End," 1961].

Part A: Fiction

New York: Berkley, 1972 [paper; subtitle changed to "The Great Science Fiction of J.G. Ballard"].

1972

A112 Love and Napalm: Export USA. See The Atrocity Exhibition, 1970 (A107).

A113 "The Greatest Television Show on Earth." Ambit, no. 53 [Winter 1972/73?], pp. 29-32.

   in Low-Flying Aircraft, 1976.

1973

A114 Crash. London: Jonathan Cape.

   New York: Farrar, Straus & Giroux, 1973.
   New York: Pinnacle Books, 1974 [paper].
   London: Panther Books, 1975 [paper].

A115 "Crash." Ambit, no. 55 [Summer?], pp. 4-9 [an extract from Crash; chapter 1 of the Cape edition].

   Penthouse 8, no. 11 (1974):62-66, 99, 108.

1974

A116 Concrete Island. London: Jonathan Cape.

   New York: Farrar, Straus & Giroux, 1974.
   London: Panther Books, 1976 [paper].

A117 "My Dream of Flying to Wake Island." Ambit, no. 60 [Autumn?], pp. 60-66.

   in Low-Flying Aircraft, 1976.

1975

A118 "The Air Disaster." Bananas, no. 1 (January/February), pp. 18-20.

A119 "Low-Flying Aircraft." Bananas, no. 2 (Early Summer), pp. 6-9.

   in Low-Flying Aircraft, 1976.
   Antaeus, no. 25/26 (Spring/Summer 1977).

A120 "Critical Mass." Ambit, no. 63 [Summer?], pp. 2-14 [an extract from High-Rise; chapter 1 of the Cape edition].

A121 "A Happy Arrangement." Science Fiction Monthly 2, no. 10 (October):17-19 [an extract from High-Rise; chapter 16 of the Cape edition].

A122 High-Rise. London: Jonathan Cape.

    New York: Holt, Rinehart & Winston, 1977.
    London: Panther Books, 1977 [paper].
    New York: Popular Library, 1978 [paper].

1976

A123 "The Life and Death of God." Ambit, no. 66 [Spring?], pp. 5-10.

    in Low-Flying Aircraft, 1976.

A124 "Notes Towards a Mental Breakdown." Bananas, no. 4 (Spring), pp. 20-21.

    An earlier, completely different story, was given the same title; see A81 and A108.

A125 "The 60 Minute Zoom." Bananas, no. 5 (Summer), pp. 18-20.

    in The Venus Hunters, 1980.

A126 "The Smile." Bananas, no. 6 (Autumn/Winter), pp. 8-10.

    in Myths of the Near Future, 1982.

A127 Low-Flying Aircraft and Other Stories. London: Jonathan Cape ["The Ultimate City," 1976; "Low-Flying Aircraft," 1975; "The Dead Astronaut," 1968; "My Dream of Flying to Wake Island," 1974; "The Life and Death of God," 1976; "The Greatest Television Show on Earth," 1972; "A Place and a Time to Die," 1969; "The Comsat Angels," 1968; "The Beach Murders," 1966].

    London: Triad/Panther Books, 1978 [paper].

A128 "The Ultimate City." In Low-Flying Aircraft, 1976 (A127).

    CoEvolution Quarterly, no. 14, Part One (Summer 1977), pp. 79-95; no. 15, Part Two (Fall 1977), pp. 92-106.

A129 "Queen Elizabeth's Rhinoplasty." TriQuarterly 35 (Winter 1976/

Part A: Fiction 1978

77):18-20.

1977

A130 "The Dead Time." Bananas, no. 7 (Spring), 12-17.

    Emma Tennant, ed. Bananas. Blond & Briggs/Quartet Books, 1977.
    in Myths of the Near Future, 1982.

A131 The Best of J.G. Ballard. London: Futura [paper; Introduction; "The Concentration City," 1957; "Manhole 69," 1957; "The Waiting Grounds," 1959; "The Sound-Sweep," 1960; "Chronopolis," 1960; "The Voices of Time," 1960; "The Overloaded Man," 1961; "Billennium," 1961; "The Insane Ones," 1962; "The Garden of Time," 1962; "Thirteen to Centaurus," 1962; "The Subliminal Man," 1963; "Passport to Eternity," 1962; "The Cage of Sand," 1962; "A Question of Re-Entry," 1963; "The Terminal Beach," 1964; "The Day of Forever," 1966; each story is prefaced with brief notes by the author; the title on cover and spine reads The Best Science Fiction of J.G. Ballard].

A132 "The Index." Bananas, no. 8 (Summer), pp. 24-25.

A133 "The Intensive Care Unit." Ambit, no. 71 [Summer?], pp. 3-9.

    *J. Laughlin et al, eds. New Directions in Prose and Poetry 37. New York: New Directions, 1978.
    in Myths of the Near Future, 1982.

A134 "Theatre of War." Bananas, no. 9 (Winter), pp. 21-25.

    in Myths of the Near Future, 1982.

1978

A135 "Having a Wonderful Time." Bananas, no. 10 (Spring), pp. 24-25.

    Emma Tennant, ed. The Saturday Night Reader. London: W.H. Allen, 1979.
    in Myths of the Near Future, 1982.

A136 "One Afternoon at Utah Beach." In Anticipations. Edited by Christopher Priest. London: Faber & Faber.

    in The Venus Hunters, 1980.

A137   "Zodiac 2000." <u>Ambit</u>, no. 75 [Summer?], pp. 4-10.

Maxim Jakubowski, ed. <u>Twenty Houses of the Zodiac</u>.
London: New English Library, 1979 [paper].
in <u>Myths of the Near Future</u>, 1982.

A138   "Motel Architecture." <u>Bananas</u>, no. 12 (Autumn), pp. 34-37.

in <u>Myths of the Near Future</u>, 1982.

A139   <u>The Best Short Stories of J.G. Ballard</u>. New York: Holt, Rinehart & Winston [Introduction by Anthony Burgess; "The Concentration City," 1957; "Manhole 69," 1957; "Chronopolis," 1960; "The Voices of Time," 1960; "Deep End," 1961; "The Overloaded Man," 1961; "Billennium," 1961; "The Garden of Time," 1962; "Thirteen for Centuarus" (sic), 1962; "The Subliminal Man," 1963; "The Cage of Sand," 1962; "End-Game," 1963; "The Drowned Giant," 1964; "The Terminal Beach," 1964; "The Cloud-Sculptors of Coral D," 1967; "The Assassination of John Fitzgerald Kennedy Considered as a Downhill Motor Race," 1966; "The Atrocity Exhibition," 1966; "Plan for the Assassination of Jacqueline Kennedy," 1967; "Why I Want to Fuck Ronald Reagan," 1968].

1979

A140   <u>The Unlimited Dream Company</u>. London: Jonathan Cape.

New York: Holt, Rinehart & Winston, 1979.
London: Triad/Granada Books, 1981 [paper].

A141   "From the Unlimited Dream Company." <u>Ambit</u>, no. 80 [Autumn?], pp. 2-12 [an extract from <u>The Unlimited Dream Company</u>; chapters 1 to 4 of the Cape edition].

A142   "Flight." <u>Antaeus</u>, no. 35 (Autumn), pp. 34-41 [extracts from <u>The Unlimited Dream Company</u>; chapters 1, 25, and 26, slightly abridged].

1980

A143   <u>The Venus Hunters</u>. London: Granada [paper; "Now: Zero," 1959; "The Time-Tombs," 1963; "Track 12," 1958; "Passport to Eternity," 1962; "Escapement," 1956; "Time of Passage," 1964; "The Venus Hunters," 1963; "The Killing Ground," 1969; "One Afternoon at Utah Beach," 1978; "The 60 Minute Zone," 1976].

This is a revised version of an earlier collection (see

Part A: Fiction 1982

A88). A statement on the copyright page reads: "Some of these stories have appeared in a previous Panther collection under the title of The Overloaded Man, 1967."

A144 "A Host of Furious Fancies." Time Out, 19 December, pp. 34-37.

> in Myths of the Near Future, 1982.

1981

A145 "Landfall, at Last." Ambit, no. 85 [Spring?], pp. 5-15 [extract from Hello America; chapters 3 to 5 of the Cape edition].

A146 Hello America. London: Jonathan Cape.

A147 "News from the Sun." Ambit, no. 87 [Autumn?], pp. 2-28.

> News from the Sun. London: Interzone, 1982 [paper; in an edition limited to 750 copies].
> in Myths of the Near Future, 1982.

1982

A148 "Memories of the Space Age." Interzone 1, no. 2 (Summer):3-13.

A149 Myths of the Near Future. London: Jonathan Cape ["Myths of the Near Future," 1982; "Having a Wonderful Time," 1978; "A Host of Furious Fancies," 1980; "Zodiac 2000," 1978; "News from the Sun," 1981; "Theatre of War," 1977; "The Dead Time," 1977; "The Smile," 1976; "Motel Architecture," 1978; "The Intensive Care Unit," 1977].

A150 "Myths of the Near Future." In Myths of the Near Future, 1982.

> Fantasy and Science Fiction 62, no. 4 (October), pp. 50-76.

Part B: Miscellaneous Media

1967

B1 "Homage to Claire Churchill." Ambit, no. 32 [Summer?], back cover.

New Worlds, no. 176 (October), inside front cover.
An "Advertiser's Announcement." The first of a series of advertisements of Ballard's ideas; consists of a photograph and a brief text.

B2 "Does the Angle Between Two Walls Have a Happy Ending?" Ambit, no. 33 [Autumn?], back cover.

New Worlds, no. 178 (December), back cover.
Ambit, no. 60 [Autumn 1974?], inside front cover.
"Advertiser's Announcement."

1968

B3 "The Bathroom: A Film in Progress by Steve Dwoskin." The Running Man 1, no. 2 (July-August):pages not numbered.

A short introduction by Ballard, and a three-page impressionistic text to accompany stills from this underground movie by Dwoskin.

B4 "A Neural Interval." Ambit, no. 36 [Summer?], back cover.

New Worlds, no. 185 (December), back cover.
"Advertiser's Announcement."

B5 "Love: A Print-out for Claire Churchill." Ambit, no. 37 [Autumn?], p. 9.

Concrete poetry.

53

1969

B6   "How Dr Christopher Evans Landed on the Moon." New Worlds, no. 187 (February), p. 49.

   Computer print-out.

1970

B7   "Placental Insufficiency." Ambit, no. 45 [Autumn?], back cover.

   "Advertiser's Announcement."

B8   "Venus Smiles." Ambit, no. 46 [Winter 1970/71?], back cover.

   "Advertiser's Announcement."

1972

B9   "The Side-Effects of Orthonovin G." Ambit, no. 50 [Spring?], pp. 26-27.

   Satirical verse monologues, supposedly by members of the Department of Sociology, Yale University.

1976

B10 "The Invisible Years: A Series of Apocalyptic Texts Written for Ambit by Varying Hands." Ambit, no. 67 [Summer?], pp. 5-12.

   The first of a number of texts contributed by Ballard to "The Invisible Years," a series of drawings by Ronald Sandford. Other writers for this series (in other issues of Ambit) include Martin Bax and George MacBeth. This piece is almost a short story.

1977

B11 "The Invisible Years." Ambit, no. 69 [Winter 1976/77?], pp. 73-80.

   Almost a short story.

B12 "The Invisible Years." Ambit, no. 72 [Autumn?], pp. 41-48.

Part B: Miscellaneous Media

Computer print-out. "This year Ballard answers the questions of Chris Evans and a Computer."

1978

B13 "The Invisible Years." Ambit, no. 73 [Winter 1977/78?], pp. 22-29.

Prose poetry.

B14 "The Invisible Years." Ambit, no. 75 [Summer?], pp. 87-94.

Prose poetry.

B15 ["Zero Synthesis."] New Worlds, no. 213 (Summer), pages not numbered.

Collage, or concrete poetry, apparently produced in 1958. There is no title; "Zero Synthesis" is the first phrase. If one looks carefully at the photograph of Ballard on the front cover of New Worlds 42, no. 126 (January 1963), one can see this material pinned to a board behind his head.

1979

B16 "The Invisible Years." Ambit, no. 78 [Spring?], pp. 57-64.

Almost a short story.

Part C: Nonfiction

1962

C1 "Which Way to Inner Space?" New Worlds 40, no. 118 (May):2-3, 116-18.

   A guest editorial, in which Ballard first uses the term "inner space." Argues against space fiction and in favor of stories set on "the only truly alien planet . . . Earth." Wishes to see sf "becoming abstract and 'cool,' inventing completely fresh situations and contexts that illustrate its theme obliquely."

1963

C2 "Time, Memory and Inner Space." Woman Journalist, (Spring), pp. 10-11.

   An article about the genesis of The Drowned World and other stories. Very briefly describes Ballard's childhood in Shanghai.

1964

C3 "Myth Maker of the 20th Century." New Worlds 48, no. 142 (May-June):121-27.

   A lengthy review of Dead Fingers Talk by William Burroughs--more of an article on Burroughs's work in general than a review of a specific work. Describes Burroughs as "true genius and first mythographer of the mid-20th century."

1965

C4 "Down to Earth." Guardian, 9 April, p. 15.

1965

Reviews of Spectrum IV edited by Kingsley Amis and Robert Conquest; Telepathist by John Brunner; I Love Galesburg in the Springtime by Jack Finney; and The Arthur C. Clarke Omnibus.

C5 "The Elephant and the Quasar." Guardian, 21 May, p. 9.

Reviews of Anomalous Phenomena by Jules Verne; The Old Die Rich by H.L. Gold; The Best SF Stories of James Blish; Connoisseur's SF edited by Tom Boardman; and Lambda 1 edited by John Carnell.

C6 "Into the Drop Zone." Guardian, 23 July, p. 7.

A review of Beyond Time by Michel Siffre.

C7 "Made in USA." Guardian, 8 October, p. 14.

Reviews of The View from the Stars by Walter M. Miller; The Dragon Masters by Jack Vance; The Reefs of Space by Frederik Pohl and Jack Williamson; The Specials by Louis Charbonneau; and Somewhere a Voice by Eric Frank Russell.

C8 "The Demolition Squad." Guardian, 12 November, p. 8.

Reviews of A Wrinkle in the Skin by John Christopher; New Writings in SF 6 edited by John Carnell; and Bill, the Galactic Hero by Harry Harrison.

C9 "The Old Guard." Guardian, 26 November, p. 17.

Reviews of Of Worlds Beyond edited by Lloyd Arthur Eshbach; Best SF Stories of Brian W. Aldiss; and Worlds Without End by Clifford Simak.

1966

C10 "The Transistorised Brain." Guardian, 28 January, p. 9.

A review of Human Robots in Myth and Science by John Cohen.

C11 "Visions of Hell." New Worlds 49, no. 160 (March):148-54.

    Michael Moorcock, ed. New Worlds Quarterly 2. London: Sphere, 1971 [paper].
A reassessment of The Human Age trilogy by Wyndham Lewis. Begins: "Hell is out of fashion--institutional hells at any rate." And concludes: "The hells that face us now are more abstract, the very dimensions of time and space, the phenomenology of the universe, the fact of our own consciousness."

Part C: Nonfiction   1966

C12   "What to Do Till the Analyst Comes." Guardian, 31 March, p. 6.

      Reviews of The Three Stigmata of Palmer Eldritch by Philip
K. Dick; The Worlds of Robert F. Young; Impulse, no. 1 and New
Worlds, no. 160; and The Anything Box by Zenna Henderson.

C13   "Terminal Documents: Burroughs Reviewed." Ambit, no. 27
      [Spring?], pp. 46-48.

      An article on William Burroughs which repeats many of the
points made in "Myth Maker of the 20th Century" (C3).

C14   "Strange Seas of Thought." Guardian, 3 June, p. 9.

      Reviews of Fantastic Voyage by Isaac Asimov; The Saliva
Tree by Brian Aldiss; Best SF 6 edited by Edmund Crispin; and
The 8th Galaxy Reader edited by Frederik Pohl.

C15   "Notes from Nowhere." Guardian, 1 July, p. 9.

      Reviews of Future Perfect by H. Bruce Franklin; Park by
John Gray; and A Robert Heinlein Omnibus.

C16   "La Jetée, Academy One." New Worlds 50, no. 164 (July):2-3.

      Billed as a "Guest Editorial": a review of La Jetée
directed by Chris Marker.

C17   "The Coming of the Unconscious." New Worlds 50, no. 164
      (July):141-46.

      in The Overloaded Man, 1967.
      An article on surrealism, cast in the form of a review of
Surrealism by Patrick Waldberg and The History of Surrealist
Painting by Marcel Jean. States that "the images of surrealism
are the iconography of inner space. . . . To move through these
landscapes is a journey of return to one's innermost being."

C18   "Death Wish Anonymous." Guardian, 19 August, p. 6.

      Reviews of All Fools Day by Edmund Cooper; Dune by Frank
Herbert; and The Fury Out of Time by Lloyd Biggle, Jr.

C19   "All in the Mind." Guardian, 23 September, p. 8.

      A review of The Changing Mind by John Roddan.

C20   "Circles and Squares." Guardian, 30 September, p. 7.

      Reviews of Inner Circle by Jerzy Peterkiewicz; New Writings
in SF 9 edited by John Carnell; and Spectrum V edited by Kingsley

59

Amis and Robert Conquest.

C21 "Notes from Nowhere: Comments on Work in Progress." New Worlds 50, no. 167 (October):147-51.

    An article written in the style of a mock interview, with "answers" to unasked questions. Deals primarily with his latest series of stories, beginning with "You and Me and the Continuum." States: "this new narrative technique seems to show a tremendous gain in the density of ideas and images. In fact, I regard each of them as a complete novel."

C22 "Waste of Beauty." Guardian, 7 October, p. 12.

    A review of Diary of the Discovery Expedition to the Antarctic, 1901-1904 by Edward Wilson.

1967

C23 "Red Stars and Sickle Moons." Guardian, 17 March, p. 7.

    Reviews of Path Into the Unknown: The Best Soviet SF; Time Probe edited by Arthur C. Clarke; Antic Earth by Louis Charbonneau; and The Egg-Shaped Thing by Christopher Hodder-Williams.

C24 "Afterword to 'The Recognition.'" In Dangerous Visions. Edited by Harlan Ellison. Garden City: Doubleday.

    Brief comments by Ballard on his short story "The Recognition." States that the story illustrates "the paradox that the only real freedom is to be found in a prison. Sometimes it is difficult to tell on which side of the bars we really are--the real gaps between the bars are the sutures of one's own skull."

C25 "The Year's Science Fiction." Guardian, 29 December, p. 4.

    Reviews of Nebula Award Stories 2 edited by Brian Aldiss and Harry Harrison; This Immortal by Roger Zelazny; Babel 17 by Samuel R. Delany; and An Age by Brian W. Aldiss.

1968

C26 "How Ariel Turned Into Prospero." Times, 2 March, p. 20.

    Reviews of The Great Computer by Olaf Johannesson; The Caltraps of Time by David I. Masson; The Starlit Corridor edited by Roger Mansfield; Analog 4 edited by John W. Campbell; and The Tenth Galaxy Reader edited by Frederik Pohl.

Part C: Nonfiction 1969

C27 "Comment on 'End-Game.'" In <u>Backdrop of Stars</u>. Edited by Harry Harrison. London: Dobson [published in America as <u>SF: Author's Choice</u> (New York: Berkley, 1968)].

A short article which describes Ballard's childhood experiences in a civilian prisoner-of-war camp near Shanghai during World War II, and relates them to the theme of his story "End-Game."

C28 "Does the Future Still Exist?" <u>Times</u>, 20 April, p. 23.

Reviews of <u>Chocky</u> by John Wyndham; <u>The Dream Master</u> by Roger Zelazny; <u>Backdrop of Stars</u> edited by Harry Harrison; <u>The Best SF Stories of C.M. Kombluth</u>; and <u>The Year's Best Science Fiction</u> edited by Harry Harrison and Brian Aldiss.

C29 "Where Have All the Space Ships Gone?" <u>Times</u>, 29 June, p. 24.

Reviews of <u>Camp Concentration</u> by Thomas M. Disch; <u>The Reproductive System</u> by John Sladek; <u>Report on Probability A</u> by Brian Aldiss; and <u>The Einstein Intersection</u> by Samuel R. Delany.

1969

C30 "The Thousand Wounds and Flowers." <u>New Worlds</u>, no. 186 (January), p. 54.

A review of <u>The Voices of Time</u> edited by J.T. Frazer [a collection of essays about time theory; it bears no relation to Ballard's own story of the same title].

C31 "An Interview with J.G. Ballard." <u>Speculation</u> 2, no. 9 (February):4-8.

An interview conducted by Jannick Storm. The emphasis is mainly on Ballard's "Atrocity Exhibition" series, his "advertisements" and his views of the 1960s media landscape.

C32 "Salvador Dali: The Innocent as Paranoid." <u>New Worlds</u>, no. 187 (February), pp. 25-30.

Michael Moorcock, ed. <u>Best SF Stories from New Worlds 8</u>.
London: Panther Books, 1974 [paper].
A copiously illustrated article on the paintings of Salvador Dali.

C33 "Dreams and Surrealism." <u>Sunday Times Magazine</u> (16 February), pp. 26-29.

A short illustrated article on surrealist painting.

1969

C34 "Use Your Vagina." New Worlds, no. 191 (June), pp. 58-60.

A review of How to Achieve Sexual Ecstasy by Stephan Gregory.

C35 "Pieces from an Interview with J.G. Ballard." International Times 60 (18 July):21, 25.

SF Commentary, no. 19 (January 1971), pp. 111-13.
An interview conducted by Robert Lightfoot and David Pendleton. The questions are not printed, just fragments of Ballard's replies. The SF Commentary version is reprinted directly from International Times. For another version of this interview, see C43.

C36 "The New Science Fiction: A Conversation Between J.G. Ballard and George MacBeth."

In The New SF. Edited by Langdon Jones. London: Hutchinson.
An interview which was first broadcast by BBC radio in 1967. It deals mainly with Ballard's "Atrocity Exhibition" series of stories.

C37 "Science Fiction Cannot Be Immune from Change." In SF Symposium. Edited by José Sanz. Rio de Janeiro: Instituto Nacional do Cinema [paper].

Algol, no. 21 (November 1973), pp. 36-37 [slightly abridged; retitled "A New Metaphor for the Future"].
A transcript of a talk first delivered at an sf symposium in Rio de Janeiro. The sense is badly mangled; the slightly edited version printed in Algol is also corrupt.

C38 "Alphabets of Unreason." New Worlds, no. 196 (December), p. 26.

A review of Mein Kampf by Adolf Hitler.

1970

C39 "The See-Through Brain." Guardian, 12 February, p. 9.

A review of We by Yevgeny Zamyatin.

C40 "J.G. Ballard." Books and Bookmen (July), p. 6.

A short piece by Ballard in response to being asked which writers have influenced him.

C41 "Sci-Fi Seer." Penthouse 5 [September?]:26-30.

Part C: Nonfiction

An interview conducted by Lynn Barber. One of the best interviews with the author yet published, this ranges very widely and deals with the moon landings, heart transplants, the disaster theme, science journalism, Ballard's childhood, the media landscape, car crashes, and future sex.

C42 "Twentieth Century Vox." Guardian, 11 September, p. 8.

An interview conducted by Michael McNay. It deals with The Atrocity Exhibition, Ballard's attitudes towards contemporary Britain, and architecture.

C43 "Inner Landscape." Friends, no. 17 (30 October), pp. 16-17.

An interview conducted by Robert Lightfoot and David Pendleton. This appears to be the full version of the International Times interview (C35). It deals with The Atrocity Exhibition, the media landscape, Freud, car crashes, and other topics.

C44 Foreword to J.G. Ballard: A Bibliography. Compiled by James Goddard. Milford on Sea: James Goddard [paper].

A brief foreword by Ballard to this amateur bibliography. The pamphlet also contains a brief "Special Introduction" by Ballard.

C45 "Lost in Space." Guardian, 26 November, p. 12.

A review of A Fire on the Moon by Norman Mailer.

C46 "Interrogation: J.G. Ballard Answers Questions." Cypher, no. 3 (December), pp. 23-27.

An interview conducted by James Goddard.

1971

C47 "Spacing Out." Times Educational Supplement, 29 January, pp. 17-18.

A short interview/profile by Brendan Hennessy. Concentrates on The Atrocity Exhibition and Ballard's attitudes to science and the media.

C48 "Fictions of Every Kind." Books and Bookmen (February).

A review of The Shattered Ring by Lois and Stephen Rose--more of a polemical piece on sf in general than a review of the book in hand. Repeats many of the points made in James Goddard's interview (C46), including the statement that "everything is becoming science fiction."

C49 "Ballard at Home." Books and Bookmen (April), pp. 11-12, 41.

    An interview/profile by Douglas Reed. Covers Ballard's views on modern fiction and his activities in the avant garde.

C50 "J.G. Ballard." Transatlantic Review, no. 39 (Spring), pp. 60-64.

    An interview conducted by Brendan Hennessy. Discusses surrealist painting, The Atrocity Exhibition, William Burroughs, and other subjects.

C51 "The Consumer Consumed." Ink, 5 June.

    A speculative article on Ralph Nader as a possible future dictator of the United States.

C52 "The Car, the Future." Drive [magazine of the Automobile Association] (Autumn), pp. 102-9.

    A speculative article on the future of automobiles and driving.

C53 "Speculative Illustrations: Eduardo Paolozzi in Conversation with J.G. Ballard and Frank Whitford." Studio International, no. 183 (October), pp. 136-43.

    A three-way discussion of surrealism, pop art, and the work of Eduardo Paolozzi. Ballard also describes his exhibition of crashed cars at the New Arts Laboratory in 1970.

1973

C54 "J.G. Ballard Interviewed." Writer (June).

    Corridor: New Writings Quarterly, no. 5 (1974), pp. 4-7 [a shorter version of the Writer interview].
An interview conducted by Peter Linnett. Ballard discusses how he started out as a writer, his working habits, etc.

C55 "Ballard on Crash: Answers to Some Questions." Cypher, no. 10 (October), pp. 53-54.

    A short interview conducted by James Goddard, concentrating on the novel Crash.

C56 Preface to Vermilion Sands, A110 [not included in the American edition, 1971].

Frederik Pohl, M.H. Greenberg, and J.D. Olander, eds. The Great Science Fiction Series. New York: Harper & Row, 1980 [a slightly abridged version of the above preface to accompany Ballard's story "The Cloud-Sculptors of Coral D"].

C57 "I Had a Crash 18 Months Ago and It was a Case of Nature Imitating Art." Radio Times, 15 December, p. 10.

A brief interview/profile by Mike Bygrave. Ballard describes how he suffered a car crash after writing the novel Crash. However, "I'm a creature of habit now. I watch the 5.45 pm news headlines every night, then take the dog out and go for a drink in The Bell."

1974

C58 "Spaced Out." New Society 28 (18 April):146-47.

A review of The Next Ten Thousand Years by Adrian Berry.

C59 Introduction to Dali. Edited by David Larkin. London: Pan Books [paper].

An introduction to the paintings of Salvador Dali; a much-revised version of the New Worlds essay on Dali (C32).

C60 "A Personal View." Cypher, no. 11 (May), pp. 7-11.

A review of Billion-Year Spree by Brian Aldiss.

1975

C61 "J.G. Ballard's Science Fiction for Today." Science Fiction Monthly 2 (October):9-11.

An interview conducted by James Goddard with David Pringle. For a much fuller version of this interview, see C63.

C62 "Some Words About Crash!" Foundation: The Review of Science Fiction, no. 9 (November), pp. 45-54.

A translation of Ballard's introduction to the French edition of Crash, together with a short interview conducted by Robert Louit.

1976

C63 "An Interview with J.G. Ballard." Vector, no. 73/74 (March), pp. 28-49.

> James Goddard and David Pringle, eds. J.G. Ballard: The First Twenty Years. Hayes, Middlesex: Bran's Head Books, 1976.

An interview conducted by James Goddard and David Pringle on 4 January 1975. A much shorter version was published in Science Fiction Monthly (C61). This is a wide-ranging interview, covering Ballard's childhood, his beginnings as a writer, the influences on his writing, his relations with New Worlds, and much else.

C64 Letters. Foundation: The Review of Science Fiction, no. 10 (June), pp. 50-52.

Two letters from Ballard, dated 11 December 1975 and 16 January 1976, commenting on Peter Nicholls's article "Jerry Cornelius at the Atrocity Exhibition" (D107).

C65 "Down to Earth." New Statesman 91 (18 June):821-22.

Reviews of The Lives and Times of Jerry Cornelius by Michael Moorcock; The Stochastic Man by Robert Silverberg; The Prayer Machine by Christopher Hodder-Williams; The Space Machine by Christopher Priest; and Universe 2 edited by Terry Carr.

C66 Introduction to J.G. Ballard: The First Twenty Years. Edited by James Goddard and David Pringle. Hayes, Middlesex: Bran's Head Books.

A brief introduction to the bibliographical section of the above book. Mentions two of his favorite stories--"The Voices of Time" and "Passport to Eternity."

C67 "Package Tours." New Statesman 92 (17 December):879.

Reviews of Martian Time-Slip by Philip K. Dick; Bring the Jubilee by Ward Moore; Galactic Empires, Vols. I and II edited by Brian W. Aldiss; Skyfall by Harry Harrison; and The Feast of St. Dionysus by Robert Silverberg.

1977

C68 "Zap Code." New Statesman 93 (25 March):405-6.

Reviews of Approaching Oblivion by Harlan Ellison; Shadrach in the Furnace by Robert Silverberg; and Medusa's Children by Bob Shaw.

Part C: Nonfiction 1978

C69 "French Polish." <u>New Statesman</u> 93 (15 April):499-500.

Reviews of <u>Travelling Towards Epsilon</u> edited by Maxim Jakubowski; <u>The Martian Inca</u> by Ian Watson; and <u>Man Plus</u> by Frederik Pohl.

C70 Introduction to <u>The Best of J.G. Ballard</u> (A131).

A short piece in which Ballard asserts that sf "now enjoys enormous freedom, and is one of the most vital forms of modern fiction." He cites Anthony Burgess, William Burroughs, and Kingsley Amis as three mainstream authors who have turned to sf, and points out how much sf has changed since Ballard himself started writing. This collection also contains brief comments by Ballard on each of the seventeen stories.

C71 "Closed Doors." <u>New Statesman</u> 93 (3 June):755.

A review of <u>The Hughes Papers</u> by Elaine Davenport and others.

C72 "Grope Therapy." <u>New Statesman</u> 94 (15 July):89.

A review of <u>Travels in Inner Space</u> by John St. John.

C73 "The Future of the Future." <u>Vogue</u> 134 (November):213-14.

A speculative article on domestic life in the year 2000 A.D. Concentrates on the impact of computers and communications technology.

C74 "Cataclysms and Dooms." In <u>The Visual Encyclopaedia of Science Fiction</u>. Edited by Brian Ash. London: Trewin Copplestone Publishing [paper].

A short introduction to the section of this encyclopedia which deals with disaster stories. Traces cataclysmic themes from "the deluge in the Babylonian zodiac myth of Gilgamesh" to modern sf, and asserts that disaster stories are "a constructive and positive act by the imagination rather than a negative one, an attempt to confront the terrifying void of a patently meaningless universe by challenging it at its own game."

C75 "Hobbits in Space?" <u>Time Out</u>, 16 December, pp. 14-15.

A review of <u>Star Wars</u> directed by George Lucas.

1978

C76 "Candide Camera." <u>New Statesman</u> 95 (14 April):502-3.

A review of The Alchemical Marriage of Alistair Crompton by Robert Sheckley.

C77 "J.G. Ballard." New Review 5, no. 1 (Summer):19-20.

A brief contribution by the author to a symposium on the future of the novel. Ballard states that he feels "extremely optimistic" about the future of fiction, though he does not name any authors.

C78 "Manbotching." New Statesman 96 (20 October):512.

A review of The Body in Question by Jonathan Miller.

C79 "J.G. Ballard." Search and Destroy: Rebel Youth Culture, no. 10 (n.d.), pp. 20-21.

An interview conducted by Jon Savage. Discusses High-Rise, sf, William Burroughs, films, rock music, and much else.

1979

C80 "The Space Age Is Over." Penthouse 14 [April?]:39-42, 102, 106.

An interview conducted by Dr. Chris Evans. Covers space travel, the communications explosion, and the computerization of everyday life in the near future. In most copies of the magazine the text of page 102 is missing due to a collation error.

C81 "Not a Step Beyond Tomorrow." Time Out, 2 November, pp. 18-19.

An interview/profile by Giovanni Dadomo. Discusses surrealism, The Atrocity Exhibition, Crash, and The Unlimited Dream Company. The cover of the magazine features a photograph of Ballard at the front door of his house in Shepperton, with the large caption: "Semi-detached dreams. J.G. Ballard and the science fiction of the ordinary."

C82 "Killing Time Should Be Prime-Time TV." Guardian, 15 November, p. 18.

A review of The Executioner's Song by Norman Mailer.

C83 "Kings of Infinite Space." Guardian, 29 November, p. 8.

A review of The Right Stuff by Tom Wolfe.

C84 "Writers' Choice for Christmas Reading." Guardian, 13 December, p. 10.

Part C: Nonfiction 1980

A brief contribution by Ballard, among others, to a symposium on the best books of the year. He discusses Emma Tennant's Wild Nights, Christopher Evans's The Mighty Micro, and Ian Gibson's The Assassination of Frederico Garcia Lorca.

1980

C85 "Unlimited Dreams--J.G. Ballard Interviewed." Vector, no. 96 (December 1979/January 1980), pp. 4-9.

An interview/profile by Alan Dorey and Joseph Nicholas. Concentrates mainly on the science fiction scene, New Worlds, and the latest novel, The Unlimited Dream Company.

C86 "Disasters." Listener 103 (14 February):208-9.

Extracts from a BBC radio interview conducted by Rodney Smith. Deals briefly with Ballard's upbringing, his beginnings as a writer, and his views on technology and the modern landscape.

C87 "Interview with J.G. Ballard." Thrust: SF in Review, no. 14 (Winter), pp. 12-19.

An interview conducted by David Pringle on 14 July 1979. Deals with Ballard's attitudes to literary criticism, New Worlds, Bananas, the near future, space flight, microprocessors, and other topics. (Full version reprinted in this volume, pp. 1-23.)

C88 "J.G. Ballard." In Dream Makers: The Uncommon People Who Write Science Fiction, by Charles Platt. New York: Berkley [paper].

An interview/profile by Charles Platt. Ballard describes the Shanghai of his childhood at some length; he goes on to talk about his discovery of science fiction and of pop art in the 1950s, and his reasons for writing "condensed novels" in the 1960s.

C89 "Brian W. Aldiss." In Novacon 10 Programme Book. Birmingham: Birmingham Science Fiction Group [paper].

A brief appreciation of Brian Aldiss, who was guest of honor at the "Novacon 10" sf convention held in Birmingham, 31 October through 2 November 1980. States that there is "no better ambassador for science fiction. . . . I'm happy to leave the convention in the good hands of Brian Aldiss; great heart, wise, witty and good companion, the best man in the world to spend an evening with in a bar on Copacabana Beach, or even, just conceivably, at the Royal Angus Hotel, Birmingham."

1981

C90 "First Things Last." Tatler 276, no. 3 (March):111.

A review of Other People by Martin Amis.

C91 "J.G. Ballard." In The Imagination on Trial: British and American Writers Discuss Their Working Methods. Edited by Alan Burns and Charles Sugnet. London and New York: Allison & Busby.

An interview conducted by Alan Burns. From internal evidence it appears the interview was tape-recorded circa 1975. Ballard discusses his home town, Shepperton, and his attitudes to other places. Justifies his methods in The Atrocity Exhibition and Crash, and talks about the critical reception of those books.

C92 "New Means Worse." Guardian, 26 November, p. 21.

A review of The Golden Age of Science Fiction edited by Kingsley Amis.

C93 "Fallen Idol." Guardian, 3 December, p. 8.

A review of Elvis by Albert Goldman.

C94 "Writers' Reading in 1981." Guardian, 10 December, p. 14.

A brief contribution to this review of the year's books. Ballard commends A Confederacy of Dunces by John Kennedy Toole and Cities of the Red Night by William Burroughs.

C95 "Things I Wish I'd Known at 18." Sunday Express Magazine, no. 38 (27 December), p. 34.

A short interview conducted by Lynn Barber and cast in the form of an autobiographical statement. Deals with Ballard's time as a student at Cambridge, contrasting it with his present-day domestic existence.

1982

C96 "The Profession of Science Fiction, 26: From Shanghai to Shepperton." Foundation: The Review of Science Fiction, no. 24 (February), pp. 5-23.

An interview conducted by David Pringle on 24 July 1981, arranged as a chronological narrative with questions omitted. Ballard describes his childhood in China and his early years in Britain. Recounts how he first became interested in psycho-

Part C: Nonfiction 1982

analysis, surrealism, science fiction, and pop art.

C97 "Legend of Regret." Guardian, 4 February, p. 18.

A review of Some Sort of Epic Grandeur: The Life of F. Scott Fitzgerald by Matthew J. Bruccoli.

Secondary Bibliography

Part D: Critical and Bio-Bibliographical Studies

1956

D1 ANON. "J.G. Ballard, London." <u>New Worlds</u> 18, no. 54 (December):inside front cover.

A short profile, with a photograph of the young author. States that Ballard "was born in Shanghai 25 years ago and has spent most of his life travelling." Says that "after winning the annual short story competition at Cambridge in 1951 he wrote his first novel, a completely unreadable pastiche of <u>Finnegans Wake</u> and <u>The Adventures of Engelbrecht</u>. James Joyce still remains the wordmaster, but it wasn't until he turned to science fiction that he found a medium where he could exploit his imagination, being less concerned with the popular scientific approach than using it as a springboard into the surreal and fantastic." Adds that Ballard gets most of his inspiration from painters, and that "outwardly, at any rate, he lives quietly in Chiswick with his wife and baby son Jimmie. He admits that though she doesn't actually write his stories his wife has as much to do with their final production as he has himself. She hopes to have his novel <u>You and Me and the Continuum</u> finished by the end of this year."

1959

D2 ANON. "J.G. Ballard, Middlesex." <u>New Worlds</u> 30, no. 88 (November):inside front cover.

A brief profile, with the same author's photograph as in D1. States that "a sure sign of the present health of sf is the continued emergence of writers . . . more interested in experimenting with the imaginative and stylistic possibilities of the medium than in the conventional short story set against an interplanetary or futuristic background. Among these writers is J.G. Ballard, who returns to <u>New Worlds</u> with 'The Waiting Grounds' in this month's issue." Ballard is then quoted as saying that sf gives him the opportunity for "experimenting with scientific or psycho-literary ideas. . . . Just as psychologists are now building models of anxiety neuroses and withdrawal states in the form of verbal diagrams--translating scientific hypothesis into literary construction--so I see a good sf story as a model of some psychic image, the truth of which gives the story its merit. Examples are <u>The Incredible Shrinking Man</u>, <u>Limbo '90</u> and Henry Kuttner's 'Dream's End.' In general stories with interplanetary backgrounds show too little originality, too much self-imitation." Of "The Waiting Grounds," his first story with an interplanetary setting, Ballard is quoted as saying: "seen as a psycho-literary model, perhaps it represents the old conundrum of the ant searching hopelessly for the end of an infinite pathway around the surface of a sphere. 'The Waiting Grounds' offers it a solution, implies that instead of crawling on and on it will find the pathway's end if it just sits still."

1961

D3   ANON. "J.G. Ballard, Shepperton, Middx." <u>New Worlds</u> 37, no. 111 (October):inside front cover.

A brief profile, with the same (out-of-date) photograph used in D1 and D2. States that "Storm-Wind," concluded in this issue, is "a shortened version of Jim Ballard's first book-length novel." Ballard is quoted as saying that "the cataclysmic story is particularly interesting. . . . Perhaps because of their climate, English writers seem to have a virtual monopoly of the genre. . . . Anyone wondering why I've chosen to destroy London quite so thoroughly should try living there for ten years. I'm only sorry that I couldn't call it <u>Gone With the Wind</u>."

1962

D4   ANON. "J.G. Ballard, Shepperton, Middx." <u>New Worlds</u> 40, no. 118 (May):inside front cover.

A short profile, with the same (out-of-date) photograph used in D1, D2, and D3. Informs readers of a BBC radio program, broadcast on 18 March 1962, entitled "The Realm of Perhaps," which featured Ballard among other speakers. "Jim Ballard's particular approach was that the advent of space travel was now something our writers should get away from and advocated more research into stories dealing with the Earth." Mentions "two new short stories coming by him shortly," and: "we especially recommend 'The Cage of Sand.'"

D5   COTTS, S.E. "The Spectroscope." <u>Amazing Stories</u> 36, no. 6 (June):139-40.

Review of <u>The Voices of Time</u>. States he first became acquainted with Ballard's work by reading "The Sound-Sweep" in a Judith Merril anthology. Compares it with Carson McCullers's <u>The Heart Is a Lonely Hunter</u>. Complains that the other stories in the collection are "almost completely dark and grim." Only

Part D: Critical and Bio-Bibliographical Studies

one of the stories matches "The Sound-Sweep" in "its perfect blend of ideas and realization of them"--"Deep End." Complains of "grandiose prose" in the remaining stories, but concludes "I suspect that time and the maturing process will solve this problem for Mr Ballard."

D6 _____. "The Spectroscope." Amazing Stories 36, no. 8 (August):122.

Review of The Wind from Nowhere. Asks if this can really be "the work of our J.G. Ballard whose promising short stories were reviewed here in June." Finds the novel "reeking with ominous portents, a plot that begs for a few great ideas, and it all comes to nothing." Describes the plot, in jocular tone, pointing out that the eponymous wind "just kind of stops of its own accord!" Concludes: "Here is a book that is better left unread."

D7 MILLER, P. SCHUYLER. "The Reference Library." Analog 70, no. 1 (September):157-58.

Review of The Voices of Time. States "this is the best one-man collection we are likely to see in 1962." The seven stories are all from English magazines but "they are as good as anyone is writing now." Gives a brief run-through of the plots. "These are all stories with intense emotional drive behind them. . . . Like Brian Aldiss, the author's short stories are still better than his longer fiction. I hope he will not grow away from us too fast."

1963

*D8 AMIS, KINGSLEY. Review of The Drowned World. Observer [27 January?].

The review which launched Ballard's literary reputation in Britain. Amis states: "Ballard is one of the brightest new stars in post-war fiction. This tale of strange and terrible adventure in a world of steaming jungles has an oppressive power reminiscent of Conrad." He adds: "In J.G. Ballard's book we have something without precedent in this country, a novel by a science-fiction author that can be judged by the highest standards. Mr Ballard may turn out to be the most imaginative of Wells' successors. . . . The book blazes with images, striking in themselves and yet continuously meaningful. He triumphantly achieves his object."

[Source: jacket copy on the Gollancz edition of The Terminal Beach.]

*D9 ALDISS, BRIAN [W.]. Review of The Drowned World. Oxford Mail [January or February?].

Describes the book as "one of the most powerful and beautiful and clever science fiction stories it has ever been my pleasure to read. Science fiction suffers a sea-change into something rich

and strange. Ballard's potent symbols of beauty and dismay inundate the reader's mind. It's most haunting and hallucinatory."
[Source: jacket copy on the Gollancz edition of The Terminal Beach.]

D10 ANON. "Floods and Flares." Times Literary Supplement, 1 March, p. 157.
Review of The Drowned World, among others. Says the novel "starts very promisingly," and describes the plot. "The reader's hopes that this is going to be more than traditional sf are, however, not fulfilled. . . . Vague talk of a new Adam and Eve is never developed and we are left wondering how Man would really cope with this emergency."

D11 FLOOD, LESLIE. "Book Reviews." New Worlds 43, no. 129 (April):128.
Review of The Drowned World. Says "it is pleasant to be able to record an instance of 'local boy makes good.' . . . Jim Ballard is a 'Nova-nurtured' writer whose early promise has almost matured in this, his second novel." Agrees that it is "one of the best sf novels to appear for many years," but feels that it shows some lack of discipline. Describes the plot, then concludes: "It is not often that the genre is rewarded by a writer of such obvious talent and I look forward to his next book with much anticipation."

*D12 AMIS, KINGSLEY. Review of The Four-Dimensional Nightmare. Observer [May?].
"This volume confirms his standing as an imaginative talent of great depth and originality."
[Source: jacket copy on the Gollancz edition of The Terminal Beach.]

*D13 ALDISS, BRIAN [W.]. Review of The Four-Dimensional Nightmare. Oxford Mail [May or June?].
Ballard's new collection "shows that unforced strangeness in which he effortlessly excels. 'The Garden of Time' is a wonderful fantasy, the most magical of metaphors."
[Source: jacket copy on the 1974 edition of The Four-Dimensional Nightmare.]

D14 FLOOD, LESLIE. "Book Reviews." New Worlds 45, no. 133 (August):124.
Review of The Four-Dimensional Nightmare. Says that it consolidates Ballard's reputation as "the first serious writer emerging in the genre in England since Arthur C. Clarke." Points out that "all but one of these eight stories first appeared in these pages" [i.e., in one or other of the Nova magazines, New Worlds and Science Fantasy]. Refers to "the undisciplined exuberance of his sometimes outrageous pseudo-technicalities" and cites such stories as "The Sound-Sweep" and "Studio 5, the Stars."

Part D: Critical and Bio-Bibliographical Studies 1965

To read Ballard's stories "is an experience akin to reading Baudelaire after a diet of the romantics, a whiff of marijuana after plain virginia." Concludes "Ballard's sf can confidently be accepted at the highest level of any contemporary fiction. Good for Jim!"

D15 ANON. "Future Indefinite." Times Literary Supplement, 2 August, p. 593.
 A leading article on futuristic fiction in general. Mentions "a recently published collection of stories," The Four-Dimensional Nightmare. Claims that Ballard "depicts life on a dying earth, in a universe running down to a predictable finish. . . . In story after story we see human beings overtaken by a creeping inanition, a pointlessness, until they even write poetry by electronic computer." Concedes that "Mr Ballard's writing is of a higher order than most in this field, and in many of his stories there is a strong taste of Kafka," but claims he illustrates the fact that much sf is fundamentally pessimistic.

1964

D16 MILLER, P. SCHUYLER. "The Reference Library." Analog 73, no. 3 (May):87-88.
 Review of Passport to Eternity. "Any story by this talented British writer is stamped with a nightmare quality that is unmistakable. He has the bizarre point of view of the early Ray Bradbury. . . ." Claims that five of the nine stories are not sf, and describes each story briefly.

D17 MOORCOCK, MICHAEL. "No Short-Cuts." New Worlds 48, no. 144 (September/October):119-20.
 Review of The Terminal Beach. The first sentence is a resounding affirmation: "There can be no question now that J.G. Ballard has emerged as the greatest imaginative writer of his day." Describes various stories in the collection, reserving highest praise for the title story. Points out that the "poetry" in Ballard "is implicit in his choice of images" and does not reside in "'fine writing' of the Bradbury type." Compares Ballard to William Burroughs, and asserts that "there is nothing obscure in Ballard's work." Concludes by advising the reader to buy the book "as an investment if nothing else, for there will come a time when a Ballard first edition will be valuable."

1965

D18 WHITE, PETER. "Ballard's Terminal Beach." Vector, no. 31 (March), pp. 9-10, 14.
 A short essay on Ballard's story "The Terminal Beach." Begins by citing the actual results of a biological survey of the

Pacific island Eniwetok (used for atomic bomb tests). Describes Ballard's story, saying that it "combines a sophisticated imaginative response to the Bomb, and all its associations, with the chilly jargon of the nuclear age technology." Ballard "creates the ironic language of holocaust, the scarifying lyricism of doomsday." Describes the structure of the story, and states that the figure of the dead Japanese doctor reminds us of "another symbol of betrayed Mankind, Bartok's miraculous mandarin." Says it is possible to enjoy Ballard's work without being aware of "the allegorical content." The story "succeeds because its allusiveness is never mere obscurity." Cites the case of Eatherly, whose name has passed into the legend surrounding Hiroshima, and says: "Ballard's Eniwetok may be a mythical island, but it is one of the most real places on Earth."

*D19 AMIS, KINGSLEY. Review of The Drought. Observer [May?].
Describes the novel as "another excursion into this remarkable author's private country. . . . This is literature—without that high-cocked little finger."
[Source: jacket copy on the Cape edition of The Atrocity Exhibition.]

*D20 BOWEN, JOHN. Review of The Drought. Sunday Times [May?].
"The experience Mr Ballard offers is mystical. It is weird; it is grotesque; it is magnificently gothic."
[Source: jacket copy on the Cape edition of The Crystal World.]

D21 MAYNE, RICHARD. "Ventriloquism." New Statesman 69 (28 May): 846.
Review of The Drought, among others. Finds most sf boring, but "J.G. Ballard is one of the exceptions: his fantasies are explored with a maniac's logic and an artist's sensibility." Describes the plot, and adds: "The result is apocalyptic; but it's described so matter-of-factly that it's powerfully credible, a compulsive nightmare if you once accept its premise."

D22 WORDSWORTH, CHRISTOPHER. "The Psychic Dustbowl." Guardian, 28 May, p. 11.
Review of The Drought, among others. Describes the novel as "a strange and rather wonderful book full of haunting landscapes, phantasmagoria, and disaster." Adds: "this is an impressive novel at any level, faulted occasionally by overexplanatory passages. . . . He makes spiritual voortrekkers of his readers." Describes the plot, concluding: "The imaginative intensity is that of 'The City of Dreadful Night.' . . ."

D23 MOORCOCK, MICHAEL [James Colvin]. "Quick Reviews." New Worlds 49, no. 151 (June):117.
Review of the paperback edition of The Drowned World, among others. States that it "seems to bear dozens of re-readings.

Part D: Critical and Bio-Bibliographical Studies 1965

Every time I read it I seem to get more from it than I did last time." Describes the plot, and adds: "On another level comes Ballard's obsession with Time. . . . This is perhaps the first novel to deal with Time, Space and Man in a way that concerns the deep metaphysical link existing between these forces. . . . It is a tribute to Ballard's powerful talent that he manages to tell both a gripping, haunting tale and at the same time make this final, total merging a convincing reality."

D24 ANON. "Style Out in Space." Times Literary Supplement, 10 June, p. 469.
Review of The Drought, among others. Describes the plot, then says "Mr Ballard paints some staggering imaginary landscapes . . . but his people and their motivations are so steeped in the atmosphere of 19th Century French symbolism that the reader often finds that they provide a curtain, rather than a key, to the author's meaning." Adds: "Mr Ballard is sometimes intoxicated by the temptations of verbal impressionism into phrases so imprecise as to be virtually meaningless. . . ." Concludes "but this is a very impressive book by a deeply serious writer, the originality and power of whose vision can be felt."

D25 MERRIL, JUDITH. "Books." Fantasy and Science Fiction 29, no. 1 (July):79-82.
Review of The Drowned World and The Wind from Nowhere. States that while "The Wind from Nowhere is a good standard sf magazine-serial novel, well-handled and excitingly told," it "is quite unrepresentative of the main line of Ballard's work, and stands in relation to The Drowned World rather as a first-rate Hercule Poirot novel does to Crime and Punishment." Continues: "Ballard is well on his way toward becoming the first truly conscious and controlled literary artist sf has produced." Describes the plot of The Drowned World, adding: "the technical-scientific aspects of the novel are intriguing and thoughtful. The human aspects are confusing, terrifying, fascinating, and all too often brilliantly credible." Concludes: "Perhaps the most effective and striking virtue of this novel is its texture: the very prose has the weight of the waters in it, and its rhythms swell somehow with the slow tempo of the inexorably rising tide."

D26 MOORCOCK, MICHAEL [James Colvin]. "Cutting Past the Defences." New Worlds 49, no. 154 (September):124-25.
Review of The Drought, describing it as "an intellectual and visionary novel of marvellously sustained power and conviction, resembling in some ways Patrick White's Voss." The novel cuts past the defences of the outer mind, "reaching the core of the inner mind." The characters are figures of deep, archetypal fantasy.

D27 ALDISS, BRIAN [W.]. "British Science Fiction Now: Studies of Three Writers." SF Horizons, no. 2 (Winter), pp. 13-37.

Thomas D. Clareson, ed. SF: The Other Side of Realism.
   Bowling Green, Ohio: Bowling Green University Popular
   Press, 1971 [extract, as "The Wounded Land: J.G.
   Ballard"].
James Goddard and David Pringle, eds. J.G. Ballard: The
   First Twenty Years. Hayes, Middlesex: Bran's Head
   Books, 1976 [extract, as "The Wounded Land: J.G.
   Ballard"].

   An examination of three writers: Lan Wright, Donald Malcolm, and J.G. Ballard. The long section on Ballard concentrates on the way "he replaces sensationalism with wit." Referring mainly to The Terminal Beach and The Drought, Aldiss points out that "critics have not noticed how witty Ballard is." His wit is like that of the metaphysical poets, which "can surprise and delight by its juxtaposition of hitherto separate ideas." Compares passages from "The Terminal Beach" and "The Delta at Sunset" to one from Thomas Hardy's A Pair of Blue Eyes: "Ballard, in using symbols to convey massively passing time in a somewhat cumbrous prose, sounds remarkably like the great Victorian novelist."

   Describes, and approves, Ballard's "dethronement of the Hero" and his eschewal of other sf conventions. "There are frequent signs in Ballard's work that he is parodying or mocking . . . all the bad things of the medium in which he has chosen to write." Adds that Ballard "likes to regard himself as something of an outcast among the sf fraternity." Quotes from the New Worlds guest editorial (C1), and points out that Ballard practices what he preaches. "His central characters, sensitive, sinful, defeated, wounded, wry, are poles away from Heinlein's swaggering heroes. . . ." Claims that Ballard's subjects are becoming more oblique: "the examination now is less of failure than of the private glories often enshrined in failure."

   Discusses Ballard's prose, pointing out that his "techniques are much more conservative than [William] Burroughs's." Rather, Ballard "attempts to 'write well' as, say, Sir Arthur Quiller-Couch would have defined the term. He enjoys encrusting his sentences with adjectives and rare words. . . ." Mentions Kingsley Amis's review of The Drowned World (D8), adding: "Conrad's men of action are not Ballard's; he traffics with the sedentary, encapsuled men of our proto-space age."

   Compares Ballard with Ray Bradbury, but points out that "children are absent from Ballard's stories, sometimes obtrusively." Nevertheless, many of the protagonists are in search of a childlike vision. "Ballard is a sensitive writer, and it is hard sometimes not to feel that his stories are written in a perverse spirit." His work is full of derelict spacecraft and abandoned buildings, making him a "literary luddite." Comments on the "collage" technique of The Drought, but suggests that in this novel Ballard "seems momentarily to be copying himself." Compares the cryptic dialogue to the plays of Harold Pinter.

   Expresses regret that Ballard no longer seems to be writing "city stories" like "Billennium" and "Chronopolis"--"at times,

Part D: Critical and Bio-Bibliographical Studies   1966

subtopia seemed almost like a patent Ballard invention." Mentions scientific inaccuracies, and Ballard's apparently careless attitude to facts. However, finds these faults forgiveable, and concludes: "Despite some shortcomings, his stories are one of the few stimulating forces in contemporary sf."

1966

D28   MILLER, P. SCHUYLER. "The Reference Library." Analog 76, no. 5 (January):148.
Review of Terminal Beach. "J.B. Ballard [sic] is, for my money, the most outstanding of the new English sf writers. . . . In some respects, and in some moods, you could call him an English Cordwainer Smith." Describes each story briefly, commending "The Time-Tombs" for its "deftly suggested etching of a Mars as delicately beautiful as anything Bradbury ever suggested, and far more hauntingly real." Calls "The Venus Hunters" "by far the best serious flying saucer story I've read." Concludes: "there are no bad Ballard stories, just as there are no bad Cordwainer Smith stories."

D29   MERRIL, JUDITH. "Books." Fantasy and Science Fiction 30, no. 1 (January):39-45.
An article on the British sf scene, which incorporates a review of The Drought. Asserts that "Ballard, starting in the American market, would probably have left sf before he entered it; not one in ten of his early stories would have sold in the States in the late 50s." States that "he reviles the inadequacies of sf endlessly; but he directs his criticism primarily at other writers, reviewers and editors inside the field. Stylistically, he allies himself with the avant garde, with experimental techniques, and surrealism. But his subject matter, his preoccupation with the metaphysics and biophysics of time and space-time conformations, his 'ontological' explorations of psychic and sur-realities, his deep awareness of the inextricable relationship between mind and matter, organism and environment, are directly on the main line of speculation in serious sf. . . ."
Says of The Drought: "It is becoming almost impossible to review a new book of Ballard's all by itself. The author is building from book to book, and from story to story, in such a way that although each unit is meaningful on its own terms, it assumes full dimensions only in the context of the whole body of work." Describes the plot, and says it is "a more easily readable book than The Drowned World, and almost certainly a better novel. . . . The significance seems to keep seeping up to the surface of the mind for a long time after the book is closed."

D30   MOORCOCK, MICHAEL [James Colvin]. "Mainly Paperbacks." New Worlds 49, no. 160 (March):154-55.
Review of the paperback edition of The Four-Dimensional

Nightmare, among others. Claims it is "barely possible" some
readers haven't read the book, in which case "they should be
ashamed of themselves." States that when "Prima Belladonna" appeared in 1956 "very few people could believe that this was the
work of a new writer, but, when this was followed up by a succession of similarly brilliant short stories, everyone admitted
that here was the finest British talent to emerge since Brian W.
Aldiss." Claims that Ballard's "blend of hard and soft science,
splendid imagery and polished style, the depth of his vision,
were the best things to happen to sf in a very long time." Describes Ballard as "deeply concerned with man's distortion of
nature" and "almost convinced that this century is the last we'll
know." Describes his characters as "primarily myth-figures."
His plots are "subtly constructed--so subtly, in fact, that some
try to claim that Ballard is not interested in plots. This is
sheer nonsense," as a study of "The Voices of Time" will show.
Describes that story as "the zenith of Ballard's first period,"
while "The Watch-Towers" is representative of the start of his
"next phase." Although Ballard has progressed since, "the collection is still one of the best we have had since sf began."

D31 MOORCOCK, MICHAEL. "The Image and the Actuality." New Worlds
49, no. 161 (April):2-3.
An editorial, commenting on Ballard's story in this issue,
"The Assassination Weapon." States that "the concern of the
serious writer is . . . to separate the truth as he sees it from
the false supposition." Claims that in his latest story Ballard
"questions the validity of various popular images and modern
myths. . . . All the images that fill the mind of modern man are
seen through the eyes of a fictional spiritual descendant of
Eatherly--the landscape of a nuclear explosion, flyovers, advertising hoardings, oil derricks, radio telescopes, and wrecked
and abandoned machines." Concludes that "Ballard's fusion of
fact and fantasy succeeds in creating a kind of reality far re-
moved from the 'reality' of the events reported and analysed in
the popular press and elsewhere, but in our view he comes up with
a far more real view of these events than has hitherto been published."

D32 ANON. "Sums and Scrubbers." Times Literary Supplement, 14
April, p. 332.
Review of The Crystal World, among others. States that
Ballard "is already well known for his series of beautifully conceived and delicately written variations on a time-theme." In
his latest novel, "which contains in its atmosphere so much of
Conrad's Heart of Darkness, in its characters so much of Graham
Greene and in some of its situations so much of Edgar Allan Poe,
his descriptive powers do not fail him." Towards the end a
number of issues are left "floating in a rather vague cosmic
teleology with which they have never been quite satisfactorily
interfused." Concludes: "Nevertheless he has established himself

as one of the most sensitive and enigmatic novelists of the present day."

*D33 ALDISS, BRIAN [W.]. Review of The Crystal World. Oxford Mail [April?].
"Ballard has produced some of the most interesting writing of the past five years; his style glitters darkly and reduplicates itself like jewels encasing the saturnine forests in his new novel."
[Source: jacket copy on the Cape edition of The Atrocity Exhibition.]

D34 BURGESS, ANTHONY. "Parallel Spatial Matrix." Guardian, 15 April, p. 9.
Review of The Crystal World. The crystallizing forest is "beautifully rendered, Ballard the poet in full ecstatic blast. . . ." Describes the central idea of the novel, then says: "it is a stimulating and frightening concept, and Ballard expends all his considerable suggestive and descriptive gifts on its detailed incarnation. . . . Unfortunately, all this is, though enough for a poem, not enough for a novel. . . . Ballard's characters are mere areas of deliquescence bearing names. It is this lack of human interest that deeply wounds all of our best science fiction."

D35 MORGAN, EDWIN. "Unconcerned." New Statesman 71 (15 April): 545.
Review of The Crystal World, among others. The novel "excels in atmosphere, action, visualization" and is "brilliantly imagined. . . . As a human adventure in a suddenly alien and frightening environment, the book is convincing and powerful." But "its deeper purposes come off less well."

D36 LEVIN, MARTIN. "Reader's Report." New York Times Book Review, 15 May, p. 41.
Review of The Crystal World. Describes Ballard as "the most elegant of dark fantasists." States that he has "effectively streamlined the archetypal frame of the adventure story, which subsists on sharp moral contrasts, with anti-matter cabalistics."

D37 MOORCOCK, MICHAEL [James Colvin]. "Landscape Without Time." New Worlds 50, no. 164 (July):146-48.
Review of The Crystal World. Describes it as perhaps Ballard's "best novel to date." The images are "strong and clear and as thoughtfully conceived as the images in the Max Ernst jacket that so marvellously complements the book." Describes the plot and adds: "as with Conrad or Graham Greene, Ballard's characters are described more in terms of their moral qualities and inner lives than physical appearance or behaviour." Concludes that The Crystal World may be regarded as the last book in a

trilogy begun with The Drowned World. "The three books represent a tour de force of imagination and intellect and undoubtedly form a major contribution to post-war literature."

D38 SIMAK, CLIFFORD. "When an Area's Plants, Animals Turn to Crystal. . . ." Minneapolis Tribune, 24 July.
Review of The Crystal World. Calls it "a strange book." Briefly describes the plot, then adds: "there are none of the wild, frantic overtones of the ordinary catastrophe novel; rather, the attention of the reader is focused upon the response of a small group of people. . . ." Finds that the writing is "heavy with imagery" and that at times it "approaches what one might call a tone poem." Although "there is some muted horror," the novel "cannot be called a horror story." Instead, there is "something of a terrible and brittle beauty." Concludes that although the book "is meant, at least in part, as an allegory . . . the allegorical framework is buried so deeply that this reviewer was unable to discover it."

D39 MERRIL, JUDITH. "Books." Fantasy and Science Fiction 31, no. 2 (August):57-69.
Review of The Crystal World and The Impossible Man (in reality more of a general essay on Ballard's work). States that "at least one fully qualified writer has now developed to occupy the position for whose description we have as yet no adequate critical language--a literary outpost rather closer to the lonely prominences of the Argentinian, Borges, the Parisian, Jarry, the Swede, Martinson, than to his closest English-language neighbours." With these two books, "Ballard climaxes his first decade as a writer . . . at a point where the criteria of genre criticism are totally inadequate to judge his work; and while most of what he has done in the last two years comes off satisfactorily (and occasionally brilliantly) under examination by the established rules of 'serious' literary criticism, those rules are themselves far short of satisfactory for examination of most of his work." Describes The Crystal World as one of a "curious thematic trilogy" (and "emphatically the best novel of the three"): "Where Drowned World examined time-past in terms of psychophysical and geophysical evolution . . . and Drought explored the drying-up of life in time-future . . . CW presents us with a (literally, physically) crystallized pattern of time-now. . . ." Analyzes the roles of the characters in the three books, commending The Crystal World as a "brilliant success." Adds that its "larger and deeper statements are to be found only in the dynamics of its relationships with the other two books." Turning to The Impossible Man, she finds in it "a near-complete sampling of Ballard's work of the last four or five years." Describes some typical elements of Ballard's fictional landscapes: "the sand beach and desert, the waiting ocean, patient river basin, echoing wind-carved rock galleries, dark grottoes and sunlit gardens; the crumbling mansions and abandoned hotels; streaming high-speed highways and

jostling crowd bodies; the stalled ship-turned-dwelling, the sand-drifted ruins." Every "major theme" is to be found here, "almost all of them interwoven with symbols, ideas, images relating to the three novels."

Finds the least "related" story to be "The Drowned Giant," although this is "probably (technically and artistically) Ballard's best short story to date." Evokes Kafka and Melville, and points out that the story is definitely not sf. On "the opposite end of the spectrum" are "The Gioconda of the Twilight Noon" and "The Impossible Man." These are "powerful, ugly, fragmentary, and unforgettable." Describes them as belonging to "a string of . . . irritating, fascinating, almost and a-bit-too-much stories, going back at least six years to 'Manhole 69' and 'The Waiting Grounds.'"

Asserts that the main focus of Ballard's early work was on "Time--most specifically, man's orientation in the universal flow of event, the place of the hour, or flower, or single human consciousness, in the birth-to-death,movement of cosmos, planet, species, culture." Claims "The Reptile Enclosure," "The Delta at Sunset," "Storm-Bird, Storm-Dreamer," and "The Day of Forever" are all "directly in this central flow." Compares "Storm-Bird" to The Drought, claiming the similarities leave "a slight double-vision blur whose net effect is somehow to intensify credibility. . . ." Says she has read "The Delta at Sunset" six times-- "and I still do not know what it is, in a story that seems unextraordinary between readings, that moves me as strongly each time."

Devotes much space to "The Screen Game" and the Vermilion Sands stories in general: "Ballard once described Vermilion Sands as an 'exotic suburb' of his mind; if so, he is an exotic suburbanite . . . because here above all is where we find the merging place of all the extremes and opposites in the sand-sea, light-dark, freezing-burning alternatives of Ballard's 'inner landscape.'" Concludes by returning to The Crystal World and quoting two passages. Mentions Ballard's debts to Hawthorne and the surrealists, "but these are trivia--the sort of things scholars may find it worth saying in 20 years, if Ballard goes ahead as he now seems to be going."

D40 CAWTHORN, JAMES. "I Love You, Semantics." New Worlds 49 [i.e., 50], no. 165 (August):144-45.
Review of reprints of The Wind from Nowhere and The Voices of Time, among others. States that these reissues "attest the growing reputation" of the author. Briefly describes The Wind from Nowhere and adds: "Filled with his customary vivid imagery, the novel is however badly weakened by some unconvincing melodrama centred upon a megalomaniacal constructor resolved to defy the elements." The stories in The Voices of Time "explore the heartland of Ballard country where small communities crouch on the fringes of ancient deserts. . . . The two-fisted technologist of Astounding's heyday is replaced, in this setting, by a figure which it is tempting to label The Dissolving Hero. Faced with

the breakup of the Universe he does not fight, but instead seeks, literally, to be absorbed." Briefly describes some of the stories, commending "The Sound-Sweep" as "possibly the best story in the collection."

D41 MOORCOCK, MICHAEL. "Ballard: The Voice." New Worlds 50, no. 167 (October):2-3, 151.

An editorial, in which Moorcock claims that Ballard "is the first clear voice of a movement destined to consolidate the literary ideas--surrealism, stream of consciousness, symbolism, science fiction, etc., etc.--of the 20th century, forming them into something that is prose, but no longer fiction (as the term is generally understood) and that is a new instrument for dealing with the world of the future contained, observedly, in the world of the present." Refers in particular to "You and Me and the Continuum," "The Assassination Weapon," "You: Coma: Marilyn Monroe" and "The Atrocity Exhibition." Says that there now exists, around New Worlds, a group of writers and critics who "enthusiastically support the work Ballard is doing."

D42 BUDRYS, ALGIS. "Galaxy Bookshelf." Galaxy Science Fiction 25, no. 2 (December):128-31.

Review of The Genocides by Thomas M. Disch. Invokes Ballard in comparison with Disch. "A story by J.G. Ballard, as you know, calls for people who don't think." Asserts that Ballard's characters have no knowledge of science, and "when the world disaster--be it wind or water--comes upon you, you are under absolutely no obligation to do anything about it but sit and worship it."

1967

D43 CAWTHORN, J. "Ballard of a Whaler." New Worlds 50, no. 170 (January):157.

A brief parody of Michael Moorcock's The Ice Schooner as it might have been if Ballard had written it. Concludes: "the harpooner's eyes were sombre and brooding and when he spun his 18-foot lance end-over-end in a characteristic gesture and drove it splinteringly into the ice, he betrayed by no flicker of a muscle that he had impaled his left foot."

D44 ELLISON, HARLAN. "Introduction to 'The Recognition.'" In Dangerous Visions. Edited by Harlan Ellison. Garden City: Doubleday.

Comments that Ballard writes "peculiarly Ballardian stories." States that his works are less revolutionary individually than "in totality." Ballard's writing is, "in some ways, serene, as oriental philosophy is serene. Resigned yet vital." Asserts that "The Recognition" is "immensely entertaining" and "thought-provoking."

Part D: Critical and Bio-Bibliographical Studies   1968

D45 HOLMES, RICHARD. "Inner Space." Times, 14 October, p. 23.
        Review of The Disaster Area. States that Ballard's "obsessional concerns" with time and landscape and "symbolic images of feeling" have given sf a new direction, relevant to contemporary thinking: "he orbits in the same system as R.D. Laing and McLuhan." Cites Ballard's extraordinary descriptive gift, an eye for the mood and code of the visual environment that is like Poe's, but steadier." Provides a brief run-through of earlier works, then states that The Disaster Area "comprises nine stories of the modern urban complex, the mental home, the surgical and technological Research Departments of today." Complains that the stories are "still weakened in places by his reliance on ... a thriller denouement," but concludes that the stories " reach us with the lonely disturbing brilliance of messages in bottles cast afloat, demanding a response."

D46 ANON. "J.G. Ballard: Advertising Is the Medium." Sunday Times, 19 October.
        A brief article about Ballard's "advertising" campaign. "He last upset people with a piece in Ambit called 'Plan for the Assassination of Jacqueline Kennedy.'" Ballard is quoted as saying: "Jacqueline Kennedy and Elizabeth Taylor are today's fictional characters, like Orpheus and Ulysses in other ages. I exploit these global fictional characters, letting my imagination play over them. These are people who are rich enough to buy mass media, publicity, television, to project themselves as fictional characters. . . ." The piece continues: "Ballard asked the Arts Council for £1,000 to back a personal advertising campaign in which he hopes to feature a nude on Westminster Abbey's high altar, a motor crash, and Princess Margaret's left armpit." Ballard is quoted as saying: "Advertising is the medium that people are tuned into. But they were just considering my application when the Kennedy piece appeared." The article concludes: "It took them a very short time to say no."

*D47 GREENE, GRAHAM. Comment on The Disaster Area. Observer [December?].
        Greene's choice as one of the three best books of the year. Describes The Disaster Area as "one of the best science fiction books I have read."
        [Source: jacket copy on the Cape edition of The Atrocity Exhibition.]

1968

D48 MOORCOCK, MICHAEL [James Colvin]. "A Literature of Acceptance." New Worlds, no. 179 (December 1967/January 1968), pp. 59-61.
        A polemical article on the current sf scene, which incorporates a review of The Overloaded Man. Describes Ballard as one of the "most important exponents and greatest talents" of the new

"subjective" school of sf. "There is no whit less concern and sense of engagement in Ballard than there was in Wells. . . . Far from dealing in straightforward philosophical ideas à la Kafka and Hesse, Ballard is involved with the detailed physical and psychological reality of the immediate present and near future." But finds The Overloaded Man, "unfortunately, a poor representation of some of his early work--some of it clumsily written and consisting principally of raw subject matter that is worked in only the simplest and most obvious ways." Adds: "There is a powerful talent here, of course, and as horror stories the collection succeeds excellently (far surpassing Bradbury in this respect), but most of these stories lack the purpose and involvement and intellectual toughness of Ballard's current work. . . ." Finds the most worthwhile item in the book--"which, I hasten to add, is considerably better than almost anything else to hand this month"--to be the essay on surrealist painting, "The Coming of the Unconscious."

D49 ARMYTAGE, W.H.G. Yesterday's Tomorrows: A Historical Survey of Future Societies. London: Routledge & Kegan Paul.
Discusses Ballard's work briefly in conjunction with that of William S. Burroughs, labeling them "The New Left." Describes The Drowned World, and comments: "Ballard's heroes seem so occluded from science that one might regard them as literary incarnations of the helpless intellectual in a world hurried along by technocrats." Quotes Algis Budrys's strictures from Galaxy (D42) with apparent approval.

D50 ANON. "Pooter." Times, 11 May, p. 21.
An article describing a science-fiction conference in Brighton, accompanied by a photograph showing Ballard, Brian Aldiss, Michael Moorcock, and others present at the event. States that Ballard, "ironically better known for The Crystal World than for his wonderful Terminal Beach," has found "an idiosyncratic path" once more in his writing. Quotes Ballard's opinion of Stanley Kubrick's 2001: A Space Odyssey: "A Pan-Am instructional film for stewardesses." Describes the speeches made by various writers, saying "Ballard's intervention resembled that of an official receiver at a bankruptcy." Quotes him as saying: "Given that the future is no more inherently interesting than the past, the problem is to write fiction that makes sense for the present. Linear techniques are just not adequate. . . . Surrealism and pop-painting techniques provide a means for expanding a narrative space. . . . People are living in the present. They want it now."

D51 SLADEK, JOHN. "The Sublimation World." Fantasy and Science Fiction 35, no. 1 (July):103-5.
A parody, as by J.G. B******. Divided into seven brief chapters, with titles like "The Eternal Grocer," "The Parsee of the Cobra Casino," and "The Bloody Fool," it describes a world in

which: "For years, decades, man had poured black, oily fumes into the atmosphere. Some of these fumes descended as solids, to soak into the earth once more, to polarize its proteins. Other matter had risen, faster during the warm days and slower at night, until it reached the sun, altering it slowly and subtly. For over a hundred years, the sun had been getting dirty; now its purplish glow turned the sensitive proteins of earth into iodine."

1969

D52 DISCH, THOMAS M. "Opinion 20: Impressed with Ballard." Speculation 2, no. 8 (January):17.
A brief quotation from an interview with Thomas M. Disch, first published in Vector, no. 51 (1968). Disch says: "I didn't really get to read any Ballard until I got to England. I started to read one of his anthologies on the boat, on the way over here, when I knew I was going to meet him. I was just astonished. I was just so impressed that somebody, in the context of science fiction, was doing work that was obviously first-rate, and as good as, if not better than, anything being done anywhere at just that moment."
[The same "Opinion" column in this issue of Speculation contains a comment by Richard Delap: "Worst short story of the year has to be J.G. Ballard's 'The Assassination of John Fitzgerald Kennedy Considered as a Downhill Motor Race.' Ballard's story presents the ultimate in poor taste and sheer, stabbingly mindless stupidity. The author has absolutely no respect for the mechanics of the English language or literary form."]

D53 KINGSTON, JEREMY. "At the Theatre." Punch, 20 August, pp. 313-14.
"The ICA Theatre in the Mall is showing a remarkable programme called 'The Assassination Weapon.' . . . In the centre of the room a large white disc slowly rotates. Projectors in the four corners flash images on to this double screen while a voice sonorously reads passages by the ex-science-fiction writer J.G. Ballard. . . .
"The superimposed photographs, surrealist paintings, charts and mandalas coupled with Ballard's dense distressed sentences have the texture of an unhappy dream. A Max Ernst worldscape of mighty fragments--flyovers, deserts, dark reservoirs, radio-telescopes--following the private logic of an hallucinating mind. Puzzling, frequently powerful, devised and invented with ingenuity and skill."

D54 ANON. "Lead-In." New Worlds, no. 194 (September/October), p. 1.
A brief profile, with a photo of the author holding a copy of Ambit, to accompany Ballard's story "A Place and a Time to Die." Describes him as "one of England's leading experimental

writers," whose influence on New Worlds writers has been "vast." Commends his series of stories which began with "The Assassination Weapon" and states that "a collection of these pieces, The Atrocity Exhibition, will be published soon by Doubleday in the USA and by Cape in the UK." Goes on to inform us that "'The Assassination Weapon,' independently done by a group of talented young architects, designers and Lambda actors in a mixed-media form using film, photographs, live actors and light machines, was recently performed at the ICA Gallery."

1970

*D55 PERRY, NICK, and WILKIE, ROY. "Homo Hydrogenesis: Notes on the Work of J.G. Ballard." Riverside Quarterly 4 (January): 98-107.
[Source: Clareson. Digests the article as follows: "Landscape and characters are fundamental to Ballard's works; the characters' 'psychological state is reflected in their environmental circumstances.'"]

D56 ANON. "Crash Course." Sunday Times [29 March?].
A short article about Ballard's exhibition "Crashed Cars," due to be held at the New Arts Laboratory Gallery from 4 to 28 April 1970. States: "Charles Symmonds has promised he'll try to get to the opening of an art exhibition . . . next week, because the items on show have been borrowed from his knacker's yard, Motor Crash Repairs. . . . 'They don't appeal to me as art,' says Symmonds. 'I detest cars. But maybe it's a good idea to show crashed cars. It's frightening. . . .' He has hired out a smashed Pontiac, an A60 and a Mini, to J.G. Ballard, the science fiction writer, who is showing them in an Atrocity Exhibition."
The article quotes Ballard's exhibition handout: "Each of these sculptures is a memorial to a unique collision between man and his technology. However tragic they are, I believe that automobile crashes play very different roles from the ones we assign them. Behind our horror lies an undeniable fascination and excitement. . . . The 20th century has given birth to a vast range of machines--computers, pilotless planes, thermonuclear weapons--where the latent identity of the machine is ambiguous. An understanding of this identity can be found in a study of the automobile. . . ."

D57 FRANKLIN, H. BRUCE. "Foreword to J.G. Ballard's 'The Subliminal Man.'" In The Mirror of Infinity. Edited by Robert Silverberg. New York: Harper & Row. Thomas D. Clareson, ed. SF: The Other Side of Realism. Bowling Green, Ohio: Bowling Green University Popular Press, 1971.
States that "The Subliminal Man" is an unusual story for Ballard, whose "most typical fictions are apocalyptic imaginings,

beautiful and ghastly visions of decay, death, despair." In this
story Ballard goes to the source of his own "decadent imaginings"--
namely his society. The story explores the contradictions of a
capitalist system out of control, and also the psychological consequences of this superproductive consumer society. Franklin's
only regret is that Ballard "fails to recognize that more than a
lone Hathaway will see 'the signs' and revolt." In this respect
his imagination is "certainly too conservative."

D58 NYE, ROBERT. "Gerhardie Revisited." Guardian, 9 July, p. 11.
     Review of The Atrocity Exhibition, among others. States
that the book consists of "15 stories or chapters (it is not
clear whether he wishes us to consider it as a novel or what)."
Adds that it is made up of "sensational stuff--bits of newspapers,
modern myth figures, reports of disasters." Compares with
William Burroughs. Concludes: "Having admired the imaginative
quality of Ballard's earlier work while finding the actual writing
a little threadbare, I have to say of this book that he seems to
me to have thickened (but not necessarily enriched) the verbal
substance at some cost to the free play of his own imagination."

D59 CHESHIRE, DAVID. "A Talent to Burn." Times, 11 July, p. 10.
     Review of The Atrocity Exhibition. States that Ballard,
"one of the most brilliant and unnerving of science fiction
writers," has talent to burn--"and he's burning it." Finds the
book pretentious and overclinical, and full of "terrible jokes."
While "it is certainly going to find admirers," Cheshire would
"be sorry to see such a depressing exhibition become, like assassinations, addictive."

*D60 HADEN-GUEST, ANTHONY. Review of The Atrocity Exhibition.
     Sunday Telegraph [July?].
     States that it is "a powerful, uneasy book, and a thorough
attempt to use the 'New Reality.'"
     [Source: jacket copy on the Panther edition of The Atroc-
ity Exhibition.]

D61 MURRAY, ISOBEL. "Down Macondo Way." Financial Times [July?].
     Review of The Atrocity Exhibition, among others. States
that Ballard is much admired for his "powerful writing" in the
field of sf. "The possible terrors of post-nuclear life have
been made startlingly probable by his ingenious, precise, almost
clinical prose." Describes the subject matter of the book, and
says that Ballard's manipulation of it "forms a terrible kind of
poetry of violence." However, complains that "such meditations
militate against a strong narrative thread." She then describes
the "plot" with the aid of the dust-jacket description, adding:
"In the book itself, the focus is perpetually blurred; one is
never sure what--or who--is real and what imagery." The book
enacts the breakdown of its central character, and "this is
everywhere convincing and sinister." Concludes that "the

separate chapters originally published in various periodicals may have been at least as effective by themselves," but in the book there is little feeling of movement to impel the reader on.

D62 GODDARD, JAMES. J.G. Ballard: A Bibliography. Milford on Sea, Hampshire: Cypher Press [paper].
An amateur publication which contains: "Foreword" by J.G. Ballard; "Preface" by John Carnell; "Introduction" by James Goddard; "Fiction in Magazines"--a listing in alphabetical order of magazine title; "Books"--an alphabetical listing of Ballard's books and their contents; "Alphabetical Listing of Stories"; "A Special Introduction" by J.G. Ballard; "Chronological Listing of Stories"--appears to be Ballard's own list of his stories in the order in which he wrote them, as opposed to the order in which they were published.
Carnell states in his preface: "in endorsing James Goddard's presentation of the published fiction of Mr Ballard, my pleasure is manifold; as a reader, a collector, an editor, an anthologist, but above all as the discoverer of Jim Ballard." He recounts how Ballard sent him a story, "Escapement," in the summer of 1956; how he then made a personal visit to Carnell's office, bringing with him a second story, "Prima Belladonna." "Jim Ballard's literary qualities were evident from the beginning. . . ."
In his "Special Introduction" to the chronological listing Ballard states: "The list contains two stories as yet unpublished, one which Playboy bought but seems to have declined to publish, and another which is the only short story of mine, I'm happy to say, I have been unable to place, though I'm still trying." The stories in question are "The Rumour" and "The Greatest Television Show on Earth" [both subsequently published in Ambit, the former under the title of "The Life and Death of God"; see A113 and A123.]
[For an expanded and updated version of this bibliography, which also reprints Carnell's preface, see J.G. Ballard: The First Twenty Years, D117.]

1971

D63 AMIS, KINGSLEY. "Aargh!" Cypher, no. 4 (April), pp. 5-6.
A short article commenting on the interview with Ballard which appeared in the previous issue of Cypher (C46). Begins by saying "I have known Jim Ballard for years and have always been a great admirer of his earlier--though never of his most recent--work." Goes on to berate Ballard's current opinions as "inflated nonsense" and attempts to refute seven of his points. Takes particular exception to Ballard's claim that sf must be "relevant," and asks: "By the way, what the roaring hell is inner space?" Concludes: "No offence, I hope, Jim. For you, the true way forward is the way back."
[See also the letter column in this issue of Cypher, which

Part D: Critical and Bio-Bibliographical Studies   1972

contains comments on the Ballard interview by Mark Adlard, James Blish, Cy Chauvin, and others. The letter column in the following issue of <u>Cypher</u> (no. 5, July 1971) contains comments on the Amis piece by Brian Aldiss and Christopher Priest, among others. Aldiss remarks: "Jimmy Ballard's critical utterances are often so wild and irresponsible that of course he invites attack." Priest says: "Amis's response to the Ballard interview struck me as being precisely the kind of thing that Ballard half-consciously intends to provoke. . . ."]

<u>1972</u>

D64 STURGEON, THEODORE. "Galaxy Bookshelf." <u>Galaxy Science Fiction</u> 32, no. 4 (January/February):116-18.

Review of <u>Chronopolis</u>. Calls Ballard "a writer's writer, surely, and a reader's writer too. . . ." Singles out "The Terminal Beach" for praise--"provocative in its content and effective in its mode." Quotes from the <u>New Worlds</u> guest editorial (C1). Laments the absence from this collection of any Vermilion Sands stories. Concludes: "I know Ballard has made waves; I know he will not stop; I am most pleased to watch where he is going."

D65 HARTWELL, DAVID G. "Thrilling Wonder." <u>Crawdaddy</u>, 16 April.

An account of the American publishing vicissitudes of <u>The Atrocity Exhibition</u>. "It was scheduled to be published in this country by Doubleday a year or so ago. But it suddenly disappeared from the Doubleday list. I investigated the disappearance (I think Ballard is a major contemporary writer) by asking someone at Doubleday and I found that the company had printed the book and then destroyed all copies on the advice of their lawyers. Then, a couple of months ago, the book was announced by Dutton for this winter. I called Dutton recently and was told that the book had been dropped because Ballard had used proper names of public figures and the lawyers were scared." Hartwell regards it as a milestone for sf that it should have produced a book "too hot for any establishment to touch."

Gives a brief resumé of Ballard's career, commending <u>Vermilion Sands</u> as "a brilliant collection of linked short stories about an imaginary surrealistic landscape in mod America which contains some of the best short sf pieces written anywhere in the 60s." Proceeds to review the British edition of <u>The Atrocity Exhibition</u>. Says that several of its parts have appeared in sf anthologies in the United States, "no one suspecting that Ballard was creating one large, coherent and fiendishly perceptive indictment of contemporary American society." Describes the book at length, adding: "The Daliesque surrealism . . . enhances the bizarre and grotesque experiences that Ballard contrasts to the level, academic tone. In his own black manner, Ballard can be quite funny." Stresses: "Because Ballard's work is good and because it is important in its examination of the group psyche of the American people, it should be printed in this country and made available to aware readers." Concludes by condemning the "insidious economic and political censorship" which Ballard has suffered in America.

D66 BOWERS, FREDERICK. "Ballard, J(ames) G(raham)." In Contemporary Novelists. Edited by James Vinson. London: St. James Press, and New York: St. Martin's Press.
 States that Ballard's works "go well beyond the limits" of sf. "They reveal a powerful and sensuous imagination which reinforces a serious and universal concern with human despair in the universe of Nature." His fiction has "a distinctly 17th century flavour," reminiscent of Browne, Burton, and Donne. His "cities of Hell" are presented "as sharply as their visual parallels in Delvaux, Dali and Ernst." Describes Ballard's novels up to The Crystal World and claims that they are "thematically . . . concerned with the delicate natural equipoise upon which our existence depends." However, none of the novels are "mere environmentalist propaganda." Describes The Crystal World as "compellingly hopeful" and essentially about finding "an ultimate, total stillness out of time." Concludes by claiming that Ballard's work "explores those particular zones of the wasteland whose approach routes were mapped by T.S. Eliot . . . both derive their strength from their underlying concern about man in his universe."

D67 PRINGLE, DAVID. Review of Vermilion Sands. Speculation, no. 31 (Autumn), pp. 31-33.
 The book "shows us Ballard in his lightest vein." Nevertheless, the stories are "central to Ballard's oeuvre--they contain the characteristic dune-filled landscapes, the glimpses of decaying technologies, and the characters who obey every obscure psychological impulse." Points out that The Atrocity Exhibition was set in contemporary Britain, whereas Vermilion Sands is set "somewhere in what Aldous Huxley once called 'the antipodes of the mind.'" Goes on to discuss the position of these stories within Ballard's work as a whole, and states that "Vermilion Sands takes its place alongside The Drought as one of Ballard's explorations of aridity." The stories outline a "moral future." Describes the stories, and claims: "There are landscape descriptions of great beauty. . . . Ballard's painter's eye has rarely been more sharp." Points out that each story has "essentially the same hero," although they were written over a period of sixteen years. "There is little discontinuity of tone, a testament to the impressive consistency of all Ballard's writing, and only one story falls conspicuously below standard--'Venus Smiles.'"

D68 BURROUGHS, WILLIAM S. Preface to Love and Napalm: Export USA (A112).
 States that this work is "profound and disquieting." In it,

Part D: Critical and Bio-Bibliographical Studies 1973

"the nonsexual roots of sexuality are explored with a surgeon's precision." The distinction between inner and outer landscapes is breaking down and, like the painter Robert Rauschenberg, Ballard is "literally <u>blowing up</u> the image," making of this "an explosive book."

D69 THEROUX, PAUL. "The Auto Crash as Sexual Stimulation." <u>New York Times Book Review</u>, 29 October, p. 56.
Review of <u>Love and Napalm: Export USA</u>. Describes it as "a cold-blooded fantasy of aberrant proportions." Gives a brief description, stating in passing that the character Dr. Nathan is "a less crazed and more ponderous version of Burroughs's Dr. Benway." Finds in the book "a kind of toying with horror, a stylish anatomy of outrage. . . ." The narrative "shoves the reader aside and shambles forward on leaden sentences. . . . It is a horrible book, and it is even in parts a boring and pointless book." Although it is "unpersuasive as a whole, the details have an undeniable ring of pathological truth." Theroux proceeds to make a side-swipe at Ballard's earlier short stories, "his rather silly tales of giants and futuristic weirdos with funny names, dramatized in laughable sentences. . . ." Concludes by stating that "if Mr. Ballard was an American he might have found it more difficult to misrepresent a war which, far from arousing us sexually, has made us impervious to suffering. It is not his choice of subject, but his celebration of it, that is monstrous."

D70 KRIM, SEYMOUR. "A book that demands a very strong stomach." <u>Chicago Sun-Times</u>, 24 December.
Review of <u>Love and Napalm: Export USA</u>. Advises readers to remember Ballard's name. "You're going to hear it more often on the counter-culture network, and from there it's going to surface right into American mass culture." Claims that "after a decade of the most drastic criticism of the USA, any man who can still scare the hell out of us is a rare boogyman indeed. Such a one is J.G. Ballard." Describes the book at some length, terming it a "monsterpiece," and says: "an incredible amount of disturbing emotional dynamite is packed in these unemotionally written 157 pages. It is the images that drain us, not any rhetoric in the almost scientifically neutral writing itself." Warns that the book cannot be read for its "story" and compares it with the work of Alain Robbe-Grillet. Concludes: "What Ballard has done is to shake us to the very toes by piling image on image of a world we never consciously made but must live in. . . . His job as artist, word-painter, idea-innovator, is to present his vision with maximum effectiveness. He succeeds beyond your wildest bad dreams."

1973

D71 RYAN, ANTHONY. "The Mind of Mr J.G. Ballard." <u>Foundation</u>:

The Review of Science Fiction, no. 3 (March), pp. 44-48.
   Compares Ballard's achievement in sf to that of Patricia Highsmith and John Le Carré in the thriller. Contrasts Ballard's work with routine sf, exemplified by the novels of Keith Laumer. Quotes Ballard on surrealism, and asserts that his prose has "a peculiar mesmeric power." Attempts to analyse Ballard's four novels of the 1960s in terms of the four ancient elements--Air, Water, Fire, and Earth--then reasserts that "the hypnotic prose disarms criticism." Quotes Gabriel Josipovici to the effect that the purpose of modern art is "the creation of a structure that will allow us to understand what it means to perceive, and will thus, in a sense, give us back the world." Claims that this is "precisely the effect of a walk through Ballard's haunted landscapes."

D72 TARSHIS, JEROME. "Krafft-Ebing Visits Dealey Plaza: The Recent Fiction of J.G. Ballard." Evergreen Review 17, no. 96 (Spring):137-48.
   An article accompanying a reprint of "The Assassination of John Fitzgerald Kennedy Considered as a Downhill Motor Race." Incorporates some interview material.
   [This issue of Evergreen includes publicity for the Grove Press edition of Love and Napalm: Export USA; the advertisement carries an endorsement by Susan Sontag: "I have admired Ballard's work for many years. He is one of the most important, intelligent voices in contemporary fiction."]

D73 PERRY, NICK, and WILKIE, ROY. "The Undivided Self: J.G. Ballard's The Crystal World." Riverside Quarterly 5, no. 4(April):268-77.
   A close reading of the novel, comparing it with Ballard's earlier work. Describes the plot at length, with numerous quotations. Analyses the character of Ventress, claiming similarities with Hardoon (The Wind from Nowhere) and Strangman (The Drowned World), and showing his relationship to the central character, Dr. Sanders. Asserts: "Sanders and Ventress can more meaningfully be seen as two aspects of a single character." Goes on: "This, together with the division of the book into two parts and the persistent reiteration of the black/white motif, suggests that The Crystal World is a study of a 'divided self.'" Analyses the other characters, pointing out that they all "pair off."
   Comments on the power of the crystal symbol, invoking Ernst Fischer's The Necessity of Art and the theories of C.G. Jung. "The crystal as self . . . suggests that we see The Crystal World as a novel of self-discovery." Sanders's "final journey into the forest becomes, on this view, an affirmative, even an optimistic act. It is an act of mysticism, and the optimism of spiritual enlightenment." Concludes by invoking Shelley's "Adonais," a poem quoted in the novel.

D74 NYE, ROBERT. "The Beautiful and the Damned." Guardian, 28

June, p. 14.
Review of <u>Crash</u>, among others. Says: "I've never been a J.G. Ballard fan, but I can see why other people are." Describes the book as "a grindingly earnest and scrupulous attempt to understand why we are all obsessed with accidents on the road." Sketches the plot, referring to the novel as a "horrific and certainly memorable exercise in controlled surrealism." Concludes: "As with earlier texts by Ballard, I could grasp why he sees a need to create a modern mythology out of technology gone mad, but I have to say that the <u>tone</u> strikes me as hellish."

D75 AMIS, MARTIN. "Auto-Perversion." <u>Observer</u>, 1 July.
Review of <u>Crash</u>, among others. Begins by stating that "the apocalyptic-epiphanic mode in fiction is not for minor talents." Mentions <u>The Atrocity Exhibition</u>, then adds "<u>Crash</u> doesn't pontificate; here Ballard isn't out to rationalize but to actualize. . . ." Compared to the perversion Ballard deals with here, "Joyce's penchant for excrement and Burroughs's interest in scaffolds seem sadly unliberated, almost quaint." Describes the plot, then points out that Ballard uses the word "perverse" sixteen times; "geometry" twenty-one times; "stylized" twenty-six times. Adds: "the glazed monotony of its descriptions and the deadpan single-mindedness of its attitudes aren't designed to convert or excite the reader, merely to transmit the chilling isolation of the psychopath." In addition, <u>Crash</u> is "heavily flawed," with loose construction, "a perfunctory way with minor characters, and a lot of risible over-writing." Concludes: "In sf Ballard had a tight framework for his unnerving ideas; out on the lunatic fringe, he can only flail and shout."

D76 QUINTON, ANTHONY. "Three-lane Lucifers." <u>Sunday Telegraph</u>, 1 July.
Review of <u>Crash</u>, among others. "By far the best" of the four novels under review is <u>Crash</u> . . . "a prose poem in the manner of Rimbaud on the scenery of the M4 and A40 as they approach London . . . flyovers and slip-roads are the scene of this remarkable work." States that "the whole undertaking is developed with splendid consistency and in that style of magical realism in which the hallucinatory character of the subject-matter is never used as an excuse for amorphous raptures in the writing." Says he found the novel "extremely comic, although the blurb invites the reader to shock and disturbance. With its force and enthusiasm it redeems, rather than condemns, the wasteland it describes."

*D77 SEYMOUR-SMITH, MARTIN. Review of <u>Crash</u>. <u>Oxford Mail</u> [July?].
Describes it as Ballard's "latest and by far best novel." Calls it "one of the more outstanding of recent warnings against the dehumanized eroticism and the brutality that are part and parcel of the new technology. . . . Here we see the 19th-century myth of the 'mad scientist' turned into frightening future reality; this is true madness, and it will exercise anybody to say exactly

how long it will be before it is no longer fantasy. An impressive book."
[Source: jacket copy on the Panther edition of Crash.]

D78 ANON. "Bumper Fun-Book." Times Literary Supplement, 13 July, p. 797.
Review of Crash. Mentions The Atrocity Exhibition and states that the new novel is "a much simpler, more obsessive work." Describes the plot, then adds that it is "a fetishist's book . . . a frantic litany, grotesque mantras in a private meditation."

D79 PRINGLE, DAVID. "The Fourfold Symbolism of J.G. Ballard." Foundation: The Review of Science Fiction, no. 4 (July), pp. 48-60.
James Goddard and David Pringle, eds. J.G. Ballard: The First Twenty Years. Hayes, Middlesex: Bran's Head Books, 1976.
Analyses Ballard's fiction in terms of "four main 'elements'" or "primary images"--Water, Sand, Concrete, and Crystal. Claims that the "Water" stories (e.g., The Drowned World) deal with the psychological past; the "Sand" stories (e.g., The Drought) concern the future; the "Concrete" stories (e.g., The Atrocity Exhibition) deal with the present; and the "Crystal" stories (e.g., The Crystal World) project images of eternity. Mentions other symbols in passing--for example, the beach and the crashed spacecraft. Deals with the apocalyptic imagery in "The Waiting Grounds" and "The Voices of Time" and comments on Ballard's attitudes towards space travel and alien beings. Concludes: "I have pursued the theme of Ballard's symbolism with an earnestness that is perhaps out of keeping with the irony, ambivalence and wit of all his writing. His work adds up to an exploration of various states of the modern mind, not a new scripture."
[For a considerably expanded and updated version of this essay see Pringle's Earth is the Alien Planet: J.G. Ballard's Four-Dimensional Nightmare, D148.]

D80 JAKUBOWSKI, MAXIM. Review of Crash. New Scientist 59 (2 August):280-81.
Describes it as "the first pornographic book dominated by 20th century technology." Describes Ballard's exhibition of crashed cars in 1970, and claims the subject is reflected, "as an extreme hypothesis," in this book. Describes the plot, calling it "repetitive and insistent." Claims Crash is not sf. "Just as Bertolucci's Last Tango in Paris created a scandal among the righteous, so will this disturbing book." Unlike the fantasists Burroughs, Vonnegut, and Pynchon, "Ballard restricts himself to the narrow corridors of today's increasingly technology-conscious world."

D81 MANO, D.K. Review of Crash. New York Times Book Review, 23

Part D: Critical and Bio-Bibliographical Studies   1973

September, p. 7.
Describes it as "hands down, the most repulsive book I've yet to come across." However, it is "well written; credit given where due." But "no one needs this sort of protracted and gratuitous anguish." Describes the plot, complaining of repetitiousness, and concludes: "Perhaps J.G. Ballard was traumatized at a drive-in theatre. One would like to be sympathetic: the man has talent. But a partial list of his previous titles doesn't reassure: The Disaster Area, The Terminal Beach, The Atrocity Exhibition. Though it is dangerous to infer creator from character . . . I don't think I'd care to meet J.G. Ballard. I certainly won't read further in the Ballard oeuvre."

D82 BRADY, JOHN. "Ballard's Autogeddon." Cypher, no. 10 (October), pp. 52-53.
Review of Crash. Says that the novel "has been received with a uniform howl of anguish by the critics." Claims that this is "one sure sign of both the book's power and closeness to the bone." Briefly describes the plot, calling the book "one of the most important novels of the 20th century." Points to the significance of the subject-matter—"one person is killed every hour on Britain's roads"—and praises the depiction of the character Vaughan, comparing him to Wells's Dr. Moreau. Quotes Céline to the effect that "no art is possible without a dance with death." Describes the climax of the novel as "a brilliantly sustained journey into inner space," and concludes with a three-paragraph quotation.

D83 ALDISS, BRIAN W. Billion Year Spree: The History of Science Fiction. London: Weidenfeld & Nicolson.
Discusses Ballard in the context of New Worlds under Michael Moorcock's editorship. Praises Moorcock's "courage and foresight" for seizing on the "unsettling Ballardian quality" and crying its virtues. Adds: "Moorcock's energy and Ballard's imagery attracted a new audience to science fiction." Ballard, "perhaps made slightly frenzied by having been so firmly nailed to the masthead of Moorcock's pirate ship," rejected linear fiction and began writing "condensed novels." Quotes a section from "The Death Module" and states that it powerfully conveys "some of the dislocations and unexpressed connections of its time." Discusses Ballard's earlier work and praises The Crystal World, but adds "the central problem of writing a novel without having the characters pursue any purposeful course of action . . . is not resolved. Ballard has never resolved it." Remarks that the short stories are "far more successful," and perhaps the stories of the "Terminal Beach period . . . will last the longest. His ferocious intelligence, his wit, his cantankerousness, and, in particular, his extraordinary rendering of the perverse pleasures of today's paranoia, make him one of the grand magicians of modern fiction."

D84   NICHOLLS, PETER. "An ABC of British Science Fiction: Apocalypse, Bleakness, Catastrophe." In Beyond This Horizon: An Anthology of Science Fact and Science Fiction. Edited by Christopher Carrell. Sunderland: Ceolfrith Press [paper].
A study of British sf, highlighting the tradition of "disaster" stories. Picks out Arthur C. Clarke, Brian Aldiss, John Brunner, and J.G. Ballard as the most important living authors. Ballard is "perhaps the most extraordinary of the four." Discusses The Drowned World, citing the influence on Ballard of Conrad and Jung. "Ballard is a superb writer--perhaps a great writer--at least as far as the local organization of his prose is concerned." But his novels are less satisfactory than his short stories--in the latter form "he has few peers in literature as a whole." Moves on to discuss his recent writing, which "comes close to toppling over into obsession." Crash is "an ugly but memorable novel."

D85   ANON. "Dusty Answer." Times Literary Supplement, 30 November, p. 1466.
Review of Vermilion Sands. Gives a brief synopsis of Ballard's career, saying "Vermilion Sands marks a return to familiar territory." Describes the locale and states: "Of the nine stories in this book none feels very different from the next. . . . The real theme is the place." Calls Ballard "one of the most accomplished creators of evocative landscapes in modern fiction. . . . He achieves his effect partly by painting his desert in the manner of Dali, a mixture of appalling clarity and the exotic." Complains that the style is sometimes overopulent, "nearer to Wilde than to wilderness." But this suits the effect of "recession." Concludes: "The aftermath of atrocity is beach-fatigue on a shore at the end of time, just before the waters again cover the earth."

D86   STRAUB, PETER. "Last Resort." New Statesman 86 (7 December): 874-75.
Review of Vermilion Sands, among others. Begins by condemning sf in general. "By contrast J.G. Ballard, along with Kurt Vonnegut Jr., and younger Americans like Thomas Disch, once seemed capable of rescuing the genre from the mountain of fifth-rate hackwork it had become." Gives a resumé of Ballard's career, saying that recently he "changed his manner and became altogether more inventive and modernist. . . . In Vermilion Sands, however, he is back in the old harness. . . . He is coasting along on the strength of one idea, twisting all his material into one repetitive pattern, and the slickness and indulgence of the stories makes them difficult to remember an hour after the book's been closed." But he finds the actual writing "creamy and precise, almost always delightful." Concludes: "The limpness of the stories in Vermilion Sands is that of a poet going lax and complacent. . . ."

Part D: Critical and Bio-Bibliographical Studies 1974

*D87 Review of Vermilion Sands. Sunday Times, 9 December, p. 38.
"J.G. Ballard is a marvellously accomplished stylist with a weirdly creative imagination. . . . He has managed the physical setting with phosphorescent brilliance. . . . This aspect of a beautifully written book is weirdly effective, the sense of evil is all-pervasive, a valid expression of the author's fundamental criticism of human society."
[Sources: jacket copy on the Panther edition of Vermilion Sands, and the Times Index, 1973.]

D88 HUTCHINSON, TOM. "Science Fiction." Times, 13 December, p. 14.
Review of Vermilion Sands, among others. "Some of these stories have glowed for us before; the lustre of the others is here undimmed for the first time. . . . J.G. Ballard is still the most remarkable conjuror of a future so alien as to have little to do with anything of contemporary consequence except, of course, and often forgotten in any consideration of his work, the projection of the agony of love requited or unrequited. . . ." Recommends "a visit with this book, where the aching landscape of the idea contains wit and irony to shade us from the anguished sun, like the heaped cumulus in that lovely story, 'The Cloud-Sculptors of Coral D.'"

1974

D89 WATSON, IAN. "SF Idea Capsules for Art Students." Foundation: The Review of Science Fiction, no. 5 (January), pp. 56-62.
An article on Watson's experience of teaching an sf course at Birmingham Polytechnic. Describes the various "idea capsules" which he uses in classes. One is a "Ballard-based capsule focusing upon The Media Environment and The Automobile as Popular Icon." States that he uses extracts from The Atrocity Exhibition and Crash, together with Ballard's Penthouse interview (C41). Says that Ballard's "concept of the technological environment as representing a set of coded messages which are 'read' by the participants" can be approached from two standpoints--the psychoanalytic (cites Norman O. Brown) and the semiotic (cites Roland Barthes). The concern with auto design, gestures, and contours of the human body "isn't merely a quirk of Ballardian psychopathology, but on the contrary an increasing preoccupation of designers, particularly of architects." Cites Herbert Marcuse and Reyner Banham on the significance of automobiles, and refers briefly to Ballard's article on Ralph Nader (C51).

D90 SAGE, LORNA. "King of the Dust-Heap." Observer, 21 April.
Review of Concrete Island, among others. Claims that Ballard's "narrow, specialized vision picks out unerringly any promising gaps in normality." Describes the plot, adding: "what's best about Concrete Island is not the hypothesis, but the

documentary meticulousness, Ballard's obsessive attention to the changing texture of the experience." He has "his own brand of frozen, dehydrated eloquence--a vocabulary pared down to primitive perceptions (brick, hard, greasy); speech reduced to commands, pleas, soliloquies; an appropriately alienated use of names and reflexive pronouns (so that, for instance, 'himself,' as in 'he picked himself up,' really means 'it'). The result is a style rigid with distaste, fit to survive in the flat, grey, man-made labyrinth of urban design."

D91 SMITH, GODFREY. "A Pattern of Islands." Sunday Times, 21 April, p. 39.
Review of Concrete Island, among others. Says that Ballard's new novel "comes so soon after the success of his last, Crash, that at first you could almost confuse them." But the new book has "its own sharp identity." Describes the plot, and concludes: "Mr Ballard writes with taut and precise economy, and the moral of his brilliantly original fable is plain: the interstices of our concrete jungle are filled with neglected people, and one day those people could be ourselves."

D92 WAUGH, AUBERON. "Motorway Crusoe." Evening Standard [London], 23 April.
Review of Concrete Island. Claims that the "exact message" of this novel escapes him. Perhaps it is about loneliness, or about "the extreme gap between accommodated and unaccommodated man in our society." But the important factor is "how it stands up as a novel." Describes the plot, comparing it to Robinson Crusoe. Concludes that the book is "perfectly enjoyable within the horror comic tradition, and Mr Ballard is exceptionally skilful when he describes the unpredictability of psychotics."

D93 JACKY. "Fiction." Times, 25 April, p. 13.
Review of Concrete Island, among others. Remarks that allegories have to be probable "in their own terms, but those terms have to be strictly observed and for this reason J.G. Ballard's wonderfully rich and well-worked image in Concrete Island suffers . . . from one or two minimal lapses in that observance." Describes the plot, pointing out some unlikelihoods, then says: "the complexity and range of themes explored is immense." Points to the theme of "isolation within the crowd, of the helplessness at the heart of technology." Concludes: "It is a very clever, subtle and misanthropic book."

D94 ANON. "Off the Road." Times Literary Supplement, 26 April, p. 433.
Review of Concrete Island. Describes Ballard as "a compulsive re-visitor of a few evocative landscapes." Describes the plot and points out that the "island" in this novel "has an unreality about it which is a recognizable Ballard characteristic: it is suspended. Just as Vermilion Sands was a location suspended

in time, so Maitland's island is suspended in place." Concludes that the novel is "a most intelligent and interesting book" and that Ballard is "our foremost iconographer of landscape."

D95 AMIS, MARTIN. "Hard Shoulder." New Review 1, no. 2 (May):92.
Review of Concrete Island. Claims the novel "will seem ridiculously slight." Describes the plot, adding: "the interpersonal set-to is preposterously remote as Ballard always is in his dealings with the human race." Describes the last page of the novel as "disastrously ambiguous." Goes on, "in fairness," to point out that "Ballard is one of the few living writers who could get much out of his hero's half-delirious self-identification with the island, an adept as he is of the language of heightened, dislocated consciousness." But "despite these small felicities," finds the book "distanced by an oddly wilful negligence." Complains about repetition of the adjective "strong" in describing the girl. Comments: "Essentially, his fiction does not propound, it embodies; the prose is simply the rhetoric of an obsession, as dense, one-colour and arbitrary as the obsession requires it to be. . . ."
Amis then gives a brief run-through of Ballard's earlier fiction, quoting from Crash. He says "Crash remains a mournful and hypnotic tour de force, possibly the most extreme example in modern fiction of how beautifully and lovingly someone can write 70,000 words of vicious nonsense." Continues: "Ballard is the rarest kind of writer--an unselfconscious stylist: it is the measure of his creative narcissism that he has his eye on no audience." Ballard has "nothing coherent to 'say,' and his plots are merely gateways to exotic locales." Ballard's "raison . . . is his awesome visual imagination and the complementary verbal intensity with which to realize it."

D96 TENNANT, EMMA. "Accident." New Statesman 87 (10 May):669.
Review of Concrete Island. Quotes Gertrude Stein on time and identity, then says: "J.G. Ballard has concerned himself in much of his work with problems of time and identity, and in Concrete Island, a modern Robinson Crusoe, he shows the effect of one upon the other. . . ." Describes the plot in detail. "Ballard's talent, as a novelist writing in the last third of the 20th century, is to show us what we refuse to see . . . and to prove that it is only by knowing ourselves that we can understand the technology we have created." Describes the "island" in the novel, adding: Maitland comes to understand this strange, neglected place, invisible to the million eyes which see it daily because it is too clear a symbol of the real identity of the present." Concludes: "Ballard, psychoanalyst of the high-rise and prophet of the six-lane, proves in this brilliant novel that although 'to know what one knows is frightening,' it is not, in the end, as frightening as not knowing can be."

D97 JAKUBOWSKI, MAXIM. Review of Concrete Island. New Scientist

62 (16 May):426.
"Ballard now enlarges his dispassionate analytical vista of technology gone awry." Describes the plot. "Ballard's progress from book to book has the very logic of madness, but I find it hard to fault." Concludes that the novel reminds him "somewhat of the brilliant French film Themroc by Claude Faraldo . . . where a whole section of working-class Paris reverts to the stone age."

D98 PRINGLE, DAVID. "An Honest Madness." Foundation: The Review of Science Fiction, no. 6 (May), pp. 83-86.
  James Goddard and David Pringle, eds. J.G. Ballard: The First Twenty Years. Hayes, Middlesex: Bran's Head Books, 1976.
  Review of Crash. Discusses sf and pornography, and describes Crash as "an insane new novel." Quotes a passage of Ballard's prose and talks of its "strange and at times beautiful blend of the poetic and the clinical." But also claims that "the book is tedious to a certain degree." Describes Ballard's apparent "impatience with character," adding that Crash is "an admonitory work," a "warning . . . against this dehumanization." Concludes: "Ballard sees this as a time when only the extreme will do, hence the extreme metaphor of Crash."

D99 MOORCOCK, MICHAEL. "Modern Metaphors." Books and Bookmen 19, no. 10 (July):37.
  James Goddard and David Pringle, eds. J.G. Ballard: The First Twenty Years. Hayes, Middlesex: Bran's Head Books, 1976.
  Review of Concrete Island and the paperback reissue of four earlier books: The Wind from Nowhere, The Terminal Beach, The Drowned World and The Drought. Like the surrealist painters whom he admires, Ballard "works with a large vocabulary of images which he transmutes and reuses over and over again in different permutations, to accomplish his various literary intentions, in pursuit of a recognizable range of moral concerns." Mentions Ballard's use of "Freudian symbolism become private metaphor" and points out that his prose is not "poetic"--rather, "his methods . . . are often those of the poet." Describes Ballard's career and earlier work in brief. States that Crash "shocked and bewildered the majority of critics" who "could not see the strong, almost puritanical, moral line running through it." Describes Concrete Island as "almost a sequel" to Crash. Although "imaginative," the novel has "much more in common with the work of Beckett than it has, say, with Blish. . . ." Concludes by seeing Concrete Island as indicating "a fruitful new opening up of form and subject matter in Ballard's work."

D100 HARDING, LEE, and TURNER, GEORGE. "One Novel--Two Reviews." SF Commentary, no. 38 (September), pp. 4-9.
  Two reviews of Crash. Lee Harding begins by glancing back at Ballard's early work, then says: "Crash is a remarkable

return to form, an apocalyptic linear novel with a beginning, middle and end, told in clear, precise prose, and a style haunted by elusive shades of Genet." The book has "extraordinary impact." Says that "anyone who feels intimidated and at times terrorized by traffic will respond to Ballard's vision." Asks: "is it sf? Ballard has made the label redundant. . . . He is the truest sf writer of his time." Concludes that Crash is "arguably Ballard's best book."

George Turner professes to find it "the supreme novel of the death-wish triumphant." Describes the plot and characters in some detail, commenting on the "remarkable writing" at the climax. Remarks on the "coolness" of Ballard's language: "The result of this patrician use of language is to throw a clinical aura over the proceedings." Asks: "why did this extraordinary, incandescently-written novel bore me to tears?" The theme is overstated and "repellent." Ballard "celebrates the unfit," and Turner has no sympathy for the characters. Concludes by speculating on Ballard's motives for writing the book, claiming to find several parallels between narrator and author [some of them false]. Believes Ballard "has been regurgitating highly personal and revoltingly dangerous ideas from his psychic system."

D101 LEVIN, MARTIN. Review of Concrete Island. New York Times Book Review, 1 December, p. 78.
Comments that Ballard "plays two themes in this compact little book." One is the "Robinson Crusoe gambit," the other is the "search-for-self motif." Describes the plot briefly. Concludes: "Mr. Ballard raises some tantalizing questions, even if he doesn't answer them satisfactorily."

1975

D102 WATSON, IAN. "The Greening of Ballard." Foundation: The Review of Science Fiction, no. 7/8 (March), pp. 188-92.
James Goddard and David Pringle, eds. J.G. Ballard: The First Twenty Years. Hayes, Middlesex: Bran's Head Books, 1976.
Review of Concrete Island. Compares with novels of William Golding. Quotes from Reyner Banham's Los Angeles: The Architecture of Four Ecologies and from Roland Barthes's Mythologies. Asserts that The Atrocity Exhibition and Crash had been much concerned with "signs," but that the present novel contains an "apparent return to Nature" as the hero is "forcibly decanted out of the mechanical sign world of polymorphous perversions into a free, liberated territory." The book spawns "other subliminal echoes"--invokes Beckett, Defoe and Kobo Abé. Raises the question of whether the novel is "a trifle too literary," but adds: "Personally I don't think so. Ballard's island means more to me than any of William Golding's. It is our contemporary nightmare island."

D103 SAMUELSON, DAVID. <u>Visions of Tomorrow: Six Journeys from Outer to Inner Space</u>. New York: Arno Press.
Book version of a thesis, originally entitled "Studies in the Contemporary American and British Science Fiction Novel," for which Samuelson was awarded a Ph.D. in 1969. Consists of detailed analyses of novels by Arthur C. Clarke, Isaac Asimov, Theodore Sturgeon, Walter M. Miller, Algis Budrys, and J.G. Ballard. The chapter on Ballard concentrates on <u>The Crystal World</u>.

Begins by quoting the <u>New Worlds</u> guest editorial (C1), then goes on to analyse "The Venus Hunters," a story in which Ballard "elaborated his position in both practice and precept." Claims "the theme of the story is the nature of science fiction." Adds that Ballard "has not been preaching anything new . . . only in the conservative reaches of popular fiction could his style and narrative method be considered innovative." Describes his career, pointing out that J.B. Priestley first used the term "inner space" in 1953. Briefly deals with <u>The Wind from Nowhere</u>, <u>The Drowned World</u>, and <u>The Burning World</u>, before moving on to a full consideration of Ballard's "latest, and perhaps best novel, <u>The Crystal World</u>." Describes the critical reaction to the book, quoting from Judith Merril (D39) and others. Also quotes from "Algis Budrys' attack on Ballard" (D42), commenting: "Viewed as sf, Ballard's novels . . . may well seem inane, but Ballard's relationship to sf is somewhat ambivalent. Although he depends on the sf audience for his livelihood, he uses the sf cosmos as he sees fit, drawing from it images, figures, conventions and rationalizations subordinated to the 'subtle interplay of character and theme.'"

Describes the plot and characters at great length, commenting in passing: "Like Ray Bradbury . . . Ballard gives aid and comfort to the enemies of science by suggesting magical relations and causation. . . . But whereas Bradbury writes little morality plays about man's potential for good or evil determining his use of science, Ballard tells of spiritual odysseys for which science is irrelevant. . . ." Claims that none of the characters "seems to have any real existence except in relation to Sanders," and Ballard's main concentration is on "the description of things." Points out that "the theme of immortality is underscored by reference to a painting, 'Island of the Dead,' by Arnold Böcklin" and adds that "this is a familiar gambit of Ballard's," citing paintings by Delvaux, Ernst, and Tanguy used in earlier novels. "Ballard frequently spells out his implications with excruciating thoroughness, as if not trusting the average sf reader to get the point." Comments on Ballard's "slow, almost meandering sentences . . . deliberate attempts at increasing aesthetic distance." Quotes some examples of "awkward" sentences, pointing to Ballard's use of the conjunction "but" in a seemingly irrelevant way. Comments on vocabulary, showing how Ballard describes the forest by using "relatively uncommon terms: palisade, minaret, jasper, mandalas, glace, basalt, panoply, lattices, enclave, fleur-de-lis, bifurcated, aureoles, iridescent, pilasters, friezes, annealed,

lapis lazuli, vestigial, cuirass, and armorial" (all from a five-page section of the novel).
  Finds "allusions to Conrad's Heart of Darkness" implicit in the book, and also echoes of Coleridge. Suggests the crystal forest "represents the immortality offered by art." Concludes: "On the level of novelistic realism, The Crystal World is not wholly successful. . . . To be sure, Ballard does not offer the same faults we see in most writers of pulp fiction, but he, too, is hampered by many of the same restrictions. And the fact that he has so humanized some old conventions, creating a fictional world in which old dreams and images come true and man's ambiguous and contradictory desires can be embodied, is a genuine, if minor, artistic accomplishment."

D104 "Ballard, J(ames) G(raham) (November 15, 1930-)." In World Authors, 1950-1970. Edited by John Wakeman. New York: H.W. Wilson Co.
  A biographical/critical entry which incorporates autobiographical statements by Ballard. He is quoted as saying: "My first 16 years were spent in this large polyglot city [Shanghai] . . . and it seems likely that the influence of this bizarre landscape was greater than that of any emotional experiences of my childhood. I was brought up largely by servants--my father was a prosperous businessman--and my memories of childhood are of wandering around the Chinese areas of the city on my own or of being driven out by the Russian chauffeur to visit the abandoned battlefields a few miles away. . . ." Ballard goes on to describe his internment in a Japanese civilian POW camp: "The camp was adjacent to a Japanese airfield, and in the last year of the war we had a close view of the continuous American bombing raids." He adds: "During [the] return to peace Shanghai was one of the most exhilirating places in the world. . . . England, after this, was a great shock. I find that even after 20 years I still regard it as a foreign country. From the beginning it was clear to me that whatever talents I had were those of an imaginative writer and that the landscape of England would never provide me with a subject matter to which I could respond. This in fact has proved the case. . . ."
  The critical part of the entry states that "Ballard's novels can be read on several levels. They are adventure stories, full of exciting, strange and often repellent incident; they are biological fantasies about human evolution and devolution; and they are attempts to construct a timeless world of the psyche." Describes The Drowned World, adding: "This strange world is evoked with great skill and power, and a characteristic mastery of visual effects, sometimes weakened by a self-indulgent use of language." Describes The Drought and The Crystal World, quoting from the TLS review of the latter (D32). Mentions some of the short story collections, and quotes from Paul Theroux's harsh review of Love and Napalm (D69). States that Ballard's views "'hang heavy over almost every page' of the literary journal Ambit. In

1967 Ballard stirred up much controversy when he offered in that magazine a prize for 'the best creative work . . . written under the influence of drugs.'" [The source of these quotations is not made clear.] Mentions Ballard's "private advertising campaign," and concludes with the following biographical information: "Ballard has three children by his 1953 marriage to Helen Mary Matthews, who died in 1964, and one child by his second wife, Claire Churchill."

D105 PERRY, NICK, and WILKIE, ROY. "The Atrocity Exhibition." Riverside Quarterly 6, no. 3 (August):180-88.
A close study of The Atrocity Exhibition. Comments on the fact that parts appeared in Ambit, Transatlantic Review, Encounter, etc., and says: "Ballard was seeking a wider or different audience for his short stories." Remarks on the break-up of the text into brief sections and says that the beginning of this tendency was visible in The Drought. Says "the first nine 'stories' in this collection convey a feeling of continuity," and comments on the identity, through various name-changes, of the central character. Analyses a short passage from "You and Me and the Continuum" and concludes that the central character is all-important: "in the relationship between subject and object, between the knower and what he knows, Ballard's attention is on the subjective, on the knower." Says that in the book's obsession with the visual media there is a "nod in the direction of McLuhan, but a McLuhan transformed by a metaphysic that is peculiarly Ballard's."

Compares the book to The Drowned World, claiming that despite all differences in the imagined situation "Ballard's epistemology remains constant." Analyses the so-called "psycho-logic" of the book, and compares it to Genet's play The Balcony. "For Genet as for Ballard the meaning of public events, the trappings of responsibility, must be re-evaluated and their connections with private fantasies made manifest." Claims Ballard's sympathies are with his central character, and this is testified by the author's "readiness to act the part of Traven in a short film called Crash that the BBC screened in early 1971. . . ." Analyses other characters in the book, deploring the fact that Dr. Nathan is characterized largely in terms of his smoking habits. Points out that the girl Coma appeared in Ballard's fiction as early as "The Voices of Time." Compares and contrasts The Atrocity Exhibition with the last-named story, claiming that "what is still at work is the quest for some kind of mystical unity."

D106 ROTTENSTEINER, FRANZ. The Science Fiction Book: An Illustrated History. London: Thames & Hudson.
Deals briefly with Ballard as the leading exponent of New Wave sf. Refers to his "dense, richly symbolic stories" and his "passive, almost autistic heroes." Quotes from Ballard's "Notes from Nowhere" (C21).

D107 NICHOLLS, PETER. "Jerry Cornelius at the Atrocity Exhibition: Anarchy and Entropy in New Worlds Science Fiction, 1964-1974." Foundation: The Review of Science Fiction, no. 9 (November), pp. 22-44.
 Discusses the work of Brian Aldiss, J.G. Ballard, and Michael Moorcock, expressing reservations about the "aesthetic distancing devices" used by these writers. Quotes three paragraphs from Crash and states: "the whole point of the passage is that it is devoid of emotional connotations. . . . The attention is clinical, aesthetic." Adds: "the whole thing can be seen as a gigantic metaphor, a kind of scream of pain deliberately muffled by sound-proofing." Disagrees with this view, and believes that "Ballard's world is the world we all live in, with this difference: that the worst of its minglings of flesh and technology, advertising and death, are accepted and welcomed by him with a placid, Buddha-like smile. . . . Ballard's triumph in Crash is to have correctly analysed the disease from within, while simultaneously being its most obvious symptom."

D108 BLUMBERG, MYRNA. "Fiction." Times, 13 November, p. 17.
 Review of High-Rise, among others. Refers to it as "J.G. Ballard's new and finest novel. . . . His writing here is vibrant with irony and images, a triumph of artistry and feeling." Describes the plot and characters.

D109 QUIGLY, ISABEL. "Crumbling Towers and Dreams." Financial Times, 13 November, p. 23.
 Review of High-Rise, among others. Calls it "a modern fable . . . a commentary on the hideous possibilities of advanced technology. . . ." But "Ballard writes less about the collapse of technology than about the boil-like bursting of original sin across a glass-and-chrome landscape." Describes the plot, and invokes Bunuel, Golding, and Godard. "The writing is cool, the observation exact, the idea bold and well developed," but "one is left unsatisfied . . . perhaps because the theme seems to demand, not so much greater artistry, as a bigger artist; grandeur rather than competence."

D110 AMIS, MARTIN. "Up!" New Statesman 90 (14 November):618.
 Review of High-Rise, among others. Claims the novel is "a harsh and ingenious reworking" of the theme of The Ascent of F6 by Auden and Isherwood. Describes the plot, commenting: "Eventually the high-rise takes on the quality common to all Ballardian loci: it is suspended, no longer to do with the rest of the planet, screened off by its own surreal logic." Says the closing pages of the novel are "as hauntingly wayward as anything Ballard has written." Adds: "I hope no one wastes their time worrying whether High-Rise is prescient, admonitory, sobering, and whatnot. For Ballard is neither believable nor unbelievable . . . : he is abstract, at once totally humourless and entirely unserious. The point of his visions is to provide him with imagery, with

opportunities to write well, and this seems to me to be the only way of getting the hang of his fiction." Concludes: "the book is an intense and vivid bestiary, which lingers unsettingly in the mind."

D111 SUTHERLAND, JOHN. "Return of the Native." Times Literary Supplement, 5 December, p. 1438.
Review of High-Rise. Provides brief descriptions of earlier novels, and states the new book is "the familiar Ballardian journey back to primal states." Describes the plot, then quotes Brian Aldiss (D83) to the effect that Ballard has difficulty handling long fictions. Nevertheless, the novel is "carefully paced," even if it contains "nagging improbabilities." Concludes that "the whole novel is dedicated to creating unease."

D112 DURRANT, DIGBY. "Squibs and Rockets: A Note on J.G. Ballard." London Magazine 15, no 5 (December 1975/January 1976):69-73.
A critical run-through of Ballard's career. Describes "Prima Belladonna," adding: "It would be unfair to imply Ballard always writes at this comparatively trivial level, far from it." Describes High-Rise at length. "If you compare the short story and the novel I've mentioned it becomes clear there are two Ballards." States that in short stories "his extraordinary inventiveness is given full rein, and, dazed by it, admiring it, our critical faculties are suspended. . . ." But the novels are "often repetitive" and obsessed with "violence, destruction, machines, time, boredom and technological sex." Complains some of Ballard's novels fail because he doesn't develop characters. But "his humour is of a paradoxical and ironic turn." Describes various earlier novels, and says: "It is easy to over-simplify Ballard. Reading him sometimes is like trying to understand a foreign language . . . he sometimes irritates by his apparent pretentious elusiveness."

1976

D113 BRADSHAW, STEVE. "Psychic Landscape." New Society 35 (22 January):169-70.
An article examining Ballard's fiction in general. Claims that he is perhaps "the only British writer since the war to make his own langauge." Describes him as having been "a fairly conventional genre writer" during his first decade as an author. Deals with the early novels in a slightly derogatory tone, but adds "there are hints of the masterpieces of the 70s." Mentions "the surprisingly visual quality of the prose," but complains that Ballard's characters remain "nervous and hesitant." Reserves greatest praise for The Atrocity Exhibition and Crash, in which "the characters take over." In Crash "Ballard uses apparently banal English place-names . . . Western Avenue, the Oceanic Terminal, the reservoirs around Heathrow, and makes them sound as distant and new as Godard's Alphaville, Tokyorama, Nueva York."

Part D: Critical and Bio-Bibliographical Studies

Concludes that High-Rise is less effective, but that Ballard should be read: "He may be the best we've got."

D114 GODDARD, JAMES. Review of High-Rise. Vector, no. 72 (February), pp. 21-22.
Synopsizes Ballard's career, saying "he can safely be regarded as a major novelist, and a writer of such originality that he is--currently--without equal." Describes the plot, saying "this is not a novel in which readers will easily identify with the protagonists. . . . It speaks well for Ballard's skill that we want to shout warnings to these demented people, but his narrative holds us spellbound, motionless. . . ."

D115 HAYMAN, MARTIN. "Future Perfect: The Crystalline World of J.G. Ballard." Street Life, no. 8 (7 February), pp. 16-17.
An essay/profile which incorporates some interview material. Describes Ballard as "the uncrowned king of sf in Britain, an intrepid explorer of inner space and an influence on practically all experimental fiction written in Britain since the early 60s." Describes the early work, and claims that "Ballard was not taken seriously until he published The Atrocity Exhibition." Describes a visit to the author's home and quotes from a conversation with him. Comments that, although the subject-matter of the last three novels is "vitally important, I feel that it has led to a coarsening and degrading of the quality of Ballard's imagination and the stultification of his lucid prose style." Looks forward to the publication of a new short-story collection.

D116 NICOL, CHARLES. "J.G. Ballard and the Limits of Mainstream SF." Science-Fiction Studies 3, no. 2 (July):150-57.
Attempts to distinguish between the conventions of "mainstream fiction" and sf, and states that Ballard mingles those conventions. Analyses two short stories in depth. "The Drowned Giant" is "mainstream sf," while "The Voices of Time" is "'merely' sf," though "both are stories of superlative quality." Argues this case in considerable detail, quoting from the stories. Concludes that in "The Voices of Time" Ballard "has used science fiction to fulfill the traditional role of the poet: to meditate on time and death." But, unlike "The Drowned Giant" and despite the fact that it is "literature," this story "is unavailable to a reader experienced only in mainstream fiction."

D117 GODDARD, JAMES, and PRINGLE, DAVID, eds. J.G. Ballard: The First Twenty Years. Hayes, Middlesex: Bran's Head Books.
Contains: "Introduction: J.G. Ballard, Our Contemporary" by James Goddard and David Pringle; "An Interview with J.G. Ballard, 4th January 1975" by James Goddard and David Pringle (C63); "The Wounded Land: J.G. Ballard" by Brian Aldiss (D27); "The Fourfold Symbolism of J.G. Ballard" by David Pringle (D79); "Modern Metaphors" by Michael Moorcock (D99); "An Honest Madness" by David Pringle (D98); "The Greening of Ballard" by Ian Watson

(D102); "Concrete Island: A Review" by Peter Linnett; "The Incredible Shrinking World: A Review of High-Rise" by David Pringle; "Preface to the First Edition" by John Carnell (D62); "Introduction" by J.G. Ballard (C66); "Chronological Bibliography of Published Fiction"; "Alphabetical Index"; "Books in Translation, 1963-1971"; "Non-Fiction Bibliography."
    The introduction gives an outline of Ballard's career and concludes: "Ballard is one of the very few writers of today who is attempting to produce a fiction for now--a body of work which does not employ any of the escape routes into convention, fantasy or history used by so many other writers of merit (from Anthony Powell to John Fowles)." The bibliography endeavors to be complete up to the end of 1975; in fact, one story is missing from the fiction list, and the nonfiction list is far from complete. The volume contains four line drawings by Carol Gregory (purporting to illustrate scenes from Ballard's stories) and a photograph of Ballard by Mark Gerson.

D118   MALZBERG, BARRY N. "Books." Fantasy and Science Fiction 51, no. 3 (September):30-36.
    Review of Love and Napalm: Export USA, among others. Notable for what is perhaps the most extreme commendation of Ballard's work yet published: "The pain in this book is overwhelming, the impact devastating. . . . Like 'The Terminal Beach' it is absolutely cold, contained, final and sui generis. In short, it is a masterpiece." Concludes: "it is impossible not to realize confronting it that one is in the presence of perhaps the major figure in western literature of our time."

D119   BARRON, NEIL, ed. Anatomy of Wonder: Science Fiction. New York: R.R. Bowker.
    Joe de Bolt and John Pfeiffer annotate The Burning World, Chronopolis, The Crystal World, The Day of Forever, The Disaster Area, The Drowned World, The Impossible Man, Love and Napalm: Export USA, The Overloaded Man, Vermilion Sands and The Wind from Nowhere. They assert that The Burning World is "worthy of comparison with Melville and Conrad"; Chronopolis contains "the crème de la crème of Ballard's short fiction"; and The Crystal World is "perhaps his best [novel]; it captures the poetry of his short fiction."

D120   JAKUBOWSKI, MAXIM. Review of Low-Flying Aircraft. New Scientist 72 (2 December):547.
    "Ballard's work over the past few years has convinced me unambiguously that he is today's only truly British novelist primarily concerned with science and its massive impact on our age." Claims this volume would serve as a good introduction to Ballard's work. "The style is taut, clinical, precise, and the imagery stunning," but points out that "Ballard's technique sometimes runs the risk of becoming repetitive and verging on self-parody." Claims Ballard's position is not antiscience: "he is

Part D: Critical and Bio-Bibliographical Studies 1976

much too fascinated by the logical lunacy of certain developments to allow himself to be prejudiced that way." Concludes: "This is a compulsive read for anyone in the slightest bit curious about the bumpy road we are travelling on to the future. . . ."

D121 NYE, ROBERT. "Disaster Area." Guardian, 2 December, p. 14.
Review of Low-Flying Aircraft, among others. The collection is "as stylish as anything he has done, and told with that meticu- is a writer who can be relied upon. He rarely writes much below his best." In this book "the prose is cleverly controlled, the effects are powerful and earnest." Claims that images of derelic- tion and disaster are most typical of Ballard and that in this book they find "urgent expression" in "The Ultimate City"--"the whole piece has the pressure and authority of Ballard at his most inspired, which is also his most disillusioned."

D122 MAHON, DEREK. "Crash." New Statesman 92 (3 December):812-13.
Review of Low-Flying Aircraft, among others. Says "entropy" is the "recurrent theme of J.G. Ballard's remarkable fictions." His method "is that of H.G. Wells," but he has little interest in characterization. Says some of these stories are jeux d'esprit (cites "The Greatest Television Show on Earth") and "all of this is good fun, though not on the same level as the powerful novella, 'The Ultimate City.' . . . Here we have Ballard at his best-- genuinely inventive, sharply observant and highly plausible."

D123 TOTTON, NICK. "Gems and Ruins." Spectator 237 (4 December): 26.
Review of Low-Flying Aircraft, among others. The collection is "as stylish as anything he had done, and told with that meticu- lously apocalyptic sobriety which is scarcely to be characterized as whimsical or sentimental. But Dr Ballard [sic] has kissed the blarney stone. He is whimsical--though admittedly he has a whim of iron." Refers to the author throughout the review as "Dr Ballard," claiming one of his "major symptoms is repetition com- pulsion." States Ballard writes the same stories over and over again.

D124 DISCH, THOMAS M. "The Eternal Invalid: A Celebration of Life with the Author of Rash." In New Worlds 10. Edited by Hilary Bailey. London: Corgi Books [paper].
A parody, in which Disch interviews "G.G. Allbard," author of "The Wounded World and Day of the Diabetic." Mr. Allbard is an invalid who writes, clinically, about his own diseases and operations: "What they refuse to understand, you see, is that a literature of extremity, like mine, is therapeutic. By revealing the hidden significance of our ailments it allows us to live in harmony with them. Illness opens up larger realms of being. It is the quintessentially modern experience. Hospitals are the cathedrals of the 20th century."

1977

D125 IRWIN, MICHAEL. "On the Scrapheap." Times Literary Supplement, 14 January, p. 26.
Review of Low-Flying Aircraft. States that these stories "leave haunting pictures in the mind." Ballard "taps our memories of disused railway-stations or airstrips, dumped cars, derelict cinemas or factories. The world he creates seems credible, because it has already begun to exist." Mentions the "ambivalence" of Ballard's attitudes, then describes the plot of "The Ultimate City." Concludes: "the four stories that lack background, that deal only in ideas, are no more than decently entertaining. But the remaining five, which constitute three-quarters of the volume, are works of real imaginative force, dreamlike, vivid, unpredictable in their effect."

D126 PRINGLE, DAVID. Review of Low-Flying Aircraft. Vector, no. 79 (January/February), pp. 18-19.
Claims Ballard is still an sf writer, though he uses "just those elements of the genre that interest him, and distorts them to his own purpose." Many other authors now do this, "precisely because of the influence of J.G. Ballard's writing." Compares Ballard to Bob Dylan, each a "revolutionary" artist in his own field. Claims Ballard is "now past his best, which is to say his most revolutionary, period." The recent stories are "less serious than the original work, as though the artist is paying a genial tribute to his younger self with the perfect knowledge that he can never recreate the earlier passion." Describes the stories, saying most "are obsessively concerned with technology, but not so much the technology of the future as that of the present seen through the eyes of the future." Quotes from "The Ultimate City," adding: "whereas Ballard used to write primarily about the melancholy of an abandoned technology, it is now the comedy which he expresses more frequently." Talks about the humor in Ballard's work. Points out that "My Dream of Flying to Wake Island" reworks the matter of "The Terminal Beach," while "The Ultimate City" is reminiscent of "Chronopolis," and "The Dead Astronaut" echoes "The Cage of Sand." Notes the theme of "superannuation" in three stories. Finds "The Beach Murders" the least satisfactory item in the book, and points out that it leans on "a piece by George MacBeth entitled 'The Ski Murders.'" Regrets the absence of "The Air Disaster" from this collection, "my favourite Ballard story of the past five years."

D127 LEIBER, FRITZ. "Fantasy Books." Fantastic Stories 26, no. 1 (February):129-30.
Review of the paperback edition of Crash. Has a "notion" that sf writers tend to see the world in mathematical terms as they get older. "In Crash geometry is king." Describes the book as "a delirium of Euclidean eroticism." Details the plot, and talks about "our culture's" obsession with automobiles, instancing

such films as <u>Bullitt</u>, <u>Vanishing Point</u>, and <u>Duel</u>. Concludes: "Ballard is seeking to satisfy a compulsion or an imperative to visualize and set down sex acts and death (by crash), frame by frame . . . in brightest light and fullest detail. . . ."

D128 FALLOWELL, DUNCAN. "Ballard in Bondage." <u>Books and Bookmen</u> 22, no. 6 (March):59-60.
Review of <u>Low-Flying Aircraft</u>, and one of the most sustained attacks on Ballard's fiction yet published. Describes his characters as "listless biodegradable people, magazine archetypes. . . ." Compares Ballard's men to Ian Fleming's and asserts that they would "go off to the Empire somewhere and help build it with a good grace." His women are "de-sexed." Ballard's prose style is "decidedly old-fashioned" and his technical innovations have been overrated. Gives grudging praise to one story, "The Beach Murders," where the "gaucheries" are fewer, but describes "The Ultimate City" as "a pedestrian yawn degenerating from a good idea." Criticizes Ballard's "portentousness" and his "intellectual weakness," while conceding that he "still has flashes of speculative ingenuity."

D129 PRIEST, CHRISTOPHER. "Landscape Artist." <u>Ghas</u> [fanzine], no. 3 (Spring), pp. 4-8.
Michael J. Tolley and Kirpal Singh, eds. <u>The Stellar Gauge: Essays on Science Fiction Writers</u>. Carlton, Victoria: Norstrilia Press, 1980 [paper; a revised version of the essay, subtitled "The Fiction of J.G. Ballard"].
Review of <u>J.G. Ballard: The First Twenty Years</u> edited by James Goddard and David Pringle (in reality a tribute to Ballard's work in general). Describes his first encounter with a Ballard story in <u>New Worlds</u> in 1962. He sent off for every available back issue of the magazine: "I found probably a dozen or so stories by Ballard. I read them all in one sitting, and became convinced that not only was he a writer of such genius that he made the rest of the sf field look tatty and thin, but also that he was probably a writer remarkable <u>by any standards</u>." Adds that fifteen years later "I still believe that Ballard is one of the three or four best novelists of any kind working in Britain. . . . His masterpiece, in my view, is <u>Crash</u>, a book which I believe will eventually be seen as one of the most important novels of this part of the century." Discusses the content of the book under review, praising the interview ("probably the single most interesting author-interview I have ever read . . . and one of the most amusing, too"). Discusses Ballard's childhood reminiscences, and his use of landscape in his fiction. Claims: "he is an artist, in the best sense; partly because of the sustained brilliance of his prose and images, but perhaps more specifically because of the very content of his work. It is the content that most involves me . . . and I find that it speaks to me in a curiously personal voice. . . ." Comments that there is something peculiarly "inevitable" about Ballard's writing: "the man's

artistry is so consistent that whatever he touches becomes a
natural part of his private universe." Adds that "it's hell
trying to write sf with Mr Ballard in the same neighbourhood!
Sometimes, in my gloomier moments, it seems to me that he has exhausted all the worthwhile themes. . . . Write a science fiction
story now that is about motorways, automobiles, hotels, airports,
advertising, assassination, film-stars, medicine, American
bombers, Pacific islands, beach-resorts, and God alone knows what
else, you ask for and often receive comparison (unfavourable) with
Ballard. And yet these are things that are intrinsic to our
world, and are dominant images in it. It is a measure of Ballard's
artistic achievement that he has taken them so completely to himself."

D130 "Special Section: J.G. Ballard.". Delap's F & SF Review 3,
no. 5 (May):3-8.
Contains: editorial comments by Richard Delap; review by
Charles Platt of High-Rise; review by Michael Moorcock of The
Crystal World; review by Joe Sanders of The Drowned World; review
by Jeff Frane of The Wind from Nowhere. The front cover carries
a large photo of the author, with the caption: "J.G. Ballard:
where does he fit?"

Delap writes: "when Ballard's new books were no longer
marketed as sf in the US his influence on the sf-reading public
began a steady decline, and until very recently his early novels
were often out-of-print and seemed to be headed the way of the
hula hoop and the fishtail auto. . . ." Claims Ballard has yet
to find a mainstream audience in America. Credits him with much
of the most important work to appear in New Worlds, and concludes:
he "deserves to be studied closely, both for his own sake and for
his effect on a field that even today is sorely in need of literary sophistication and innovation."

Platt states that "High-Rise could be J.G. Ballard's first
major commercial success in America." Describes the novel, commenting: "The message of the book is easily understood as an
ironic, witty commentary on our man-made environment." Claims
that within the sf field Ballard "was regarded as an author who
didn't care about the genre or its readers. Yet, in a way, I
think Ballard did care. The unintelligent criticism bothered him
more than his detractors ever realized." Concludes: "Ballard's
work is now received with great critical acclaim in France and
Germany and gets good reviews in Britain. But his failure to
reach that American audience must have been a perpetual frustration. . . ."

Moorcock says he "can't pretend lack of bias" in reviewing
The Crystal World; it was the first novel he serialized when he
took over the editorship of New Worlds in 1964. "Ballard was one
of the imaginative authors I most admired then and he is one of
the few I still admire." Describes the novel as "the work of a
symbolist," and points out that the images take precedence over
plot and characters. "The dramatic tensions are maintained by a

Part D: Critical and Bio-Bibliographical Studies   1977

conflict between those who will not accept the suprareality (or surreality) of the psychic world and those who accept it but are checked either by the others or by their own 'normal' impulses. . . . This is the so-called 'pessimistic' aspect of Ballard's work, for in his books the villains are those who are trying to save the world from 'disaster' which, to Ballard's heroes, is no disaster at all, but the very reverse." Points to the influence of the surrealist painters, as well as that of Conrad and Graham Greene. Concludes that the novel contains "the message of an old-fashioned Romantic, a true surrealist, but not, as some would have it, a hopeless pessimist."

Joe Sanders calls The Drowned World "a good introduction to Ballard: a relatively accessible book. . . ." Describes the plot, commenting: "Ballard's languid style . . . throws the reader off balance by dwelling on apparently trivial things while slipping bizarre zingers into subordinate clauses." Jeff Frane finds The Wind from Nowhere "in keeping with the works of Wyndham, Christopher and others." The imagined situation is "convincing for the duration of the novel" and Ballard "possesses an extraordinary visual sense." Frane's "only grievance with the book is the highly unrealistic upbeat ending."

D131 STABLEFORD, BRIAN. "New Island Discovered in Ballard Archipelago." Foundation: The Review of Science Fiction, no. 11/12 (July), pp. 99-100.

Review of High-Rise. Traces the theme of environmental change in Ballard's fiction. States the novel is "a robinsonade which perpetually invites comparison with Lord of the Flies." Believes Ballard's view of social evolution is dialectical, though non-Marxist, and the book is not merely about "a 'return' to savagery." Instead, it is about a transformation of social relationships, though Ballard is vague about "the new reality emerging from this transcendence." Says the novel is a "careful work" and the reader should not demand too much specificity about future social forms.

D132 SCHOLES, ROBERT, and RABKIN, ERIC S. Science Fiction: History, Science, Vision. New York: Oxford University Press.

Discusses Ballard briefly in the context of 1960s New Wave sf. Quotes Aldiss on Ballard (D83), and adds that Ballard's is "clearly a fiction of extremities." States that he has been most successful in shorter forms, and goes on to describe the "condensed novels" which make up The Atrocity Exhibition.

D133 HUTCHINSON, TOM. "Blasts of Power." Times, 1 October, p. 9.

Review of The Best of J.G. Ballard. Calls him "the most poetic of British sf avant-guardians." Commends the brief introductions to the stories. However, the autobiographical clues which Ballard provides give little away. Comments on Ballard's fascination with the mandala and time. Quotes the introduction to "The Overloaded Man," saying it gives "a humorous glimpse of

what domestic uproar was caused" when Ballard's wife first read
the story. Comments on the "O. Henry-like" endings of "Manhole
69" and "A Question of Re-Entry"--these stories "come through
well enough on a popular magazine level, but I feel the ideas
explored and the ideas excited in the reader's mind deserve
better." Remarks on the "sense of isolation" which is Ballard's
"hallmark," and points out that two characters have the same name
as "the notoriously reclusive writer B. Traven." One of Ballard's
"most astonishing achievements" is his "image-making," and his
"most significant realization is that the Space Age is finished."
Ballard's novels are often seen as "studies in slow-motion dis-
integration" but these short stories, including "such marvels as
'The Sound-Sweep,'" suggest "an affirming progress from solipsism
of a kind to an acknowledgment of another's reality." Points out
that the last story in the book, "The Day of Forever," has a
hopeful ending. Concludes: "I never thought to find this most
inherently sombre of writers releasing to me such a charge of
optimism."

1978

D134 BISHOP, MICHAEL. "Evangels of Hope." Foundation: The Review
of Science Fiction, no. 14 (September), pp. 35-43.
An article in response to the view of sf put forward by
Alexei and Cory Panshin in their SF in Dimension. Claims that
the Panshins are concerned with sf's "ability to generate powerful, psychologically integrative visions" rather than with "mere
style or literary technique." Says that "given a choice between
A.E. van Vogt's shuddering spaceship travelling at one light-year
per minute and the ruined technological landscapes of J.G.
Ballard, the Panshins will spring for that clunky spaceship every
time." Bishop proceeds to attack the Panshins' view, referring
to writers such as Philip K. Dick and Ursula Le Guin. Quoting
Le Guin's essay "Science Fiction and Mrs. Brown" (on the need for
more concern with character in sf), Bishop states: "if there
were more of Mrs Brown in J.G. Ballard's arid landscapes of
quartzite and plastic, then perhaps the Panshins would not recoil
in such disgust from stories like 'The Terminal Beach' and 'You:
Coma: Marilyn Monroe.' My feeling, however, is that van Vogt
neglects Mrs Brown because mind-boggling marvels interest him
more, whereas Ballard eases the old lady aside--particularly in
his Atrocity Exhibition pieces--precisely to point out the de-
humanizing effects of our technological age. In much of Ballard's
work, Mrs Brown is present through the paradox of her absence.
Therefore, just as the Panshins admire the reckless, irrational
(or non-rational) energy of van Vogt, I admire the analytic precision of Ballard."

D135 BURGESS, ANTHONY. Introduction to The Best Short Stories of
J.G. Ballard (A139).

States that the first thing to say about Ballard "is not that he is among our finest writers of science fiction but that he is among our finest writers of fiction tout court period." Points out that Ballard accepts thematic limitations, "but they are his own." He presents human beings in credible but extreme situations. It is "too easy to call Ballard a prophet of doom." The content and energy of his stories is "too stimulating for depression." What Burgess calls "two of the most beautiful stories in the world canon of short fiction" are in this collection--"The Drowned Giant" and "The Garden of Time." "The rhythms of poignancy which animate both stories are masterly: Ballard is a moving writer." Concludes that Ballard is "restless to try new things. Through him only is sf likely to make a formal and stylistic breakthrough of the kind achieved by Joyce, for whom Vico's La Scienza Nuova was new science enough. That Ballard is already important literature this selection will leave you in no doubt."

D136 ANON. "The High Vista by J.G. B*ll*rd." Sirius [fanzine], no. 1 (November), pp. 11-14.

A parody, purporting to be the first chapter of Ballard's latest novel, "an engrossing tale about a man crawling along a window-ledge and about all the strange characters he meets there." Begins: "Later, as Dr Charles Tallack lay on the window-ledge eating his meagre breakfast of sparrow's legs and rainwater, he reflected on all the welcome changes which had overtaken his life in the past week." Continues to poke fun at High-Rise, Crash, and other Ballard novels, introducing such characters as "Quilby, the idiot younger brother of the mysterious young woman who lived in the apartment opposite," and Robert Stiffman, "this hoodlum lover . . . an old-Etonian with an MA in musicology who liked to affect the manner of an East End punk rocker." Concludes: "This immense journey across the face of an inscrutable architecture was the only sensible course of action open to him. The concrete stretched away into the sunset like some road to Xanadu. Eagerly, Tallack climbed over the sill, oblivious of the sharp glass tearing at his clothes, and lowered himself onto the welcoming ledge."

D137 WOOD, MICHAEL. "This is Not the End of the World." New York Review of Books [November?].

Review of The Best Short Stories of J.G. Ballard, among others. States that Ballard's notion of "inner space" once threatened to change the direction of sf. Comments that the word terminal "echoes mournfully through Ballard's stories and novels." Describes some typical landscapes and situations, and remarks: "It is difficult . . . to separate the private terror from the public possibility, the personal nightmare from the nightmares of history. In all the stories the stress clearly falls on the mental conditions being shown, the inner spaces of psychosis. . . . The historical places and imaginable historical disasters are figures; they are shapes and traces the psyche has found for the making of its own portrait."

Comments on the "brief and handsome introduction" by Anthony Burgess. States that Ballard is "a master of conventional sf," and describes the plots of "Chronopolis," "The Subliminal Man," and other stories. But says that "Ballard's heart, or his head, is elsewhere. He is not primarily interested in the narrative line of his stories, or in the people. . . . He is interested mainly in images of the kind I have mentioned, an abandoned Eniwetok, an earth without oceans, a universe of sand and coral or salt or concrete." Briefly describes some of the remaining stories, commenting that the writing is "often obsessive, and frequently in energetic bad taste. It evokes a mind, or a series of minds, haunted by dreams of emptiness and annihilation." Concludes, however, that "the best of Ballard's remarkable stories—'The Voices of Time,' 'The Cage of Sand,' 'The Terminal Beach,' 'The Atrocity Exhibition'—confront us with landscapes we can neither disown nor forget."

1979

D138 MOORCOCK, MICHAEL. "New Worlds: A Personal History." Foundation: The Review of Science Fiction, no. 15 (January), pp. 5-18.

A memoir of Moorcock's editorship of New Worlds from 1964 into the 1970s. There are numerous mentions of Ballard. States that Moorcock's ideas "had been given encouragement and clearer shape by my friendship with J.G. Ballard, whose enthusiasm vindicated many of my half-hearted attempts to find out what was 'wrong' with the sf genre and most modern literature. . . ." Says later: "What Ballard and I had in common was that our knowledge of sf was not profound. Neither of us had read most of the well-known writers or stories. We had no particular taste for them. Ballard enjoyed Bradbury. I enjoyed Bester. We imposed our own imagination on the rest of sf, thinking most of it was better than it actually was. . . ." Moorcock also discloses that for a few days in 1966 Ballard was editor of New Worlds' sister-magazine, Impulse, "before failing to be reconciled either with the publisher or with his assitant editor, the patient Keith Roberts."

D139 FRANKLIN, H. BRUCE. "What Are We to Make of J.G. Ballard's Apocalypse?" In Voices for the Future: Essays on Major Science Fiction Writers. Vol. 2. Edited by Thomas Clareson. Bowling Green, Ohio: Bowling Green University Popular Press.

A Marxist analysis of the phenomenon of "the apocalyptic imagination running riot in Anglo-American culture today," as evidenced in Ballard's fiction. Asserts that Ballard "thrives" because of "certain conditions of the present era"—namely, the climate of fears surrounding economic crises, alleged overpopulation, the threat of nuclear war, etc. Unifying Ballard's novels is the theme of "the global catastrophe as an external projection of a deranged inner landscape." Detects a solipsistic tendency in the stories, "a danger inherent in bourgeois ideology right from the start." However, points out that there is an instinctively anticapitalist element in some of Ballard's fiction, exemplified by the characterization of the multimillionaire Hardoon, the "villain" of The Wind from Nowhere. But "Ballard does not generally go down far enough below the unconscious to the sources of the alienation, self-destruction, and mass slaughter of our age. He therefore remains incapable of understanding the alternative to these death forces, the global movement toward human liberation which constitutes the main distinguishing characteristic of our epoch."

Mentions with approval "The Killing Ground," in which Ballard evokes an "armed peasantry" rising up against American forces in Europe. But claims that Ballard has subverted his own insight by giving the story a pessimistic ending. Provides a lengthy analysis of The Crystal World, contrasting it with actual political events in Africa in the 1960s. In dealing with blacks, Ballard uses images which are "disgustingly racist." Goes on to discuss later works. In Crash, "Ballard's brilliant imagination penetrates deeply into the symbolic significance of the automobile" but "it is determined by his class outlook and therefore operates within very narrow limits." Concludes: "Ballard accurately, indeed magnificently, projects the doomed social structure in which he exists." But what could he create "if he were able to envision the end of capitalism as not the end, but the beginning, of a human world?"

D140 MOORCOCK, MICHAEL. "My Favourite SF Writer." In Seacon '79: 37th World Science Fiction Convention [program book]. Edited by Graham Charnock. London: Seacon '79.

Bylined "M.J. Moorcock (39)," this begins as a parody of a schoolboy essay but soon develops into a serious statement of Moorcock's admiration for Ballard. "I like him because he combines exotic symbolism with psychological insight." States that in recent years Ballard has "refined his language, producing some of the most polished and concentrated prose we have in English. . . ." States that among those who owe a debt to Ballard "are Robert Nye, D.M. Thomas, George MacBeth, Giles Gordon, Bridgid Brophy, Angus Wilson, Alan Burns, Angela Carter and many others. . . . It is perhaps not insignificant that the girlfriend of Crazy Charlie, president of the local Notting Hill Hell's Angels, last year changed her name to Vermilion Sands." Goes on to describe Ballard's insight into urban experience which has led to a fiction "profoundly coherent and in harmony with the times."

D141 BRIGG, PETER. "The Drowned World." In Survey of Science Fiction Literature. Vol. 2. Edited by Frank N. Magill. Englewood Cliffs, N.J.: Salem Press.

An essay which lists the characters and describes the plot of the novel. Comments that Ballard "penetrates the heart of the apocalyptic experience by integrating the changing physical universe with a changing psychic one." Compares to Conrad's Heart of Darkness--"except that Ballard strips away any return from the dark journey and is totally unconcerned with the political and social connotations of the earlier novel. Kerans' 'descent into the phantasmagoric forest' shares with Marlow's quest the flickering quality of being dream at one moment and realism at another." Stresses the biological themes of the novel, refers to the "surrealistic grace and pervasive imagery of Ballard's writing." Concludes: "a very careful stoicism is at the core of Ballard's position, a stoicism strong enough to tolerate a conception of the human race being terminated by the reactions of its genetic materials to the implacable thrust of cosmic forces."

D142 GOLDMAN, STEPHEN H. "Love and Napalm: Export USA." In Survey of Science Fiction Literature. Vol. 3. Edited by Frank N. Magill. Englewood Cliffs, N.J.: Salem Press.
An essay describing the book in detail. Comments: "Ballard postulates changes and investigates their consequences," like other sf writers--"however, unlike Heinlein, Van Vogt or Asimov, he rarely suggests resolutions." Complains: "The result of the author's technique is to create a tension which works quite well when limited to a few stories, but suffers from overexposure when repeated in 15 stories. . . ." Concludes that sooner or later sf "writers and readers alike will have to come to terms with" Ballard's book.

D143 PRINGLE, DAVID. "The Crystal World." In Survey of Science Fiction Literature. Vol. 1. Edited by Frank N. Magill. Englewood Cliffs, N.J.: Salem Press.
An essay which lists the characters and describes the plot of the novel. Claims that the novel "has much of the feel of an extended short story," and none of the characters is developed into "the well-rounded and convincingly established figures one expects in a novel." A "partial exception" is the protagonist, "especially if one regards the other characters as symbolic figures, slivers of Sanders' personality. . . ." States that "the plot (particularly the sometimes rather tedious sections involving Ventress and Thorensen) is obviously of minor importance compared to the descriptions of landscape." Says that there are "numerous brilliant visual set pieces." It is "essentially a mystical novel, a type of literature peculiarly difficult to write in the present day. Ballard's uneasiness--his embarrassment, even--at finding himself dealing with such a theme is pointed up by his heavy use of irony. . . ." States that The Drowned World and High-Rise are probably stronger novels but that The Crystal World has an "important place in Ballard's canon. It is the only work in which he has dealt at length with the quasi-religious theme of 'acceptance,' of communion with the universe. . . ."

Part D: Critical and Bio-Bibliographical Studies   1979

D144   STABLEFORD, BRIAN. "The Drought." In Survey of Science Fiction Literature. Vol. 2. Edited by Frank N. Magill. Englewood Cliffs, N.J.: Salem Press.
   An essay which lists characters and describes the plot. Comments: "Ransom is an archetypal Ballard 'hero' . . . he is a spectator, emotionally and teleologically inert, passively allowing his consciousness to be molded by the changing environment." The ending is "far more ambiguous" than in earlier novels--"the rain which begins to fall at the conclusion . . . can only be seen as an ironic gesture, a whim of chance which is neither merciful nor cruel, but simply derisory." Invokes R.D. Laing and his concept of the "schizophrenic voyage." Concludes: "It is, in every way, a dry book."

D145   _____. "The Short Fiction of J.G. Ballard." In Survey of Science Fiction Literature. Vol. 4. Edited by Frank N. Magill. Englewood Cliffs, N.J.: Salem Press.
   Lists all Ballard's collections of stories. Claims that "Build-Up" first introduces "the characteristic theme of many Ballard stories: his protagonists are frequently haunted by dreams of some mysterious past, which exert a powerful psychological attraction. The 'price' of following that attraction . . . is in almost every case what we as observers would term a descent into madness, but there is a curious sense of triumph in those stories where such a resolution can be attained, while the concluding moments of those in which it cannot are frustrated and desolate. One of the most important observations to be made about Ballard's work is that stories in the former category outnumber stories in the latter quite considerably." Proceeds to describe such stories of "fulfilment" as "The Overloaded Man" and "The Gioconda of the Twilight Noon." Finds "Manhole 69" and "Deep End" to be stories of "frustration." Argues that Ballard has since brought his stories "closer to home," and cites "The Terminal Beach" as a key work--"perhaps Ballard's finest story-- economical and devastating." Points out that Ballard is fond of using a landscape of "other-worldly wilderness," even in stories set on the earth, such as "The Cage of Sand," and cites Ray Bradbury as an influence. Describes the Vermilion Sands stories-- "Ballard at his most romantic." Claims "Studio 5, the Stars" is the best of them, "a synthesis of Greek myth and Sunset Boulevard." Goes on to deal with the city stories, from "Chronopolis" to "The Ultimate City," but says: "Ballard's chief field of interest has always been private experience: cherished hopes, guilt-fantasies and aesthetic responses are the focal points of his stories." Although he "has never tried to resist classification" as an sf writer Ballard is "foremost a surrealist writer." Quotes from the essay "The Coming of the Unconscious" (C17). Concludes by describing him as "a particularly ruthless iconoclast," with "phenomenal" inventiveness and "a more powerful imagination than any other contemporary writer."

D146 _____. "The Wind from Nowhere." In Survey of Science Fiction Literature. Vol. 5. Edited by Frank N. Magill. Englewood Cliffs, N.J.: Salem Press.
An essay which lists characters and describes the plot. Points out that the novel is "within a long tradition of British speculative novels featuring disaster of various magnitudes, which extends back as far as Mary Shelley's The Last Man (1826)." Claims that characterization is not Ballard's strong point: "the landscapes of his stories are psychological landscapes, not merely reflecting but embodying mental states. . . ." States that "if Hardoon is taken to be 'the unacceptable face of capitalism,' the fable can be given a political gloss." Hardoon fails, but "his failure constitutes a judgment not that Nature is stronger than culture, but that his way of comprehending the situation is wrong." Concludes that the novel is "considerably inferior to its successors. . . ."

D147 PARRINDER, PATRICK. "Science Fiction and the Scientific World View." In Science Fiction: A Critical Guide. Edited by Patrick Parrinder. London: Longman.
Deals in passing with Ballard as the sf writer "who seems most deliberate in his reaction against the scientific outlook." Claims that in his early work he is "the poet of the scientific world-view in decline," and points out that many of his stories envisage the end of the Space Age. Mentions one of Ballard's "favourite metaphors, the 'terminal beach.'" Claims that this "apocalyptic symbol" derives from Wells's The Time Machine. Describes The Drowned World at some length. Adds that the more Ballard "extends his range to new areas of social experience, whether those of the car crash, the high-rise apartment block or the concrete deserts of the modern city, the more he eliminates the sense of wonder." Finds Ballard's universe basically determinist.

D148 PRINGLE, DAVID. Earth is the Alien Planet: J.G. Ballard's Four-Dimensional Nightmare. San Bernardino: Borgo Press [paper].
A sixty-three page monograph divided into four chapters, the second of which is an expanded and updated version of Pringle's essay "The Fourfold Symbolism of J.G. Ballard" (D79). The first chapter outlines Ballard's career, comparing and contrasting him with such writers as Bradbury and Vonnegut. Divides his work into three periods--1956-1965, a "romantic" period; 1966-1975, a "bleak" period during which he began to move away from sf; and 1976 onwards, a "mellower" phase in which "his stories are tending towards the fantastic again." Lists five accusations commonly leveled at Ballard by his detractors, and attempts to answer them. Asserts: "Ballard is a writer whose works improve on rereading. . . . Those who put most effort into reading Ballard will get most out."
Chapter 3 analyses Ballard's characters, finding them to be

variations on "the Lamia, the Jester and the King"--apart from the central characters, who are surrogates of Ballard himself. "These protagonists generally have a sense of humour, but the jokes are almost always on themselves. It is precisely this dimension of irony which redeems them from the surface clichés of their conception." The other figures in Ballard's fiction are, "to a certain degree, emblematic. . . . It is important to realize that Ballard is symbolic fantasist." Adds: "he is concerned with his own mind and impulses; with the relationship between the solitary awareness and various environments and technologies; ultimately, with the relationship between humanity and time, the fact of death, the 'phenomenology of the universe.'" Goes on to deal with the depiction of women, "natives," working-class people and the rich in Ballard's stories, finding them all to be more-or-less unrealistic, portrayed as psychological archetypes rather than believable persons. Attempts to trace the "patterns" which these characters form by invoking the terminology of Freud and Jung. Concludes: "His work is best appreciated as a symbolic whole, and his characters are best seen as figures in an inner landscape."

The final chapter endeavours to trace a number of Ballard's themes--"Imprisonment," "Flight," "Time Must Have a Stop" and "Superannuation." Sees these as balanced pairs which "are really reducible to two more fundamental themes . . . <u>consciousness</u> and <u>unconsciousness</u>, or, to put it another way, <u>individuality</u> and <u>dissolution</u>." Gives examples from many different stories and novels. Finds Ballard to be "one of the last champions of the solitary, rational awareness. One senses that much of Ballard's fiction is about the preservation (and surrender) of individuality in the face of encroaching technological and social change. To this extent, he is a representative of the humanist and liberal tradition, and his purpose is a positive one: by making us more aware of our 'desires' he is helping to free us." Concludes: "he will be seen as one of the major imaginative writers of the second half of the 20th century--an author for our times, and for the future."

D149 LEE, HERMIONE. "The Stuff of Dreams." <u>Observer</u>, 21 October, p. 39.
Review of <u>The Unlimited Dream Company</u>, among others. Describes the book as "a rich, seductive and challenging work" which "confirms his mastery of a very particular idiom." Describes the plot, saying that the novel "mysteriously but alluringly describes what might happen if archetypal dreams of eroticism and ambition were to 'come true' in the real world." Claims that there is "too much decoding to do" but this is redeemed by "Ballard's almost Melvillean eloquence."

D150 CARTER, ANGELA. "Weaver of Dreams from the Stuff of Nightmares." <u>Guardian</u>, 26 October, p. 11.
Review of <u>The Unlimited Dream Company</u>. States: "this is a

little homage to J.G. Ballard, long and dark, surreal star of English letters, now become the shaman of Shepperton. . . ." Gives a brief resumé of the history of New Worlds under Moorcock's editorship, and point out Ballard's importance to the magazine. Describes the earlier novels, and comments on Ballard's characteristic use of the word "some" as an indefinite article. This is "a verbal device used so often it becomes incantatory, a formal rhetorical sign to tell you this is not normal prose." Notes that the new novel "appears to mark the cessation of Ballard's most atrociously black period." "The Unlimited Dream Factory [sic] has its full share of idiosyncratic humour." Describes the plot and compares the subject matter to that of William Blake. However, the ending is marred by "too much psychedelic-style mawkishness."

D151 FALLOWELL, DUNCAN. "Cruising on Reality." Quarto, no. 2 (December), p. 18.
Review of The Unlimited Dream Company. Begins by quoting Anthony Burgess's dust-jacket endorsement and commenting: "he must be mad." In the same abusive vein as his earlier review of Ballard (D128), Fallowell proceeds to tear the novel apart. "Parables . . . work only vis à vis some system of belief and there is no system of belief behind Ballard's novel. Instead there is a yearning of the heart and loins of the sort which Edwardian ladies had when listening to the music of Scriabin." Ballard is "a visionary minus intellect," which means "a sentimentalist." Asserts that "writing is Ballard's big problem" and it is "the fundamental weakness of the whole modern school of British fantasy--Ballard, Aldiss, Moorcock, etc. Their writing is somehow unfledged, an inadvertent parody of what 'important writing' is supposed to sound like." Contrasts Ballard with Mervyn Peake and Gabriel Garcia Marquez, and concludes by recommending Thomas M. Disch's novel On Wings of Song--"if flying were possible he would be much better at it."

D152 BRADBURY, MALCOLM. "Fly Away." New York Times Book Review, 9 December, pp. 14-16.
Review of The Unlimited Dream Company. States that Ballard "has a notable line of credits behind him" and "more and more he looks like a leading figure in a very rich and developing field." Although his earlier work was science fiction, "he has long since worked loose from that pocket." Compares Ballard with Italo Calvino and Thomas Pynchon, who draw on sf methods "to create a magical modern fantasy. A writer of enormous inventive powers . . . he has, like Calvino, a remarkable gift for filling the empty deprived spaces of modern life with the invisible cities and the wonder worlds of the imagination." Describes the plot at some length, adding: "it is heady stuff, a dreamy pastoral, but Mr. Ballard sustains it from a well-funded imagination, a prolix style and a great mythical sense. At times, but only at times, the metaphors grow a little too thick. . . ." But finds the book

"dense and erotic and magical, a pleasure to read. And it leaves me with no doubt that Mr. Ballard is a very important fantasist."

1980

D153 DICKINSON, MIKE. "Three Aspects of Fantasy." <u>Vector</u>, no. 96 (December 1979/January 1980), pp. 10-14.

An article on three new fantasy novels, one of them <u>The Unlimited Dream Company</u>. Claims that, "despite an attitude of surgical precision and a fascination with technology," Ballard "has often trembled on the brink of fantasy." Describes the plot, adding that "Ballard's writing in this novel is as intense, visionary and sexual as it was in <u>Crash</u>." Says there has been "a growing streak of dry, understated humour in his work since <u>The Atrocity Exhibition</u> days, and here it is at its most evident." Cites the influence of "Henri (Le Douanier) Rousseau and his 'primitive' paintings of lush, highly-coloured tropical forests." Ballard's writing is "succulent but in no way obscure." Questions the point of the novel, however, claiming "we are invited to watch an amoral superman, already a criminal, play with people's lives." Likens Ballard's protagonist to that of Heinlein's <u>Stranger in a Strange Land</u>. Mentions the relevance of William Blake. Concludes that the sum of the novel's parts is "magnificently high."

D154 CLUTE, JOHN. Review of <u>The Unlimited Dream Company</u>. <u>Foundation: The Review of Science Fiction</u>, no. 19 (June), pp. 84-85.

Describes the novel as "a posthumous fantasy," that is a tale "set in some kind of afterlife." Compares it with works by John Kendrick Bangs, Ambrose Bierce, Wyndham Lewis, and others. Describes the plot, and characterizes the protagonist as "grandiloquent, paranoid, edgy with self-devouring imperious lust." Concludes that the novel's "main innovation lies in the stridency of its protagonist's coming to terms with the shape of the meaning of his life. . . . Because the epiphanies are so thoroughly owned by Blake, there is a final failure of liquidity of texture. . . . The book has no religion." Adds in a footnote that the novel contains an "homage to the painter Stanley Spencer and to the apocalyptic prelapsarian paradise further up the Thames at Cookham he returned to constantly in his works."

D155 LAFFERTY, R.A. "The Profession of Science Fiction, 21: True Believers." <u>Foundation: The Review of Science Fiction</u>, no. 20 (October), pp. 43-46.

A piece in which Lafferty states he is not a "true believer" in sf. He includes a number of short verse critiques of well-known sf writers. Most of these are very uncomplimentary. The verse headed "J.G. Ballard" is as follows:

        A beach without an ocean yet,
        A cartless horse, a plotless prating,

A dogless tail, guitarless fret.
Oh why, Oh why's he fascinating?

D156 BESTER, ALFRED. Interview. In Dream Makers: The Uncommon People Who Write Science Fiction. Edited by Charles Platt. New York: Berkley [paper].
In this interview conducted by Platt, Bester states: "there's a marvelous writer named Ballard--what is it, A.G., E.G. Ballard? Jesus Christ, that son of a bitch could write. Christ, he's written some stories I wish I had written. There's one called 'The Voices of Time'; whew! What a piece of work. It makes no sense to me at all, but I am absolutely enchanted by it, it's great. And of course The Crystal World is a hell of a novel."

D157 MALZBERG, BARRY N. Interview. In Dream Makers: The Uncommon People Who Write Science Fiction. Edited by Charles Platt. New York: Berkley [paper].
In this interview conducted by Platt, Malzberg comments: "Nobody can write with precision and passion, about anything, without being life-confirming. I believe that profoundly. That's why I think J.G. Ballard's Crash and The Atrocity Exhibition-- this is not death, this is life. To be able to write in such a poised and beautiful fashion and control it so well is affirmation, is optimistic. I'm not as good as Ballard; I wish to hell I were. But I know exactly what that man was trying to do. . . ."

D158 PUNTER, DAVID. The Literature of Terror: A History of Gothic Fictions from 1765 to the Present Day. London and New York: Longman.
Chapter 14 of this work, "Modern Perceptions of the Barbaric," discusses Ballard as a contemporary practitioner of Gothic, alongside such writers as William Burroughs, Thomas Pynchon, and Angela Carter. "In J.G. Ballard, the principal subject at issue is the conflict between the individual and a dehumanized environment." Demonstrates this through a two-page analysis of The Atrocity Exhibition: "Ballard is a self-conscious artificer, piecing together a book out of elements from newspaper reports, newsreel films, scientific documents: Burroughs's emphasis on casual violence, crossed with Robbe-Grillet's painstakingly alienated naturalism, crossed with Godard's Weekend. The book is a faulty rerun of obsessions, a search to find interconnexions between apparently inexplicable phenomena."

1981

D159 ABLEMAN, PAUL. "Desert Song." Spectator, 30 May, p. 25.
Review of Hello America. Asserts "Ballard seems to be increasingly engaged in writing strip cartoons without the cartoons." Recounts anecdote of a visit to a pop concert where "an amplified voice kept bawling aggressively that we would shortly be addressed

by 'the greatest writer in the whole world, Jimmy Ballard.' Well, I can now reveal, at lower amplification, that he isn't." Finds that the novel "displays a modest talent." Asserts Ballard "has no interest in things like personality, pain, consciousness, ambition, love or any of the other central concerns of classical fiction." Claims he has one theme: "entropy." Describes the plot, finding that "it all palls very quickly." Complains of implausible technology, and concludes: "the breezy attitude to nuclear weapons which informs this book can only enhance their sinister glamour and thus constitutes a disservice to the human race."

D160 NYE, ROBERT. "A Garden Greener than Arcadia." Guardian, 4 June, p. 8.
Review of Hello America. Surveys Ballard's career briefly, saying he has been left "in a kind of one man's no-man's land between cultures. My contention is that this is no bad place for an authentic writer to be, and that Ballard merits patient attention. . . ." Says Hello America "cannot be acclaimed as his best, but it is so very much another contribution to a fascinating oeuvre that in seeking to define its qualities I must refer readers to the Ballard phenomenon as a whole. His procedures perhaps exclude the writing of individual works of genius. He is not a masterpiece man." Compares Ballard to Edmund Spenser, "whose The Faerie Queene appears to me to have done something similar for the world as perceived by an Elizabethan Englishman. Spenser eschewed brilliance in providing a sort of garden which was greener than either reality or Arcadia. Ballard cannot write as well, but that is his game too, unless I am gravely mistaken." Finds the novel "full of sly comedy." Describes the plot, claiming that "the incidental absurdities are stronger than the overall story-line." Complains that Ballard provides comedy at the expense of the characters. Concludes: "this is a very clever fiction, and . . . another amazing improvisation on Ballard's basic theme. What is that theme? The same as Edmund Spenser's. That the world has run its time and man has had it, hurrah."

D161 AMIS, MARTIN. "Journey Without Maps." Observer, 7 June, p. 32.
Review of Hello America. States "Ballard's talent is one of the most mysterious and distempered in modern English fiction-- and it is by far the hardest to classify." Surveys Ballard's career at some length, saying of Crash that it has "a numb, luminous quality that loiters in the mind." Comments of The Unlimited Dream Company: "with Ballard, fantasy takes on a vertiginous steepness, giving the reader a sense of queasy dislocation and foreboding." Describes the plot of Hello America, finding it "in many respects . . . a simple adventure story, Buchan or Henty adrift in the time machine." States: "Ballard's work is quite unprotected by humour. His eye for the comedy of human variety is non-existent. . . . Only in the margins of the present novel

is Ballard's real strength allowed any play: the ability to invest abstract vistas with intense and furtive life." Concludes: "the novels he will write could not be written, could not even be guessed at, by anyone else."

D162 GLENDINNING, VICTORIA. "My Newfoundland." Sunday Times, 7 June, p. 43.
Review of Hello America, and others. Describes opening scene, saying "it is brilliantly done." Recounts the plot, commenting: "The working-out of the fantasy is inevitably not so exciting as the setting-up." Concludes: "It's a dream that rings true; Hello America is a collage of prevailing themes and nightmares from literature and film. . . . [Ballard] has the wit to feel the tug of kites flying in the common imagination, to pull on the strings and haul them in."

D163 STRAWSON, GALEN. "A New World Safari." Times Literary Supplement, 12 June, p. 659.
Review of Hello America. States "Ballard is renowned among writers of science fiction both for the diversity of his inventions and for the richness of his descriptive language." Describes the plot, finding many "echoes of his earlier work." Notes the motifs of desert and jungle and abandoned city: "sometimes it seems as if Ballard's oeuvre is just the systematic extrapolation . . . of an initial fixed set of possibilities, obsessions, and palmary symbols." Describes characters and incidents, concluding: "Sometimes the novel is unable to contain, in such a way as to give real force to, the crazy ballad of idées fixes. Ballard is unquestionably at his best when writing short stories, and it is hard at times not to feel that Hello America is really a set of short stories. . . . Ballard provides a wealth of images, and, if they behave like a fractious orchestra of individually acclaimed soloists, subverting strong narrative development, it is just so that they together work their unsettling and extravagant effects."

D164 RATHBONE, JULIAN. "The Ultimate Work." Literary Review 2, no. 39 (August):8-10.
Review of Hello America—in reality an extended article on Ballard's work in general. Mentions the game of "spot the real classic, the author who will be widely read in two hundred years' time" and states that Ballard is his nominee. Explains: "There are two reasons why Ballard tends to be dismissed by your common-or-garden up-market reviewer: first, he made his name as a writer of science-fiction short stories (for, you know, pulp magazines); second, and far more important, it is difficult to say what he is about . . . it is not nice to have to say 'This I loved. It was moving, revelatory, but I don't yet have the means to say what he is about.'" Proceeds to attempt to "place" Ballard, describing his work from The Atrocity Exhibition onwards in considerable detail.

Says The Unlimited Dream Company is "a rich, complex, moving book" and the theme is continued in Hello America, which is "more genial." Describes the plot at length, concluding that the novel is "a joy--witty, playful, moving, mythic, poetic (in the best, least pretentious of senses). . . . It must have been hard play to write Hello America, but play. And a play won through the hell of the earlier books."

D165 MOORCOCK, MICHAEL. Review of Hello America. Foundation: The Review of Science Fiction, no. 23 (October), pp. 78-80.
States that the novel is "probably the best sf we are ever going to get from J.G. Ballard and it is consequently inferior to his recent non-generic books such as Crash or The Unlimited Dream Company." Finds the blend of "conventional sf elements and idiosyncratic vision" unsatisfactory, although "even unsatisfactory Ballard is better than no Ballard." Hello America is an attempt at a generic book, but "if the average sf writer takes the stuff of metaphor and tries to give it the appearance of reality, then authors like Ballard take the stuff of reality and expand it into metaphor." Describes the plot at some length, criticizing various details, but adds: "to quarrel with the book's geography or the probability of its science or political events would be pointless." Summarizes: "This book does well on image, is a bit weak on mood (as in all Ballard's stories where action is substituted for metaphysical mystery) and is not very coherent in form." Comments that the ending is "surprisingly optimistic, even a trifle sentimental," and concludes: "When the dust settles we're left with the impression of the best images, some excellent prose, and we might even remember that we have read a good, tight Ballard story. In this case I think we shall have done some of the selecting and concentrating ourselves."

1982

D166 GOLDSTEIN, TOBY. "J.G. Ballard: Visionary of the Apocalypse." Heavy Metal (April), pp. 38-40.
A profile of the author, which incorporates some interview material. States that Ballard interprets "the psychological unrest pervading our society in concise, extreme language. . . . Ballard has been called, along with Jean Genet and William S. Burroughs, one of punk's major literary figures. He has inspired brilliantly reckless performers like Suicide, Joy Division, and The Normal aka Daniel Miller--composer of a paean to Ballard's apocalyptic novel Crash called 'Warm Leatherette.'" Describes a visit to Ballard's home, apparently in the summer of 1981: "Ballard, who at fifty-one resembles your favourite balding uncle, is used to the disappointment of first-time visitors. 'I feel that I should lay on a twelve-lane turnpike for them, and a huge interchange, instead of this little quiet suburban street with its happy children and pretty gardens. . . .'" Describes

Ballard's works at some length, quoting him as saying: "In writing books like Crash or The Atrocity Exhibition or High-Rise, I was exploring myself, using myself as the laboratory animal, as it were, probing around. I had to take the top off my skull when I was writing Crash and start touching pain and pleasure centres to see what happened."

(This issue of Heavy Metal also contains the following snippet of news, signed by Brad Balfour: "When British avant-rockers Siouxsie and the Banshees hit town, I stepped backstage to ask bassist-songwriter Severin what his list of favorite flights of science-fiction fancy might be. Here's his off-the-cuff reply: Crash by J.G. Ballard; Atrocity Exhibition by J.G. Ballard; The Illustrated Man by Ray Bradbury; The Green Brain by Frank Herbert; and, he emphasized again, anything else by Ballard.")

D167 DISCH, THOMAS M. Introduction to "An Italian Lesson." In The Man Who Had No Ideas: A Collection of Stories. London: Victor Gollancz.

In this introductory note to one of his own stories Disch states: "Often when prose is praised for being 'poetic,' it is not for its aural properties but for its power to project images on the camera obscura of the reading mind. J.G. Ballard, for instance, might as well have been born deaf, but few writers paint so persuasively with a typewriter."

Appendixes

1: Foreign Language Editions

The following list if incomplete, but it will serve to indicate the range of translations of J.G. Ballard's books. The list is based on the entries in the Index Translationum (Paris: UNESCO) for the years 1964 to 1976, together with information kindly supplied by Ballard's agent, John Wolfers. No attempt has been made to trace translations of individual short stories, although these are numerous and include translations into languages not represented in the list below (e.g., Russian).

DANISH

Verden under Vand (The Drowned World). Trans. Niels Erik Wille. Copenhagen: Hasselbalch, 1969.

Grusomhedsudstillingen (The Atrocity Exhibition). Trans. Jannick Storm. Copenhagen: Rhodos, 1969 [this is the first edition; it appeared more than six months before the English edition].

Krystalverdenen (The Crystal World). Trans. Finn Andersen. Copenhagen: Stig Vendelkaer, 1973.

Slutstranden (The Terminal Beach). Trans. Arne Herlov Petersen. Copenhagen: Stig Vendelkaer, 1973.

DUTCH

De brandende Aarde (The Burning World). Trans. Mieke Meuldrager-Ezelin. Amsterdam: Meulenhoff, 1967.

De verdronken Aarde (The Drowned World). Trans. Mieke Meuldrager-Ezelin. Amsterdam: Meulenhoff, 1968.

De Wind van Nergens (The Wind from Nowhere). Trans. M. Vellema. Laren: Luitingh, 1968.

De kristallen Aarde (The Crystal World). Trans. Mieke Meuldrager-

Appendixes

Ezelin. Amsterdam: Meulenhoff, 1969.

Dooplopend Strand (The Terminal Beach). Trans. Mieke Meuldrager-Ezelin. Amsterdam: Meulenhoff, 1971.

De Gruweltentoonstelling (The Atrocity Exhibition). Trans. Jet van der Mijn. Amsterdam: Bezige Bij, 1971.

De Wachtvelden (The Overloaded Man). Trans. Mieke Meuldrager-Ezelin. Amsterdam: Meulenhoff, 1973.

De zingende Beelden (Vermilion Sands). Trans. G.R. de Bruin. Amsterdam: Bezige Bij, 1973.

Eiland in Beton (Concrete Island). Trans. B. ter Laat. Utrecht/Antwerp: Bruna, 1978.

De Torenflat (High-Rise?). Trans. ? Utrecht/Antwerp: Bruna, 197?.

De Laatste stad (Low-Flying Aircraft?). Trans. ? Utrecht/Antwerp: Bruna, 197?.

De Klap (Crash). Trans. David Brisk. Utrecht/Antwerp: Bruna, 1980.

FRENCH

Le monde englouti (The Drowned World). Trans. Marie-France Desmoulin. Paris: Denoël, 1964.

Cauchemar à quatre dimensions (The Four-Dimensional Nightmare). Trans. Laure Casseau. Paris: Denoël, 1965.

Le forêt de cristal (The Crystal World). Trans. Claude Saunier. Paris: Denoël, 1967.

Billénium. Trans. Lionel Massun. Verviers: Marabout, 1970.

Crash! Trans. Robert Louit. Paris: Calmann-Lévy, 1974.

L'île de béton (Concrete Island). Trans. Georges Fradier. Paris: Calmann-Lévy, 1974.

Sécheresse (The Drought). Trans. Claude Darner. Paris: Casterman, 1975.

Vermilion Sands ou le paysage intérieur. Trans. various hands. Paris: Opta, 1975.

La foire aux atrocités (The Atrocity Exhibition). Trans. François Rivière. Paris: Champ Libre, 1976.

Foreign Language Editions

I. G. H. (High Rise). Trans. Robert Louit. Paris: Calmann-Lévy, 1976.

Le vent de nulle part (The Wind from Nowhere). Trans. Rene Lathiere. Paris: Casterman, 1977.

Cauchemar à quatre dimensions (Revised Edition). Trans. Gisèle Garson and Pierre Versins. Paris: Denoël, 1978.

Appareil volant à basse altitude (Low-Flying Aircraft). Trans. Elizabeth Gille. Paris: Denoël, 1978.

Le rêveur illimité (The Unlimited Dream Company). Trans. Robert Louit. Paris: Calmann-Lévy, 1980.

Le livre d'or de la science fiction: J.G. Ballard. Edited, introduced and part-translated by Robert Louit. Paris: Presses Pocket, 1980 [contains: "L'homme subliminal" ("The Subliminal Man"); "L'homme saturé" ("The Overloaded Man"); "Treize pour le Centaure" ("Thirteen to Centaurus"); "Chronopolis"; "Fin de partie" ("End-Game"); "Demain, dans un million d'années" ("Tomorrow is a Million Years"); "Le jour de toujours" ("The Day of Forever"); "Un assassin très comme il faut" ("The Gentle Assassin"); "Le Vinci disparu" ("The Lost Leonardo"); "Perte de temps" ("Escapement"); "Le géant noyé" ("The Drowned Giant"); "Le cage de sable" ("The Cage of Sand"); "Les statues qui chantent" ("The Singing Statues"); "Amour et napalm: export USA" ("Love and Napalm: Export USA"); Bibliography].

Le salon des horreurs (new edition of The Atrocity Exhibition). Trans. Elizabeth Gille. Paris: Lattes, 1981.

Salut l'Amérique (Hello America). Trans. ? Paris: Denoël, 1981.

GERMAN

Der Strum aus dem Nichts (The Wind from Nowhere). Trans. Gisela Stege. Munich: Heyne, 1964.

Welt in Flammen (The Burning World). Trans. Wulf H. Bergner. Munich: Heyne, 1968.

Kristallwelt (The Crystal World). Trans. Margarete Bormann. Hamburg: Schröder, 1969.

Karneval der Alligatoren (The Drowned World). Trans. Inge Wiskott. Hamburg: Schröder, 1970.

Liebe und Napalm: Export USA (The Atrocity Exhibition). Trans. Carl Weissner. Frankfurt: Melzer, 1970.

Der unmögliche Mensch (The Impossible Man). Trans. Alfred Scholz. Hamburg, Schröder, 1971.

Die tausend Träume von Stellavista (Vermilion Sands). Trans. Alfred Scholz. Hamburg: Schröder, 1972.

Der vier-dimensionale Alptraum (The Four-Dimensional Nightmare). Trans. Wolfgang Eiserman. Hamburg: Schröder, 1973.

Die Betoninsel (Concrete Island). Trans. Wolfgang Jeschke. Munich: Heyne, 1981.

Der ewige Tag (The Day of Forever). Trans. Michael Walter. Frankfurt: Suhrkamp, 1981.

Der stürzende Turm (High-Rise). Trans. ? Munich: Heyne, 1981?

GREEK

*The Crystal World has appeared in Greek. [Source: John Wolfers]

ITALIAN

Vento dal nulla (The Wind from Nowhere). Trans. Mario Galli. Milan: Mondadori, 1962.

Deserto d'acqua (The Drowned World). Trans. Stefano Torossi. Milan: Mondadori, 1963.

Essi ci guardano dalle torri (Passport to Eternity). Trans. Hilja Brinis. Milan: Mondadori, 1965.

Terra bruciata (The Burning World). Trans. Lea Grevi. Milan: Mondadori, 1966.

Condominium (High-Rise). Trans. Beata della Frattina. Milan: Mondadori, 1976.

Incubo a quattro dimensioni (The Four-Dimensional Nightmare). Trans. Hilja Brinis et al. Milan: Mondadori, 1977.

Il gigante annegato (The Terminal Beach). Trans. Beata della Frattina. Milan: Mondadori, 1978.

La zona del disastro (The Disaster Area). Trans. various hands. Milan: Mondadori, 1979.

*The Crystal World, The Day of Forever, Vermilion Sands, Crash, Concrete Island and Low-Flying Aircraft have also appeared in Italian. [Source: John Wolfers]

Foreign Language Editions

JAPANESE

Shizunda Sekai (The Drowned World). Trans. Minegishi Hisashi. Tokyo: Sogen Shinsha, 1968.

Jikan Toshi (Billenium). Trans. Uno Toshiyasu. Tokyo: Sogensha, 1969.

Kessho Sekai (The Crystal World). Trans. Mekamura Yasuo. Tokyo: Sogensha, 1969.

Toki No Koe (The Voices of Time). Trans. Yoshida Seuchi. Tokyo: Sogen Shinsha, 1969.

Eien eno Pasupoto (Passport to Eternity). Trans. Nagai Jun. Tokyo: Sogen Shinsha, 1970.

Jikan no Bohyo (The Terminal Beach). Trans. Ito Satoshi. Tokyo: Sogen Shinsha, 1970.

Kyofu Sekai (The Wind from Nowhere). Trans. Uno Toshiyasu. Tokyo: Sogensha, 1970.

Moeru Sekai (The Burning World). Trans. Nakamura Yasuo. Tokyo: Sogen Shinsha, 1970.

Oboreta Kyojin (The Impossible Man). Trans. Otani Keiji. Tokyo: Sogensha, 1971.

Bamilion Sanzu (Vermilion Sands). Trans. ? Tokyo: Hayakawa, 1980.

? (Concrete Island). Trans. Hajime Owada and Akihiko Kokuryo. Tokyo: NW-SF, 1981.

? (The Unlimited Dream Company). Trans. ? Tokyo: Sanrio, 1981.

*The Four-Dimensional Nightmare, The Atrocity Exhibition, High-Rise, Low-Flying Aircraft and The Best Short Stories of J.G. Ballard have also appeared in Japanese. [Source: John Wolfers]

NORWEGIAN

Luftspeil (Vermilion Sands). Edited and translated by Jon Bing. Oslo: Gyldendal, 1972 [contains a two-page foreword by Ballard, different to that in the later British edition; an eight-page appreciation of Ballard by Jon Bing; a bibliography; and a six-page glossary of proper names].

POLISH

*Concrete Island and The Best of J.G. Ballard have appeared in Polish. [Source: John Wolfers]

Appendixes

PORTUGUESE

Cataclismo solar (The Drowned World). Trans. Mario Augusto de Almeida Braga and Maria Isabel Morna Dias Braga. Lisbon: Livros do Brasil, 1966.

O mundo de cristal (The Crystal World). Trans. Eurico de Fonseca. Lisbon: Livros do Brasil, 1967.

Menos um (The Terminal Beach). Trans. Pedro Ramires. Rio de Janeiro: Bruguera, 1971.

Passaporte para o eterno (Passport to Eternity). Trans. Maria Emilia Ferros Moura. Lisbon: Livros do Brasil, 1976?

SPANISH

El mundo sumergido (The Drowned World). Trans. Francisco Abelenda. Buenos Aires: Sud-Americana, 1966.

El hurracan cosmico (The Wind from Nowhere). Trans. Francisco Cazorla Olmo. Barcelona: Minotauro, 1967.

El hombre imposible (The Impossible Man). Trans. Marcial Souto. Buenos Aires: Minotauro, 1972.

La sequía (The Drought). Trans. ? Barcelona: Minotauro, 197-?

Crash. Trans. Francisco Abelenda. Barcelona: Minotauro, 1979 [contains the introduction which first appeared in the French edition, Calmann-Lévy, 1974].

La exhibicíon de atrocidades (The Atrocity Exhibition). Trans. Marcelo Cohen and F. Abelenda. Barcelona: Minotauro, 1981.

*Vermilion Sands, Concrete Island, High-Rise and Low-Flying Aircraft have also appeared in Spanish. [Source: John Wolfers]

SWEDISH

Kristallvarlden (The Crystal World). Trans. Peter Stewart. Stockholm: Wahlstrom and Widstrand, 1971.

Drömbolaget (The Unlimited Dream Company). Trans. Peter Stewart. Stockholm: Almqvist and Wiskell, 1981 [includes a seven-page biographical essay on Ballard by Peter Stewart].

2: Nonfiction in French

A number of nonfiction items by Ballard have appeared only in the French language. This is evidence of the considerable interest which Ballard's work has elicited in France. The following list is probably incomplete, but contains all the French items I have been able to trace.

1974

1 "Recontre avec J.G. Ballard." Galaxie, no. 117 (February), pp. 136-42.
   An interview conducted by Philippe R. Hupp. Deals mainly with Crash and Vermilion Sands.

2 Preface to Crash! Paris: Calmann-Lévy [translated from Ballard's English by Robert Louit].
   Magazine litteraire, no. 88 (May 1974).
   This preface to the novel Crash was published in English in 1975 (see C62). It has also appeared in Spanish.

3 "Entretien avec J.G. Ballard." Magazine litteraire, no. 87 (April), pp. 34-35.
   An interview conducted by Robert Louit, dealing with The Atrocity Exhibition, Crash, etc. Published in English in 1975 (see C62).

4 "Délires à l'heure du thé." Actuel, no. 46 (September), pp. 66-68.
   A short profile/interview by Jean-Pierre Lentin. Also contains quotations from Michael Moorcock and John Sladek.

1976

5 "La révolution Ballard." L'Express, 2-8 February, pp. 28-29.
   A profile/interview by Noelle Loriot. Concerns High-Rise.

1977

6 "Nous vivons l'ère des réalismes imaginaires: recontre avec J.G. Ballard." Univers, no. 8 (March), pp. 154-67.
   An interview conducted by Stan Barets, dealing with The Atrocity Exhibition, "The Ultimate City," Crash, surrealist painting, modern China, and much else.

7 "Jim G. Ballard." Opus International, no. 64 (Autumn), pp. 52-54.
   An interview conducted by Anne Tronche. Deals with surrealism, pop art, The Atrocity Exhibition, and Vermilion Sands. Contains comments on the artists Chirico, Ernst, Richard Hamilton, Géricault, Goya, Bellmer, and Dali. Accompanied by a photograph which shows Ballard in conversation with Jorge Luis Borges.

1978

8 "Visa pour la réalité." Magazine litteraire, no. 142 (November), pp. 16-17.
   An article on Graham Greene, translated from Ballard's English by Robert Louit (it has not appeared in English).

1980

9 "J.G. Ballard." In I. G. H. Paris: Editions Rombaldi [Book Club].
   An interview conducted by Laurence Paton, concerning High-Rise.

10 Brief introductions to "End-Game," "Tomorrow is a Million Years," "The Gentle Assassin," "The Lost Leonardo," "Escapement," "The Drowned Giant," "The Singing Statues," and "Love and Napalm: Export USA." In Le Livre d'or de la science fiction: J.G. Ballard. Paris: Presses Pocket.
   Introductory matter especially written for this volume and translated from Ballard's English by Robert Louit. The book also contains Ballard's short introductions to "The Subliminal Man," "The Overloaded Man," "Thirteen to Centaurus," "Chronopolis," "The Day of Forever," and "The Cage of Sand," from The Best of J.G. Ballard (A131).

Indexes

1: The Writings of J. G. Ballard (Parts A, B, and C)

Indexed by title. References are to entry numbers, not pages (A = fiction; B = miscellaneous; C = nonfiction). In the case of interviews (and profiles incorporating substantial interview material) the interviewer's name is given in square brackets after the title.

"Afterword to 'The Recognition'" C24
"Air Disaster, The" A118
"All in the Mind" C19
"Alphabets of Unreason" C38
"Assassination of John Fitzgerald Kennedy Considered as a Downhill Motor Race, The" A79
"Assassination Weapon, The" A70
"Atrocity Exhibition, The" A77
Atrocity Exhibition, The A107

"Ballard at Home" [Douglas Reed] C49
"Ballard on Crash: Answers to Some Questions" [James Goddard] C55
"Bathroom: A Film in Progress by Steve Dwoskin, The" B3
"Beach Murders, The" A99
Best of J.G. Ballard, The A131
Best Short Stories of J.G. Ballard, The A139
"Billenium" A20
Billenium A35
"Brian W. Aldiss" C89
"Build-Up" A4
Burning World, The A62

"Cage of Sand, The" A30

"Candide Camera" C76
"Car, the Future, The" C52
"Cataclysms and Dooms" C74
"Chronopolis" A12
Chronopolis and Other Stories A111
"Circles and Squares" C20
"Closed Doors" C71
"Cloud-Sculptors of Coral D, The" A89
"Coitus 80: A Description of the Sexual Act in 1980" A103
"Coming of the Unconscious, The" C17
"Comment on 'End-Game'" C27
"Comsat Angels, The" A96
"Concentration City, The" A86
Concrete Island A116
"Confetti Royale" A68
"Consumer Consumed, The" C51
"Crash!" A100
"Crash" A115
Crash A114
"Critical Mass" A120
"Cry Hope, Cry Fury!" A84
Crystal World, The A71

"Day of Forever, The" A83
"Dead Astronaut, The" A83
"Dead Time, The" A130

Indexes

"Death Module, The" A81
"Death Wish Anonymous" C18
"Deep End" A16
"Delta at Sunset, The" A57
"Demolition Squad, The" C8
Disaster Area, The A85
"Disasters" [Rodney Smith] C86
"Does the Angle Between Two Walls Have a Happy Ending?" B2
"Does the Future Still Exist?" C28
"Down to Earth" [The Guardian] C4
"Down to Earth" [New Statesman] C65
"Draining Lake, The" A65
"Dreams and Surrealism" C33
Drought, The A67
"Drowned Giant, The" A58
"Drowned World, The" A22
Drowned World, The A34
Drowned World and The Wind from Nowhere, The A63
"Dune Limbo" A64

"Elephant and the Quasar, The" C5
"Encounter, The" A42
"End-Game" A43
"Equinox" A53
"Escapement" A2

"Fallen Idol" C93
"Fictions of Every Kind" C48
"First Things Last" C90
"Flight" A142
"Foreword" C44
Four-Dimensional Nightmare, The A41
"French Polish" C69
"From the Unlimited Dream Company" A141
"Future of the Future, The" C73

"Garden of Time, The" A25
"Generations of America, The" A95
"Gentle Assassin, The" A21
"Gioconda of the Twilight Noon, The" A59
"Great American Nude, The" A94

"Greatest Television Show on Earth, The" A113
"Grope Therapy" C72

"Happy Arrangement, A" A121
"Having a Wonderful Time" A135
Hello America A146
High-Rise A122
"Hobbits in Space?" C75
"Homage to Claire Churchill" B1
"Host of Furious Fancies, A" A144
"How Ariel Turned Into Prospero" C26
"How Dr Christopher Evans Landed on the Moon" B6
"I had a crash 18 months ago and it was a case of nature imitating art" [Mike Bygrave] C57
"Illuminated Man, The" A52
"Impossible Man, The" A74
Impossible Man and Other Stories, The A72
"Index, The" A132
"Inner Landscape" [Robert Lightfoot and David Pendleton] C43
"Insane Ones, The" A23
"Intensive Care Unit, The" A133
"Interrogation: J.G. Ballard Answers Questions" [James Goddard] C46
"Interview with J.G. Ballard" [David Pringle] C87
"Interview with J.G. Ballard, An" [Jannick Storm] C31
"Interview with J.G. Ballard, An" [James Goddard and David Pringle] C63
"Into the Drop Zone" C6
"Introduction" [Dali] C59
"Introduction" [J.G. Ballard: The First Twenty Years] C66
"Introduction" [The Best of J.G. Ballard] C70
"Invisible Years, The: A Series of Apocalyptic Texts . . ." B10-14, 16

"J.G. Ballard" [Books and Bookmen] C40

"J.G. Ballard" [Brendan Hennessy] C50
"J.G. Ballard" [New Review] C77
"J.G. Ballard" [Jon Savage] C79
"J.G. Ballard" [Charles Platt] C88
"J.G. Ballard" [Alan Burns] C91
"J.G. Ballard Interviewed" [Peter Linnett] C54
"J.G. Ballard's Science Fiction for Today" [James Goddard with David Pringle] C61
"Journey Across a Crater" A104

"Killing Ground, The" A98
"Killing Time Should Be Prime-Time TV" C82
"Kings of Infinite Space" C83

"La Jetée, Academy One" C16
"Landfall, at Last" A145
"Last World of Mr Goddard, The" A14
"Legend of Regret" C97
"Life and Death of God, The" A123
"Lost in Space" C45
"Lost Leonardo, The" A50
"Love: A Print-out for Claire Churchill" B5
"Love and Napalm: Export USA" A91
Love and Napalm: Export USA A112
"Low-Flying Aircraft" A119
Low-Flying Aircraft and Other Stories A127

"Made in USA" C7
"Mae West's Reduction Mammoplasty" A106
"Man on the 99th Floor, The" A33
"Manbotching" C78
"Manhole 69" A6
"Memories of the Space Age" A148
"Minus One" A44
"Mobile" A5
"Motel Architecture" A138
"Mr F. is Mr F." A18
"My Dream of Flying to Wake Island" A117

"Myth Maker of the 20th Century" C3
"Myths of the Near Future" A150
Myths of the Near Future A149

"Neural Interval, A" B4
"New Means Worse" C92
"New Science Fiction, The: A Conversation Between J.G. Ballard and George Macbeth" C36
"News from the Sun" A147
"Not a Step Beyond Tomorrow" [Giovanni Dadomo] C81
"Notes from Nowhere" C15
"Notes from Nowhere: Comments on Work in Progress" C21
"Notes Towards a Mental Breakdown" A108
"Notes Towards a Mental Breakdown" A124
"Now Wakes the Sea" A40
"Now: Zero" A9

"Old Guard, The" C9
"One Afternoon at Utah Beach" A136
"Overloaded Man, The" A17
Overloaded Man, The A88

"Package Tours" C67
"Passport to Eternity" A29
Passport to Eternity A46
"Personal View, A" C60
"Pieces from an Interview with J.G. Ballard" [Robert Lightfoot and David Pendleton] C35
"Place and a Time to Die, A" A102
"Placental Insufficiency" B7
"Plan for the Assassination of Jacqueline Kennedy" A80
"Preface" C56
"Prima Belladonna" A3
"Princess Margaret's Face Lift: An Intersection of Fiction and Reality" A105
"Prisoner of the Coral Deep" A49
"Profession of Science Fiction, 26: From Shanghai to Shepperton, The" C96

"Queen Elizabeth's Rhinoplasty" A129
"Question of Re-Entry, A" A38

"Recognition, The" A87
"Red Stars and Sickle Moons" C23
"Reptile Enclosure, The" A60

"Salvador Dali: The Innocent as Paranoid" C32
"Say Goodbye to the Wind" A109
"Sci-Fi Seer" [Lynn Barber] C41
"Science Fiction Cannot Be Immune from Change" C37
"Screen Game, The" A47
"See-Through Brain, The" C39
"Sherrington Theory, The" A37
"Side-Effects of Orthonovin G, The" B9
"Singing Statues, The" A32
"60 Minute Zoom, The" A125
"Smile, The" A126
"Some Words About Crash!" C62
"Sound-Sweep, The" A10
"Souvenir" A66
"Space Age Is Over, The" [Dr. Chris Evans] C80
"Spaced Out" C58
"Spacing Out" [Brendan Hennessy] C47
"Speculative Illustrations: Eduardo Paolozzi in Conversation with J.G. Ballard and Frank Whitford" C53
"Storm-Bird, Storm-Dreamer" A75
"Storm-Wind" A19
"Strange Seas of Thought" C14
"Studio 5, the Stars" A15
"Subliminal Man, The" A36
"Sudden Afternoon, The" A45
"Summer Cannibals, The" A97

"Terminal Beach, The" A51
Terminal Beach A54
Terminal Beach, The A56
"Terminal Documents: Burroughs Reviewed" C13
"Theatre of War" A134
"Things I Wish I'd Known at 18" C95
"Thirteen to Centaurus" A28

"Thousand Dreams of Stellavista, The" A27
"Thousand Wounds and Flowers, The" C30
"Time, Memory and Inner Space" C2
"Time of Passage" A48
"Time-Tombs, The" A39
"Tolerances of the Human Face" A101
"Tomorrow is a Million Years" A78
"Track 12" A7
"Transistorised Brain" C10
"Twentieth Century Vox" [Michael McNay] C42

"Ultimate City, The" A128
"University of Death, The" A93
Unlimited Dream Company, The A140
"Unlimited Dreams: J.G. Ballard Interviewed" [Alan Dorey and Joseph Nicholas] C85

"Venus Hunters, The" A55
Venus Hunters, The A143
"Venus Smiles" A82
"Venus Smiles" B8
Vermilion Sands A110
"Violent Noon, The" A1
"Visions of Hell" C11
"Voices of Time, The" A13
Voices of Time and Other Stories, The A26
"Volcano Dances, The" A61

"Waiting Grounds, The" A8
"Waste of Beauty" C22
"Watch-Towers, The" A31
"What to Do Till the Analyst Comes" C12
"Where Have All the Space Ships Gone?" C1
"Which Way to Inner Space?" C1
"Why I Want to Fuck Ronald Reagan" A92
Wind from Nowhere, The A24
"Writers' Choice for Christmas Reading" C84
"Writers' Reading in 1981" C94

The Writings of Ballard

"Year's Science Fiction, The"
    C25
"You and Me and the Continuum"
    A69
"You: Coma: Marilyn Monroe"
    A76

"Zap Code" C68
"Zero Synthesis" B15
"Zodiac 2000" A137
"Zone of Terror" A11

2: Critics, Reviewers, and Interviewers (Parts C and D)

This is an index of the authors of all the critical and bio-bibliographical works listed in Part D of the bibliography. It also contains the names of the interviewers listed chronologically in Part C. References are to entry numbers.

Ableman, Paul   D159
Adlard, Mark   D63
Aldiss, Brian   D9, D13, D27, D33, D63, D83
Amis, Kingsley   D8, D12, D19, D63
Amis, Martin   D75, D95, D110, D161
Armytage, W.H.G.   D49

Barber, Lynn   C41, C95
Barron, Neil   D119
Bester, Alfred   D156
Bishop, Michael   D134
Blish, James   D63
Blumberg, Myrna   D108
Bowen, John   D20
Bowers, Frederick   D66
Bradbury, Malcolm   D152
Bradshaw, Steve   D113
Brady, John   D82
Brigg, Peter   D141
Budrys, Algis   D42
Burgess, Anthony   D34, D135
Burns, Alan   C91
Burroughs, William S.   D68
Bygrave, Mike   C57

Carnell, John   D62
Carter, Angela   D150
Cawthorn, James   D40, D43

Chauvin, Cy   D63
Cheshire, David   D59
Clute, John   D154
Colvin, James [Michael Moorcock]   D23, D26, D30, D37, D48
Cotts, S.E.   D5, D6

Dadomo, Giovanni   C81
De Bolt, Joe   D119
Delap, Richard   D52, D130
Dickinson, Mike   D153
Disch, Thomas M.   D52, D124
Dorey, Alan   C85
Durrant, Digby   D112

Ellison, Harlan   D44
Evans, Christopher   C80

Fallowell, Duncan   D128, D151
Flood, Leslie   D11
Frane, Jeff   D130
Franklin, H. Bruce   D57, D139

Glendinning, Victoria   D162
Goddard, James   C46, C55, C61, C63, D62, D114, D117
Goldman, Stephen H.   D142
Goldstein, Toby   D165
Greene, Graham   D47

Critics, Reviewers, and Interviewers

Haden-Guest, Anthony D60
Harding, Lee D100
Hartwell, David G. D65
Hayman, Martin D115
Hennessy, Brendan C47, C50
Holmes, Richard D45
Hutchinson, Tom D88, D133

Irwin, Michael D125

Jacky D93
Jakubowski, Maxim D80, D97, D120

Kingston, Jeremy D53
Krim, Seymour D70

Lafferty, R.A. D155
Lee, Hermione D149
Leiber, Fritz D149
Levin, Martin D36, D101
Lightfoot, Robert C35, C43
Linnett, Peter C54, D117
Louit, Robert C62

MacBeth, George C36
McNay, Michael C42
Mahon, Derek D122
Malzberg, Barry N. D118, D157
Mano, D.K. D81
Mayne, Richard D21
Merril, Judith D25, D29, D39
Miller, P. Schuyler D7, D16, D28
Moorcock, Michael D17, D23, D26, D30, D31, D37, D41, D48, D99, D130, D138, D140; see also James Colvin, pseud.
Morgan, Edwin D35
Murray, Isobel D61

Nicholas, Joseph C85
Nicholls, Peter D84, D107
Nicol, Charles D116
Nye, Robert D58, D74, D121, D160

Paolozzi, Eduardo C53
Parrinder, Patrick D147
Pendleton, David C35, C43
Perry, Nick D55, D73, D105
Pfeiffer, John D119
Platt, Charles C88, D130

Priest, Christopher D63, D129
Pringle, David C61, C63, C87, C96, D67, D79, D98, D117, D126, D143, D148
Punter, David D158

Quigly, Isabel D109
Quinton, Anthony D76

Rabkin, Eric S. D132
Rathbone, Julian D164
Reed, Douglas C49
Rottensteiner, Franz D106
Ryan, Anthony D71

Sage, Lorna D90
Samuelson, David D103
Sanders, Joe D130
Savage, Jon C79
Scholes, Robert D132
Seymour-Smith, Martin D77
Simak, Clifford D38
Sladek, John D51
Smith, Godfrey D91
Smith, Rodney C86
Sontag, Susan D72
Stableford, Brian D131, D144-46
Storm, Jannick C31
Straub, Peter D86
Strawson, Galen D163
Sturgeon, Theodore D64
Sutherland, John D111

Tarshis, Jerome D72
Tennant, Emma D96
Theroux, Paul D69
Totton, Nick D123
Turner, George D100

Watson, Ian D89, D102
Waugh, Auberon D92
White, Peter D18
Whitford, Frank C53
Wilkie, Roy D55, D73, D105
Wood, Michael D137
Wordsworth, Christopher D22

3: Persons Referred to by Ballard and His Critics (Parts B, C, and D)

This is an index of the persons (mostly writers and artists) referred to in the entries for Ballard's miscellaneous and nonfiction writings (Parts B and C); and also of the persons referred to in the entries for the critical and bio-bibliographical works about Ballard (Part D). The authors of all books reviewed by Ballard are listed here. References are to entry numbers.

Abé, Kobo D102
Aldiss, Brian C9, C14, C25, C28-29, C60, C67, C89, D7, D30, D50, D84, D107, D111, D132, D151
Amis, Kingsley C4, C20, C70, C92, D27
Amis, Martin C90
Asimov, Isaac C14, D103, D142
Auden, W.H. D110

Bangs, John Kendrick D154
Banham, Reyner D89, D102
Barthes, Roland D89, D102
Bartok, Bela D18
Baudelaire, Charles D14
Bax, Martin B10
Beckett, Samuel D99, D102
Berry, Adrian C58
Bertolucci, Bernardo D80
Bester, Alfred D138
Bierce, Ambrose D154
Biggle, Lloyd C18
Blake, William D150, D153
Blish, James C5, D99
Boardman, Tom C5
Böcklin, Arnold D103
Borges, Jorge Luis D39

Bradbury, Ray D16-17, D27-28, D48, D103, D138, D145, D148, D165
Brophy, Brigid D140
Brown, Norman O. D89
Browne, Sir Thomas D66
Bruccoli, Matthew J. C97
Brunner, John C4, D84
Buchan, John D161
Buddha, Gautama D107
Budrys, Algis D49, D103
Bunuel, Luis D109
Burgess, Anthony C69, D137, D151
Burns, Alan D140
Burroughs, William S. C3, C13, C50, C70, C79, C94, D17, D49, D58, D69, D75, D80, D158, D165
Burton, Robert D66

Calvino, Italo D152
Campbell, John W. C26
Carnell, John C5, C8, C20
Carr, Terry C65
Carter, Angela D140, D158
Céline, Louis Ferdinand D82
Charbonneau, Louis C7, C23

Persons Referred to

Christopher, John C8, D130
Churchill, Claire B1, B5, D104
Clarke, Arthur C. C4, C23, D14, D84, D103
Cohen, John C10
Coleridge, Samuel Taylor D103
Conquest, Robert C4, C20
Conrad, Joseph D8, D27, D32, D37, D103, D119, D130, D141
Cooper, Edmund C18
Crispin, Edmund C14

Dali, Salvador C32, C59, D65-66, D85
Davenport, Elaine C71
Defoe, Daniel D102
Delany, Samuel R. C25, C29
Delvaux, Paul D66, D103
Dick, Philip K. C12, C67
Disch, Thomas M. C29, D42, D86, D151
Donne, John D66
Dwoskin, Steve B3
Dylan, Bob D126

Eatherly, Claude D18, D31
Eliot, T.S. D66
Ellison, Harlan C68
Ernst, Max D37, D53, D66, D103
Eshbach, Lloyd Arthur C9
Euclid D127
Evans, Christopher B6, B12, C84

Faraldo, Claude D97
Finney, Jack C4
Fischer, Ernst D73
Fitzgerald, F. Scott C97
Fleming, Ian D128
Fowles, John D117
Franklin, H. Bruce C15
Frazer, J.T. C30
Freud, Sigmund C43, D99, D148

Genet, Jean D100, D105, D165
Gibson, Ian C84
Godard, Jean-Luc D109, D113, D158
Gold, H.L. C5
Golding, William D102, D109
Goldman, Albert C93
Gordon, Giles D140

Gray, John C15
Greene, Graham D32, D37, D130
Gregory, Stephan C34

Hardy, Thomas D27
Harrison, Harry C8, C25, C28, C67
Heinlein, Robert A. D142, D153
Henderson, Zenna C12
Henry, O. D133
Henty, G.A. D161
Herbert, Frank C18, D165
Hesse, Herman D48
Highsmith, Patricia D71
Hitler, Adolf C38
Hodder-Williams, Christopher C23, C65
Hughes, Howard C71
Huxley, Aldous D66

Isherwood, Christopher D110

Jakubowski, Maxim C69
Jarry, Alfred D39
Jean, Marcel C17
Johannesson, Olaf C26
Josipovici, Gabriel D71
Joyce, James D1, D75, D135
Jung, Carl Gustav D73, D148

Kafka, Franz D15, D39, D48
Kennedy, Jacqueline D46
Kubrick, Stanley D50
Kuttner, Henry D2

Laing, R.D. D45, D144
Laumer, Keith D71
Le Carré, John D71
Le Guin, Ursula D134
Lewis, Wyndham C11, D154
Lucas, George C75

MacBeth, George B10, D126, D140
McCullers, Carson D5
McLuhan, Marshall D45, D105
Mailer, Norman C48, C82
Malcolm, Donald D27
Mansfield, Roger C26
Marcuse, Herbert D89
Margaret, Princess D46
Marker, Chris C16

Marquez, Gabriel Garcia D151
Martinson, Harry D39
Marx, Karl D131, D139
Masson, David I. C26
Matthews, Helen Mary D104
Melville, Herman D39, D119, D149
Merril, Judith D5, D103
Miller, Daniel [The Normal] D165
Miller, Jonathan C78
Miller, Walter M. C7, D103
Moorcock, Michael C65, D43, D50, D83, D107, D150-51
Moore, Ward C67

Nader, Ralph C51, D89
Nicholls, Peter C64
Nye, Robert D140

Panshin, Alexei and Cory D134
Paolozzi, Eduardo C53
Peake, Mervyn D151
Peterkiewicz, Jerzy C20
Pinter, Harold D27
Poe, Edgar Allan D32, D45
Pohl, Frederik C7, C14, C26, C69
Powell, Anthony D117
Presley, Elvis C93
Priest, Christopher C65
Priestley, J.B. D103
Pynchon, Thomas D80, D152, D158

Quiller-Couch, Sir Arthur D27

Rauschenberg, Robert D68
Rimbaud, Arthur D76
Robbe-Grillet, Alain D70, D158
Roberts, Keith D138
Roddan, John C19
Rose, Lois and Stephen C48
Rousseau, Henri D153
Russell, Eric Frank C7

St. John, John C72
Sandford, Ronald B10
Scriabin, Alexander D151
Severin [Siouxsie and the Banshees] D165
Shaw, Bob C68
Sheckley, Robert C76
Shelley, Mary D146

Siffre, Michel C6
Silverberg, Robert C65, C67-68
Simak, Clifford C9
Sladek, John C29
Smith, Cordwainer D28
Spencer, Stanley D154
Spenser, Edmund D160
Stein, Gertrude D96
Sturgeon, Theodore D103
Symmonds, Charles D56

Tanguy, Yves D103
Taylor, Elizabeth D46
Tennant, Emma C84
Theroux, Paul D104
Thomas, D.M. D140
Toole, John Kennedy C94
Traven, B. D133

Vance, Jack C7
van Vogt, A.E. D134, D142
Verne, Jules C5
Vico, Giambattista D135
Vonnegut, Kurt D80, D86, D148

Waldberg, Patrick C17
Watson, Ian C69
Wells, H.G. D8, D82, D122, D147
White, Patrick D26
Wilde, Oscar D85
Williamson, Jack C7
Wilson, Angus D140
Wilson, Edward C22
Wolfe, Tom C83
Wright, Lan D27
Wyndham, John C28, D130

Young, Robert F. C12

Zamyatin, Yevgeny C39
Zelazny, Roger C25, C28